Grandma's
Complete
Cookbook

Grandma's Complete Cookbook

More than 200 recipes with traditional tips for success

PUBLISHED BY
THE READER'S DIGEST ASSOCIATION, INC.
LONDON • NEW YORK • SYDNEY • MONTREAL

Grandma's Complete Cookbook

Project Editor John Andrews
Art Editor Julie Bennett
Editor Lisa Thomas
Designer Martin Bennett
Writers Jo Anne Calabria, Grace Campbell,
  Dixie Elliott and Tracy Rutherford
Photographers André Martin and Simon Smith
Stylists Jenny Iggleden and Gabrielle Wheatley
Home Economists Grace Campbell and
  Vanessa Horton
Food Stylist Jennie Shapter
Nutritionist Fiona Hunter
Proofreader Sarah Kaikini
Indexer Diane Harriman

FOR VIVAT DIRECT

Editorial Director Julian Browne
Art Director Anne-Marie Bulat
Managing Editor Nina Hathway
Trade Books Editor Penny Craig
Picture Resource Manager
  Sarah Stewart-Richardson
Pre-press Technical Manager Dean Russell
Product Production Manager
  Claudette Bramble
Senior Production Controller Jan Bucil

Colour origination by FMG
Printed and bound in Europe

ISBN: 978 1 78020 168 9
Book code: 400-634 UP0000-1

Grandma's Complete Cookbook
Published in 2012 in the United Kingdom by Vivat Direct
Limited (t/a Reader's Digest), 157 Edgware Road,
London W2 2HR.

First published in the United Kingdom in 2011 under the title
Grandma's Quick and Thrifty Cookbook.

Grandma's Complete Cookbook is owned and
under licence from The Reader's Digest Association, Inc.
All rights reserved.

Adapted from *Grandma's Quick & Thrifty Cookbook* published
by Reader's Digest (Australia) Pty Limited in 2010.

We are committed both to the quality of our products and
the service we provide to our customers. We value your
comments, so please do contact us on **0871 351 1000** or via
our website at **www.readersdigest.co.uk**
If you have any comments or suggestions about the content of
our books, email us at **gbeditorial@readersdigest.co.uk**

PHOTOGRAPHY CREDITS

Images supplied by The Reader's Digest Association, Inc., with
the exception of the following:

Icons (used throughout) – potato masher: ShutterStock, Inc./
Kelly Nelson; gingerbread cutter: iStockphoto.com/
Rob Eyers; wooden spoon: iStockphoto.com/Jo Unrhu; pink
timer: iStockphoto.com/Thomas Vogel; red and white gingham:
iStockphoto.com/Subjug

Front Cover Dorling Kindersley / Getty Images; Claudio Divizia
/ istockphoto; **Back Cover** azureforest / istockphoto;
Shutterstock. **15** ShutterStock, Inc./Scuddy; **19** iStockphoto.
com/Jack Kelly; **20** iStockphoto.com/Camilla Wisbauer; **21**
(bottom) ShutterStock, Inc./Rihardzz, (centre above)
ShutterStock, Inc./Mark Aplet; **28** Vivat Direct Ltd/Simon
Smith; **32** ShutterStock, Inc./Ultimathule; **35** ShutterStock,
Inc./Argunova; **81, 112, 143, 151, 177, 186, 193, 201, 262,
309, 326** Vivat Direct Ltd/Simon Smith; **362** iStockphoto.com/
Louis Hiemstra

Every effort has been made to find and credit the copyright
holders of images in this book. We will be pleased to rectify
any errors or omissions in future editions. Email us at
gbeditorial@readersdigest.co.uk

Contents

Introduction

Grandma seemed to be someone who could turn her hand to anything and make it taste wonderful. You'd find her pottering away in the kitchen, working her magic with the humblest ingredients and whipping up delicious treats and deeply satisfying, heart-warming meals. Grandma's food was made with love, care and affection and we eagerly devoured it, down to the last morsel. She usually cooked from memory and handwritten recipes passed on by family and friends. In an age when fewer women went out to work, she could spend time in the kitchen, effortlessly baking bread and cakes, turning home-grown vegetables into tasty pickles and berries into luscious jams, and pulling perfect roasts out of the oven complete with all the trimmings.

As much as we still enjoy the food of childhood memories, many of us no longer have Grandma's experience and skills, or the time required to make these dishes in the same way. And so we bring you *Grandma's Complete Cookbook*, a collection of classic recipes, adapted for the modern cook, that recall the warmth and security of childhood – food lovingly prepared and warmly offered by mothers and grandmothers; the sort of food we adored as children and often crave as adults when in need of soothing and comfort.

This beautiful book passes on Grandma's cooking wisdom, with a collection of more than 200 quick and simple recipes that evoke convivial meals and recall the charm of a time when life was a little simpler, maybe merrier and more relaxed. We show how easy it is to plan ahead and manage your kitchen, and help you to master basic techniques so you too can cook calmly and competently, just as Grandma did.

The recipes in this book are as easy on the pocket as they are welcome at the dinner table. All have been adapted to combine the best of the old ways with the advantages of modern methods, equipment and ingredients, bringing the joys of real food and home-style cooking to a new generation.

We hope this book helps you to recapture some of your favourite childhood food memories, so that you can share them with your own family for generations to come.

The Editors

About this book

All the recipes in this book have been designed to be quick to prepare, as well as economical (less than £3.50 per serving). Each recipe is labelled according to the categories below. The quickest and thriftiest recipes are listed separately on pages 8 and 9.

SPEED RATING

Express   On the table in 20 minutes

Super quick   On the table in 30 minutes

Quick   On the table in 50 minutes or less

Prepare and relax   Less than 20 minutes preparation; slow cooking – or standing or resting – with minimal input needed from the cook

THRIFT RATING

Luxury on a budget   Recipes costing £3 to £3.50 per serving

Thrifty   Recipes costing less than £2.75 per serving (most starters, soups, snacks, baked goods and desserts)

Extra thrifty   Main-course recipes that are less than £2 per serving, and snacks, desserts and side dishes that are less than £1.25

The quickest and thriftiest recipes

grandma's kitchen

'Waste not, want not' was Grandma's kitchen philosophy. Here are many of her secrets to keeping a thrifty and efficient kitchen and making the most of what you have.

Kitchen wisdom

Grandma's kitchen always seemed to run smoothly and she knew how to make the most of everything. Her tips on how to shop wisely and store your purchases correctly will also help you to save waste, time and money.

Shopping wisely

Thrifty doesn't mean stingy. Canny shopping means planning well, knowing your local shops and taking advantage of what's plentiful and good value. When you shop wisely, you'll always eat well and still be able to afford the occasional luxury. Remember though that the 'cheapest' food isn't always the best value.

Writing a good shopping list will save you time, stress and money, as you'll buy only the items you actually need for a full week's meals. While using a shopping list minimises impulse buys, look for specials that can be substituted for an ingredient on your list, or frozen for later use (see page 33). Choose carefully, as Grandma would have done: make sure the quality is good, that you'll use it all and that it fits in with your planned meals.

Shop around

Supermarkets have made shopping much more convenient than it was Grandma's day. But you'll often get better value for money if you shop around, are selective in your ingredient choices and plan what you need. If you're going further afield to shop, weigh up whether your food savings will be more than the cost of petrol and time. You can save time and transport costs by visiting the supermarket less frequently – perhaps only once or twice a month – and stocking up on staples. For fresh produce and specialist items, shop locally if you can, like Grandma did. Find a good greengrocer, butcher and fishmonger who will recommend the day's best buys.

Grocers who cater to ethnic communities often sell a wide range of more exotic foods at much cheaper prices than is the case at the supermarket – ask which fruit or veg are at their best. They are also an excellent source of good-value grains, pulses, nuts and dried fruit. Also try your local farmers' market for specialist cheeses, meats and seasonal fruit and vegetables, especially organic.

Melons, berries and peaches will smell sweet when ripe; mangoes, avocados and plums will 'give' slightly when gently squeezed.

Choosing the best

When buying fresh produce, select carefully to ensure you get the best-quality ingredients.

Fruit and vegetables

Freshly picked local produce often has the best flavour. If something looks tired or wilted, leave it on the shelf. Produce doesn't have to look perfect, but it should usually be firm and not wrinkled, bruised or soft.

Poultry

● Generally, larger birds are better value because there's a higher proportion of meat to bone. Look for plump birds that have soft, blemish-free skin (the thinner the skin, the younger the bird will be).
● Buy the best bird you can afford; although free-range and organic poultry are more expensive, the flavour is superior to cage-reared birds. Corn-fed birds have a yellowish flesh and good flavour.

Seafood

● Fish and shellfish are always best eaten really fresh. Ask your fishmonger for advice on how to cook unfamiliar varieties, and enjoy experimenting with the catch of the day.
● Choose fresh-smelling fish that have glistening skin, bright eyes and firm flesh. Fillets should be moist and firm, and shellfish brightly coloured.

Meat

● Economical cuts of meat have plenty of flavour, but usually need slow cooking or marinating in order to tenderise them. Meat bought on the bone can also be economical, especially if you keep the bones to make stock.
● In general, choose lean cuts of meat that have been trimmed of surplus fat. Weight for weight, you'll get better value because you're not paying for the fat.
● Bright red meat is not always a sign of quality – well-hung meat will be darker.

Banish bugs

If you notice moths in the pantry or weevils in packets, clean the cupboard and discard all foods with insect traces, such as cobwebs or small holes in the packaging.

To kill any insect eggs, freeze the remaining food packages (opened or unopened) for 48 hours. Then store them in sealed glass jars to prevent re-infestation – weevils can chew through plastic packets and settle in again.

Stocking the pantry

It's frustrating to run out of an ingredient and then have to buy an expensive replacement from a convenience store – a practice Grandma would have frowned on. Canned, bottled and dried goods have a long shelf life, so stock up when they're on special offer and enjoy their convenience. As well as basic seasonings and sauces, keep the following items on hand for use in a multitude of recipes.

Canned foods

Fish Canned sardines, tuna, salmon, crab and anchovies are usually more economical than the fresh equivalent and make speedy, nutritious salads, pasta dishes, pizza toppings, fishcakes, egg dishes and tasty fillings for jacket potatoes.

Fruit Canned fruit is useful for breakfast or a quick dessert, or when a certain variety of fresh fruit isn't in season or is too expensive.

Tomatoes Available whole or chopped in cans (with or without herbs) – ideal for soups, casseroles, curries and pasta sauces.

Bottled items

Oils An economical all-rounder such as vegetable, sunflower or peanut oil is perfect for shallow and deep-frying. Extra virgin olive oil and nut oils are great for salad dressings and drizzling, but burn easily when heated.

Olives Essential for Mediterranean dishes – pasta sauces, salads, stews or pizza toppings.

Sweeteners Honey can be used in sweet and savoury dishes and for glazes, marinades, sweet-and-sour recipes, salad dressings or for sauces. Golden syrup, black treacle and molasses are useful if you bake a lot. Maple syrup makes a quick topping for pancakes and ice cream.

Tomato passata Made from ripe tomatoes with the seeds removed, passata is great for soups, pasta sauces and even tomato-based drinks.

Tomato purée A small amount used in sauces, stocks, gravies, dressings and marinades adds an intense tomato-flavour boost. Once the can or tube is opened, keep it in the fridge.

Vinegars Red wine vinegar is the most versatile. Balsamic vinegar, although expensive, is rich and mellow and goes a long way.

Dried goods

Flour You'll need self-raising, plain flour and cornflour for making cakes, desserts and batters, coating meat and fish and thickening sauces. When you're making bread, strong flour is best, but you can also use plain flour. For baking, you'll also need a stock of baking powder and bicarbonate of soda.

Fruit Dried fruit is good for baking, desserts and high-energy snacks.

Grains Bulghur wheat and couscous are quick to prepare; and they can be used in warm and cold salads and to accompany meat, poultry and vegetarian mains. Serve quick-cooking fine polenta soft, like mashed potato, or allow it to set, then grill it.

Noodles Noodles are inexpensive and ultra quick to prepare. Many types need little or no cooking and can simply be softened in boiling water. Wok-ready noodles can be used straight from the packet.

Nuts and seeds Always keep a small supply of nuts (cashews, walnuts, flaked almonds and pine nuts) on hand for use in baking and for adding to stir-fries, salads or noodle dishes. Ground nuts have a much shorter life, so if possible grind whole nuts in a food processor or grinder as and when you need them. Keep some seeds in store too: add pumpkin and sunflower seeds to salads, and sesame seeds to stir-fries. Store nuts and seeds in airtight containers and use within three months.

Oats Use oats in porridge, add them to sweet and savoury crumble toppings, or use them to thicken soups or as a crumb coating.

Pasta Keep several varieties of dried pasta, and some lasagne sheets. Allow about 100g dried or 150g fresh pasta or noodles per person.

Rice Long-grain rice is very versatile; but fragrant basmati rice is the most authentic choice for Indian dishes, and will complement all Asian recipes. Risotto rice is the best for risotto and paella. Allow 75g raw rice per person when calculating quantities.

Sugar Caster sugar dissolves more quickly than granulated (white) sugar, but the two kinds are generally interchangeable. Light and dark brown sugars lend a slight caramel taste to recipes and are good in fruit cakes.

Smart storage tricks

Stackable square containers make the best use of space on your pantry shelves; you can also buy 'shelf extenders' or stackable wire racks from specialist storage shops that will do wonders to maximise your storage space

Group like items with like, storing the following foods together: baking supplies; pastas, grains and rice; oils and vinegars; herbs and spices; and cuisine-based items such as Indian, Chinese or Mexican ingredients.

Check your supplies regularly and replace items that are running low; discard any that show signs of insect infestation or have passed their dates.

Store the most frequently used items at the front, where they are easy to see and reach, with newer supplies behind older ones.

Fridge essentials

A well-stocked, well-organised fridge makes life in the kitchen so much easier. When you unpack your shopping, it's worth taking the time to position items in your fridge according to where they will keep best and how often you need them. Place raw meat or fish on the bottom shelf, in a dish or container, so that no drips can fall onto other foods and contaminate them. For ease of access, keep dairy products on one shelf, sauces on another, salads and vegetables in the drawers and all the condiments together, with their labels showing, so that those with the earliest use-by dates are consumed first.

Dairy

All dairy items should be used by their use-by date. Store **cheeses** in the warmest part of the fridge (at the top, in a door shelf if you have room). Keep them covered in a plastic container or wrapped in foil or greaseproof paper – don't use cling film as it encourages a damp surface that can become mouldy. Keep **cream**, **crème fraîche**, **soured cream** and **yoghurt**

Egg yolks, covered with water, can be refrigerated for up to five days.

covered, and store cartons of **milk** in the fridge door. Keep **eggs** in their boxes near the top of the fridge or in the egg holders in the door, stored in date order.

Storing fruit and vegetables

Some produce should be stored at room temperature: tomatoes, to develop flavour; avocados, to ripen; most fruit, except berries; and onions, potatoes and root vegetables in a cool, dark place. Oranges and lemons keep best wrapped in paper and stored in a drawer.

- **In the fridge** Berries, peppers, carrots, celery, cucumber, grapes, green beans, herbs, leeks, mushrooms (in a paper bag), radishes, salad leaves, spring onions, courgettes.
- **Out of the fridge** Avocados, garlic, onions, potatoes, pumpkin, sweet potatoes, tomatoes.
- **In the fruit bowl** Apples, bananas, kiwi fruit, mangoes, pears, stone fruit such as peaches.

Fish

It's best to eat fresh fish on the day you buy it. But if this isn't possible, remove the packaging as soon as you get home, wipe the fish with clean kitchen paper, place it on a plate and cover with cling film. Store in the bottom of the fridge, ideally for no longer than 24 hours.

Meats

Always put **fresh meats** straight into the fridge. Keep them in their sealed packs, or put unpacked meat on a plate and wrap in fresh cling film or waxed paper. Make sure raw meats are kept away from cooked food.

Bacon can be stored with the raw meats, but **sliced cooked meats**, such as ham and salami, must be stored away from raw meats. Once opened, place bacon and sliced cooked meats in a sealed container and use within a few days. A large piece of ham will keep longer in the fridge if wrapped in a muslin cloth that has been dipped in vinegar.

Garden produce

Keep **fresh vegetables** and **salad leaves** in the salad drawer, which is several degrees cooler and more humid than the upper part of the refrigerator. If you're short of space, store them in plastic bags in the main part of the fridge, away from raw meats. Also avoid the cold spots in the fridge, such as near the freezer compartment or the cold plate at the back of some fridges; if ice crystals form in salad vegetables, they will be unusable.

Store bunches of **herbs**, with the roots on, upright in a glass of water in the fridge door. Loosely wrap cut herbs in damp kitchen paper and store in the salad drawer. Either way, they will last for several days.

How long will it keep in the fridge?

Most food items these days come with a use-by date, but here are some general guidelines.

Bacon	1 week
Cheese, eggs and milk	up to 1 week
Cooked casseroles, curries and stews	2 to 3 days
Cooked deli meats and fish	1 week
Cooked rice	1 to 2 days
Cooked vegetables, pasta or grains	1 to 2 days
Green vegetables, salad and soft fruits	2 to 3 days
Raw fish	2 days
Raw meat, sausages and poultry	3 days

Avoiding common problems

• Store strongly flavoured foods (such as Gruyère or Camembert cheese) in plastic containers in the fridge so that their smell doesn't taint other foods.

• To reduce the likelihood of food becoming contaminated, cover or tightly wrap any items that have been opened, and keep lids on jars.

• Metal cans will rust in the fridge, so transfer any leftover food from opened cans into sealed plastic containers before refrigerating them.

• Remember that use-by dates apply only when a product is sealed. Once opened, most jars, cans and packs of food should be refrigerated and used within two to three days.

Fridge care

• Avoid overfilling your fridge. Air needs to circulate freely for the fridge to work efficiently and use less electricity.

• Never put hot or warm food in the fridge as this will raise the temperature. Always allow cooked food to cool completely before storing.

• Keep your fridge clean by mopping up spills immediately. Empty it regularly and wipe it out with a weak solution of bicarbonate of soda to keep it smelling fresh.

To save some time when beating cream, chill the mixer blades and bowl in the freezer first. You'll find that the cream will be much easier to whip.

Freezer essentials

Freezer foods are a boon for the busy cook, and you may be surprised at how many different foods you can freeze. Set your freezer to 'fast freeze', if it has that setting, before shopping if you're buying items to freeze in bulk.

Loaves of bread (sliced for convenience), pitta breads and naan can all be frozen. Stale bread can be made into breadcrumbs and frozen.
Chillies can be halved lengthways and frozen, then chopped while still frozen.
Citrus juices can be frozen in ice-cube trays, then transferred to plastic bags; drop a cube or two into stews and curries, or thaw to use in desserts and salad dressings.
Citrus zest can be grated, bagged and used from frozen.
Egg whites can be frozen in an ice-cube tray, then transferred to a plastic bag and used for making meringues.
Fish, meat and poultry can be bought ready-frozen, but if you're buying fresh portions to freeze, check that they are labelled 'suitable for freezing'. You can freeze food in its supermarket packaging for one month; for a longer period, open the packet and repack the food in a freezer bag, taking care to exclude all the air. If you're buying portions from a butcher or fishmonger, always check that they haven't already been frozen.

Cooking food from frozen

• Never cook raw poultry and large joints of meat from frozen as they may not cook right through. Always thaw them fully first.
• Frozen vegetables and frozen fresh pasta can be dropped straight into the pan.
• Mince and thin small sausages, such as chipolatas, can be cooked from frozen, but ensure that they are cooked right through.
• Frozen herbs, ginger, chopped chilli and grated cheese can also be added straight to dishes during cooking – there's no need to thaw them first.
• Soups, stews, casseroles, bakes and pies can be baked or cooked on the hob from frozen, but start cooking them at a low temperature to first thaw the food, then gradually increase the temperature in order to cook the dish right through.
• Prawns, seafood and thin fish fillets can be cooked from frozen.

Fresh herbs can be simply washed, dried, put into a freezer bag and frozen; crumble them into dishes during cooking.

Frozen berries are economical and handy. To freeze your own, see page 33.

Frozen vegetables are convenient and nutritious and can be bought in large, economical bags. Once opened, reseal with a clip or bag tie. To freeze your own vegetables, see page 33. Salad vegetables aren't suitable for freezing as they are too fragile.

Ginger can be peeled and frozen, then grated straight into your cooking pot. This way it stays fresh much longer.

Pastry, both bought and homemade, freezes well. Stuffed pasta and gnocchi can be frozen and then cooked from frozen.

Prepared meals such as pasta sauces, stews and soups are ideal for cooking in bulk and then freezing. Freeze in small batches or individual portions for up to three months, or one month if the food contains garlic, as the flavour deteriorates. To use, thaw them (preferably in the fridge), reheat thoroughly, then simmer for 5 minutes.

Stock, either homemade or bought, can be frozen for up to one month. Pour into freezer bags in convenient portions, leaving a little space for expansion. Vegetable stock can double up for poultry and fish dishes; beef stock is best used only for meat casseroles and gravy, as it has a meaty taste and gives a deep brown colour.

Tomato purée can be frozen in an ice-cube tray, or dolloped onto a baking tray lined with baking parchment. Once frozen, place it in a plastic bag and return to the freezer until needed.

Safely thawing frozen food

• Freeze food quickly, but thaw it slowly – preferably in the fridge, and in a container to catch any drips.

• Take large, dense items (such as meat, poultry, fish and prepared meals) from the freezer the night before and thaw them in the

Tips for safe freezing

• Always cool food before you freeze it. Putting hot food in the freezer makes the freezer warmer, and can cause other foods to start thawing. It also makes the fridge work harder and uses more electricity.

• Never refreeze anything that has been frozen and thawed, or is past its best. Raw food that has been frozen and then cooked can be frozen again.

• Wrap or seal food well before you freeze it to keep the air out so it doesn't get 'freezer burn', which affects its texture.

• Freeze raw foods in portion-sizes. Spread chicken and fish fillets on a baking tray and freeze them, then transfer the individual portions to freezer bags and seal well. You can then take out and thaw only what you need.

fridge, still wrapped, so they will be ready to cook the next evening.

• Smaller items, such as chicken breasts, can be removed from the freezer in the morning and thawed in the fridge (on a plate or in a dish) for cooking that evening.

Kitchen equipment

You don't need masses of kitchen utensils to cook well. When investing in a new kitchen purchase, it makes sense to buy the best you can afford: good-quality equipment lasts longer and will usually be easier and more pleasurable to use. If you look for items that can do more than just one job you'll also free up a lot of space in your cupboards and avoid paying for pieces you don't need. Obviously the exact utensils you need depend a lot on the type of cooking you do, but here are some points to consider when it comes to deciding on your bigger kitchen purchases.

Cookware and bakeware

- A large, ovenproof gratin dish is useful for cooking dishes such as lasagne and pasta bakes, and can be used for serving at the table.
- The most versatile frying pan is a non-stick, heavy-based one with a lid. Look for one with a heatproof handle so the pan can be transferred to the oven or under the grill, increasing your cooking and serving options.
- Buy good-quality, heavy-based saucepans, such as stainless steel pans with an aluminium base (and lid). These regulate heat more effectively than cheap pans, giving you more control over the cooking process, and will last for many years.
- A cast-iron or flameproof casserole dish is invaluable as it can be used on the hob, in the oven and for serving at the table. Although an investment purchase, it will truly last you a lifetime. A tight-fitting lid is important as it helps to retain moisture in the dish during cooking.
- A collapsible metal steamer, or metal or bamboo steamer inserts that can be tiered on top of your pans, are fabulous for steaming fish, vegetables and chicken – and take up minimal space.
- If you do a lot of baking but don't have much storage space, try silicon bakeware. Soft and pliable, silicon cake and muffin tins can be

Attractive mixing bowls can double as salad and serving bowls. Glass or ceramic bowls are more versatile than plastic and won't retain odours.

squashed into tight spaces, are nonstick, cool quickly after cooking and won't rust.

Chopping

- A set of top-quality knives makes food preparation easier, faster and safer: accidents often happen when you're trying to hack through food with a blunt knife. A stainless-steel blade is best, with a steel-lined handle. These knives are dishwasher-proof, won't rust and will last many years.
- Keep different chopping boards for raw and cooked food, especially meat. A separate chopping board for fruit will prevent strong smells such as onion and garlic being transferred to the fruit.

Some helpful gadgets

Today we have more kitchen gadgets than Grandma ever dreamed of, taking the laborious and time-consuming grind out of processes such as mincing, whisking, beating and kneading.

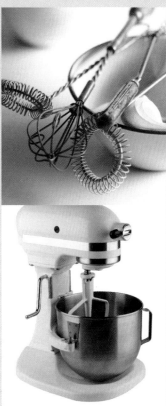

- **A microwave oven** can't be beaten for sheer speed, economy and efficiency, cooking food in a fraction of the time it would otherwise take. It's ideal for thawing food, heating leftovers, and small jobs like melting butter and chocolate. Loosely cover the microwave dish to help the food to cook more quickly and to stop it drying out or splattering the oven.

- **A food processor** will take many laborious food preparation chores off your hands. It will chop, mince, mix, purée, shred and grate, whizz up cake mixtures and make pastry and dough, giving perfect results in seconds. You can also use it for grating cheese, chopping nuts, making breadcrumbs, mixing smooth creamy sauces, dressings and dips, and puréeing or blending soups.

- **A wire whisk** is useful for small mixing jobs, such as whisking eggs or quickly eliminating lumps in sauces.

- **An electric hand mixer** is great for whipping cream, egg whites, sauces and cake batters and for making creamy mashed potatoes.

- **A hand-held stick blender** can be used as a mini food processor to quickly purée soups and sauces in the pot, and avoids having to transfer food to a food processor or blender.

- **An old-fashioned meat grinder** still deserves a place in the modern kitchen. Although you can use a food processor to mince meat and to make sausages, a meat grinder cuts through meat more cleanly, without mangling the muscle fibres, so the mince is less likely to be gluey or mushy.

- **An instant-read meat thermometer** takes the guesswork out of roasting all kinds of meat to perfection. You can opt for a dial model or a digital variety. They give an internal reading when you insert them into the roasting meat – some digital models even have an alarm telling you when the desired cooking temperature has been reached.

- **Weighing scales** are a worthwhile investment. Electronic digital scales are accurate and can switch from metric to imperial and back to zero instantly at the press of a button. An 'add and weigh' feature allows you to measure out an entire recipe in one bowl.

- **The humble crockpot or slow cooker** has made a comeback as modern cooks rediscover the delights of slowly simmered meals using economical cuts of meat. If you enjoy casseroles and make them often, a crockpot is a worthy investment. Crockpots are excellent for time-poor cooks as they create meals requiring little preparation: the ingredients are simply added to the crockpot and the dish can then be left to slowly simmer at a controlled temperature all day or even overnight, resulting in a delicious meal.

Cooking essentials

Years of practice in the kitchen allowed Grandma to find her way around a recipe with ease and to conjure up tasty dishes with minimal effort. Here we share some of her wisdom so you can follow in her footsteps.

How to read a recipe

In Grandma's day, recipes were very concise because a great deal of cookery knowledge was assumed. Modern recipes tend to give more explanation, and are written in a fairly standard way.

It's important to read a recipe right through before starting to cook, to ensure you have the right ingredients and equipment and that you understand all the techniques involved. The following notes will help you to understand the 'shorthand' for recipes in this and other books.

A note on cups

Many old recipes, and most recipes from the US, use cup measurements. In this system, the same volume of different ingredients will have different gram weights according to the density of the ingredients: 1 cup of honey weighs 350g (12oz), while 1 cup of shredded coconut weighs 60g (2¼oz). Measuring your ingredients on a set of scales to the correct gram weight will always give a more accurate result than cups, especially in baking recipes, where precision is more important.

Weights and measurements

• All cup and spoon measurements are level unless stated otherwise.
• If a recipe gives both metric and imperial measures, use one or the other – don't mix the two systems.

Temperature conversions

Celsius (°C)	Fahrenheit (°F)	Gas mark	
-18°C	0°F	–	freezer temperature
0°C	32°F	–	water freezes
82°C	180°F	–	water simmers
100°C	212°F	–	water boils
140°C	275°F	1	low oven
180°C	350°F	4	moderate oven
220°C	425°F	7	hot oven
240°C	475°F	9	very hot oven

To stop a pot boiling over on the stove, rub lard or butter on the inside rim before bringing it to the boil.

Conversion chart

If you're used to using metric measures but you come across a 'real' Grandma recipe that uses only imperial measurements, the chart below will help you to convert them.

WEIGHT		VOLUME	
Metric (approx.)	Imperial	Metric (approx.)	Imperial
10g	⅓oz	30ml	1fl oz
15g	½oz	50ml	2fl oz
25/30g	1 oz	75ml	2½fl oz
35g	1¼oz	85ml	3fl oz
40g	1½oz	90ml	3¼fl oz
55g	2oz	100ml	3½fl oz
70g	2½oz	250ml	9fl oz (1 cup)
85g	3oz	500ml	18fl oz (2 cups)
100g	3½oz	1 litre	35fl oz (4 cups)
500g	1lb 2oz		
1kg	2lb 4oz		

• Can sizes vary between manufacturers; if the can size specified in the recipe is unavailable, use the nearest equivalent. A small variation in the quantity of most ingredients is unlikely to adversely affect a recipe.

Ingredients

Unless the recipe states otherwise, assume:
• all eggs are large (60g to 70g)
• pasta is dried, and nuts are raw and unsalted
• dairy foods (milk, cream, soured cream and yoghurt) are full-fat – using a low-fat product in a recipe written for a full-fat product may give a different result
• all fruits and vegetables are medium-sized
• you should peel any fruits and vegetables that would normally be peeled before cooking, such as onions and garlic. If the skin is to be left on, the recipe will say so.

Oven temperatures

In some old recipes, you might see references to a slow, moderate or hot fire. The modern equivalents are a low, moderate or hot oven. Most recipes are written for regular ovens; if you have a convection (fan-driven) oven, reduce the temperature by 20°C (68°F).

All ovens differ; some run hotter or cooler than the temperature indicated on the thermostat. Always check or test foods 10 to 15 minutes before the end of the recommended cooking time.

All ovens have spots that are hotter than others. This is why recipes may say to put foods on a certain shelf of the oven, or to turn foods around part-way through cooking so they cook through and brown more evenly. This is less of a problem with fan ovens, as the warm air circulates more freely.

Cooking methods

Food can be ruined by poor preparation or the wrong cooking method. Conversely, using the correct preparation and cooking methods can transform more economical foods, such as cheaper cuts of meat, into delicious meals.

In general, cheaper cuts of meat are tougher than prime cuts and are best suited to gentle, slow-cooking methods, such as pot-roasting, braising and stewing. They may also be marinated to help to tenderise them. Save expensive prime cuts, such as fillet, for roasting or pan-frying; casseroling them will only dry them out and ruin them. More expensive cuts of meat can be 'stretched' to go further, for example by stuffing a boned joint. You can also supplement the meat with pulses, vegetables or dumplings, or top it with pastry.

You'll find more information on cooking techniques in the 'Basics and techniques' section (see page 352).

'Wet' cooking methods

Boiling is a fast cooking method in which foods are added to a large quantity of boiling water, and kept at a boil until cooked. In Grandma's day, vegetables, for example, were boiled for substantially longer than is recommended today, and she often added bicarbonate of soda to the cooking water. This is an old-fashioned method for preserving the vegetables' colour, but it destroys vitamin C. Meat generally becomes tough and dry if boiled, although some meats can be successfully cooked by slow simmering or poaching.

Braising is similar to stewing but generally used for larger and slightly better cuts of meat than stewing. The meat (or poultry) is usually fried briefly to brown it all over and then placed in a casserole dish on a bed of vegetables with enough stock to come about halfway up the meat. The pan is then covered tightly and the meat or poultry cooked slowly on the stove or in the oven until tender and juicy. Good-value, suitable cuts include stewing steak, blade,

To save time, marinate your meat in advance and then freeze it until the day you want to cook it. The meat will be tasty and tender.

skirt (or meat sold as braising beef), shoulder of lamb or neck fillet, pork spare-rib, chops, lamb's liver and chicken.

Poaching is a very gentle cooking method, suitable for delicate foods such as tender cuts of meat and seafood, as well as eggs and fruit. Fruit is often poached in a liquid flavoured with sugar, wine and spices, which is then served as a sauce with the fruit. When poaching, the liquid should be barely moving, otherwise the food may break up.

Pot roasting is excellent for whole large cuts or boned and rolled joints, which are more economical than roasting cuts. Pot roasts are slow-cooked in a covered casserole dish using a well-flavoured stock, often with wine or

Popular preparation methods for meat

- **Marinating** helps to tenderise meat by breaking down the fibres and is great for cheaper, tougher cuts. It also adds flavour and helps keep the flesh moist during cooking. (Vegetables and tofu can also be marinated.) A typical marinade includes oil, wine or vinegar, herbs and spices.

- **Stuffing** a boned joint with a tasty filling makes the meat go further and adds flavour and moisture. You can buy some cuts ready-boned, or ask your butcher to bone a joint for you. Stuffing is also delicious with poultry.

- **Tenderising** meat by gently pounding it with a meat mallet breaks down tough fibres and thins the meat down to a uniform thickness for quick and even cooking. Boneless cuts such as escalopes and chicken breast fillets are suitable for this treatment; place them between two sheets of baking paper or cling film before pounding.

cider, vegetables, herbs and spices. Topside, silverside, brisket and flank are good choices.

Steaming involves cooking food in a steamer or double boiler over a saucepan containing a small amount of steaming water. It's suitable for tender cuts of meat and seafood, and most vegetables. For extra flavour and to seal in juices and nutrients, foods can be wrapped (with flavourings and herbs) in foil or baking-parchment parcels before steaming. Alternatively, aromatics, such as herbs, vegetables and spices, can be added to the cooking liquid; their flavour will waft up with the steam and permeate the food.

Stewing is excellent for very tough cuts of meat. To help tenderise it, the meat is generally cut into smaller chunks of uniform size. Good beef choices include chuck and shin; these are often labelled 'stewing steak'. For a lamb stew, neck fillets are good value. Harder vegetables

are added at the start of the cooking time or partway through. Softer vegetables are added towards the end so that they don't overcook. Stews are easy to prepare and can be left to cook on a low heat for several hours.

'Dry' cooking methods

Baking is similar to roasting, but without the use of oil. It's commonly used for bread, pastry, cakes, biscuits and puddings. Foods such as meat, poultry, fish and vegetables are usually baked in foil to retain their moisture.

Roasting involves cooking meat, poultry or vegetables in the oven in a roasting tin with some oil or fat (dripping would have been Grandma's fat of choice; a healthier option is olive oil). Foods may need to be basted occasionally during roasting so that they don't dry out.

When baking a cake, place a dish of hot water in the oven. This keeps the air in the oven moist and stops the cake from scorching.

Shallow-frying is similar to pan-frying, but using enough oil so that it comes 1cm to 2cm up the sides of the pan.

Stir-frying is a quick cooking technique, typically using a wok, where thin portions of prime, tender meat and other ingredients, such as vegetables and noodles, are briefly fried over a high heat while being stirred and tossed. This is an excellent way to stretch a small amount of tender meat into a filling meal.

Frying methods

Deep-frying is a fast method in which meat, fish or vegetables are completely immersed in boiling fat or oil. The food can be first crumbed or battered to seal in moisture and give a crisp coating.

Pan-frying is a quick method in which thin or small pieces of tender meat, poultry and fish are fried on a medium heat in a small amount of oil. Non-stick pans make it possible to fry foods with a minimum of fat. Fish and meat (except for minced meat items such as sausages and patties) can be left underdone according to preference; poultry should always be cooked right through.

Cooking vegetables

Most vegetables can be cooked by a variety of methods, although softer vegetables, such as asparagus and broccoli, require less cooking than hard vegetables, such as carrots and potatoes. All vegetables, however, will turn to mush if they are overcooked. Some – for example, root vegetables – respond well to slow-cooking methods such as casseroling and braising.

Cooking vegetables as lightly as possible preserves their flavour, texture and vitamin content. Cooking them in water results in the loss of some water-soluble vitamins; this is minimised if they are steamed rather than boiled. Grilling, baking and roasting preserve water-soluble nutrients, as do casseroling and braising, because the vitamins are retained in the sauce or gravy.

Cooking fresh vegetables helps to release certain nutrients and phytochemicals, making them more available to your body. But at the same time, improper handling and cooking can destroy essential nutrients, especially vitamin C and folate. Here's how to preserve vital nutrients.

- Vitamins and minerals are often concentrated in and near the skin, so leave the skins on vegetables such as carrots and potatoes when you're cooking them, but clean them really thoroughly first.
- Cook vegetables whole whenever possible. Otherwise, cut vegetables into larger pieces to reduce the surface area exposed, thereby minimising nutrient loss.
- Cook vegetables in the minimum amount of water, and only for as long as necessary.
- Reheat leftover vegetables as quickly as possible to avoid any further nutrient loss.

The finishing touches

Grandma was a wizard at making meals look great. Here are a few quick tricks to add some magic to even the simplest dishes.

Soup garnishes include an elegant swirl of cream, a sprinkling of chopped fresh herbs, a scattering of crispy bacon pieces or chunky croûtons, or a spoonful of tangy tomato salsa.

For a quick topping for a cake lay a paper doily on top of the cake, then lightly sift icing sugar over it. Gently lift the doily off and you'll be left with a beautiful pattern.

Fresh herbs, whether sprigs, whole leaves or chopped, are one of the cheapest and easiest ways to garnish a dish.

Fry some breadcrumbs in a little melted butter until crisp and golden, then scatter them over cooked vegetables to add a lovely crunchy bite.

Use a zester to remove fine strips of citrus zest to adorn sweet and savoury dishes.

Scatter a handful of toasted nuts or seeds over a salad, or sprinkle some chopped or flaked nuts, such as almonds, over desserts.

Many dishes can be cooked or served in elegant, individual dishes. This works just as well for sweet as for savoury dishes and is particularly good if you're entertaining, as the food will look very enticing.

To top off desserts add a simple garnish: a twist of citrus fruit, a fanned, sliced strawberry or kiwi fruit, some grated chocolate or a light dusting of icing sugar.

To keep cake icing moist and stop it cracking on the cake, add a pinch of bicarbonate of soda to it.

Kitchen thrift

Making ingredients go further was one of Grandma's talents, born of necessity. It still makes sense to save money in the kitchen wherever possible, so here are some of Grandma's canny tips for modern cooks.

Making your meals go further

If you have an unexpected guest, or not quite enough of a key ingredient, there are many ways to stretch out a meal.

• If you don't have quite enough fish, cut it into pieces and use it in a chunky one-pot meal. Alternatively, poach the fish and combine it with mashed potato to make fishcakes.

• To make a small roasting chicken feed more people, stuff it with well-flavoured couscous and surround the bird with grilled sausages. Alternatively, joint the chicken and use the pieces to make a casserole or curry, and serve it with rice and a side dish.

• You can also make a dish more substantial by boosting it with extra ingredients. Most recipes can be easily doubled, but if all else fails you can stretch a dish simply by serving it with bread, potatoes or dumplings (true Grandma choices), or the healthier options of vegetables, rice, beans or pasta.

• Dress up a plain cake and make it bigger by cutting it into layers, then spreading it with cream and piling on fresh fruit.

• There are plenty of ways to make desserts go further, or to make it appear as though a small portion was intentional. Serve an elegant sliver of tart with a dollop of whipped cream or crème fraîche and dust with icing sugar, or scoop a modest portion of ice-cream into an elegant stemmed glass and drizzle with a fruit coulis or chocolate sauce (see page 355 for recipes).

Extending meals with grains, pulses and pasta

Bulghur, also known as cracked wheat, is a delicious alternative to rice and is really easy to prepare. Place it in a heatproof bowl, pour boiling water over it, then cover and leave to soak for 20 minutes. Drain it well. Enjoy the bulghur plain, or toss it with a little olive oil and lemon juice and add plenty of chopped fresh herbs. Bulghur goes well with all kinds of grilled meats and fish, roasts and casseroles.

Couscous is good with stews and casseroles, and is inexpensive, quick and easy to prepare.

Pasta or noodles are a great accompaniment to a meat, fish or poultry dish, or can be added to soups to bulk them out.

Don't throw it away

- **Heat soft or stale biscuits** in a preheated 160°C/gas 3 oven for a few minutes, then cool them on a wire rack. They will regain their crispness and will taste as good as new.
- **Use up** any leftover red or white wine for meat stock, or white wine for fish and poultry stock. It will greatly enhance the flavour. Leftover wine is also perfect for adding flavour to casseroles and stews.
- **Keep** the rinds from hard cheese, such as Parmesan, or deli meats like pancetta. Freeze them, then add them to the pan for extra flavour in your next soup or casserole; just discard before serving.
- **Save** chicken carcasses, ham bones and clean vegetable offcuts (but not peelings) to make your own flavoursome stock.
- **Don't waste** the rind from citrus fruits. Grate them and freeze them for use in breads, cakes and icings.

Pulses, such as beans and lentils, are a healthy alternative to mashed potatoes for roasts or braised and grilled dishes. They can be a little bland on their own, but it's easy to jazz them up with a little extra virgin olive oil, crushed garlic and lemon juice, or soured cream and some chopped fresh herbs.

Rice goes with all sorts of stews, casseroles, curries, stir-fries and other Asian dishes. It can also be added to soups.

Potato power

- Everyone loves mashed potato, so there will be few objections to using it to extend a meal.
- To spruce up mashed potatoes, stir a little pesto, mustard or horseradish sauce through the mashed potatoes just before serving.
- If you're short of potatoes, mash them with an equal quantity of carrots for a colourful, healthy mash. Alternatively, roast them with other vegetables such as pumpkin and parsnips.
- For mashed mixed root vegetables, boil two or three different vegetables (choose from carrots, swedes, parsnips, celeriac, potatoes or sweet potatoes) together until tender, then mash them with butter and milk, or with yoghurt and snipped fresh chives.
- To make scrumptious oven-baked chips, scrub some potatoes, leaving the skin on, then cut into thick wedges. Brush lightly with olive oil, place on a baking tray and bake for 30 to 40 minutes in a hot oven. If you like, you can also sprinkle the potatoes with dried herbs, fennel seeds, paprika or cajun seasoning before roasting them.
- As a simple but substantial side dish, toss steamed or boiled baby new potatoes with olive oil, lemon zest and chopped fresh mint.
- Make a warm potato salad by tossing sliced, boiled new potatoes with a little vinaigrette dressing and some snipped fresh herbs, such as chives or parsley.

Brilliant ways with leftovers

Throwing away leftovers is a waste of good food and money when you could transform them into new meals instead. Store any remains in a sealed container in the fridge and use them the next day, or within two days at the very latest. Most leftovers make a great addition to a chunky soup, but try these ideas too.

- **Cooked rice** Toss with chopped raw vegetables and dressing to make a salad, or turn it into fried rice by stir-frying it with vegetables and a little meat.
- **Cooked pasta** If there's enough for another serving, stir it into a tomato-based sauce, add some cooked vegetables and perhaps some chopped ham. Sprinkle with grated cheese and bake in a moderate oven until the cheese is golden and bubbling. If you have only a small amount of leftover cooked pasta, add it to a minestrone-style soup.
- **Cooked fish and shellfish** These can be added to salads, sauces, soups, stir-fries, risottos or pizza toppings, or used in fishcakes, tarts and pastry parcels. You can also use leftover cooked fish in a frittata, or mix it through croquettes or patties.
- **Cooked meat or poultry** Leftovers from a roast can be added to almost anything: sandwiches, salads, sauces, fillings for pies or pancake parcels, omelettes, hashes, and rice and pasta dishes. For instance, if you have leftover roast chicken, use it in a pie, frittata or risotto. Also, chicken scraps are great combined with mashed potato, then shaped into croquettes or patties and fried.

- **Cooked vegetables** These make a fantastic filling for an omelette, or try adding them to a tortilla or quiche. They are also tasty fried with leftover potatoes, or stirred into a sauce to go with pasta. Or you can stir them into a creamy sauce, spoon them into little baking dishes, top with breadcrumbs, grated cheese or a savoury crumble topping, then briefly grill or bake them to make a tempting gratin.
- **Stale bread** Use in bread and butter pudding (see page 264), or make into breadcrumbs for use in stuffings, gratin toppings or crispy coatings. Alternatively, cut the bread into small cubes, fry until crisp and golden and sprinkle over salads or soups for a tasty garnish.
- **Leftover uncooked pastry** Don't throw pastry away, instead gently roll it into a ball, wrap in aluminium foil and freeze it. Later, grate it over baked fruit dishes before baking for an instant, no-fuss topping.
- **Dry plain cake** Use up any leftover or stale cake as the base for a fantastic trifle (see page 287), or turn it into cake crumbs in a food processor and freeze for use in crumbles or dessert bakes.

Handy substitutes

With the exception of baking recipes, many recipes are quite flexible, so if you run out of a certain ingredient, you can often replace it with another food from the same 'family' (for example, substitute one firm white fish for another, and replace lemons with limes).

Many dishes can also be easily adapted for vegetarians by swapping tofu for meat or poultry, and by using vegetable stock instead of meat stock.

- Swordfish is a substitute for fresh tuna, and trout for salmon; chicken or turkey will stand in for pork.
- Leeks can be used instead of onions or shallots.
- Chard can stand in for spinach, while fennel makes a tasty substitute for celery.
- Peas are a great substitute for broad beans; mangetout can be used instead of asparagus.
- Pears can be substituted for apples, and peaches for mango, pawpaw or papaya.
- Dried apricots can be used instead of dried prunes or figs.
- Tangy goat's cheese can replace most kinds of blue cheese.
- Couscous can also be used if bulghur or rice are called for.
- Almonds are a cheaper alternative to pine nuts.

Saving energy costs

Inefficient cooking is a waste of money as it uses up a lot of extra electricity or gas. Use the tips below to reduce your power bill.

- Cooking in bulk saves energy and therefore money, but can also save you time in the long run. It takes just a little extra effort to cook up a double or triple batch of a soup or stew, or an extra pudding or pie. One batch can be eaten straight away, while the rest can be frozen for another meal.
- When the oven is on, you can bake several dishes at the same time. If you're roasting

Homemade soups are endlessly versatile. In a minestrone, you can use whatever vegetables are good value and currently in season.

a chicken, prepare roast vegetables as an accompaniment. Or, if you're making a baked dessert, roast a few peppers at the same time to use in a salad the next day.

- Save power when baking a number of batches of biscuits. Rather than have the hot oven waiting while you remove biscuits and re-line the baking trays, keep a couple of trays lined and ready so that you can keep the batches rolling.
- Cook several different ingredients at the same time in a layered steamer that's been placed over a single pan of simmering water. Or use a microwave to cook vegetables quickly – take care not to scorch them though.
- Invest in a set of good-quality, heavy-based pans with tight-fitting lids that will keep in the heat. Although they may cost more initially, the outlay will be well worth it in the long run.

Preserving fruits and vegetables

Grandma relied on preserving to save surplus produce for leaner times or have it on hand out of season. Homemade pickles and jams have an unbeatable flavour, and there's a pleasing sense of self-sufficiency in preserving your own food.

Freezing herbs

If you freeze herbs, much of their colour and flavour can be retained. Freezing is ideal for herbs with very fine leaves or a high moisture content, and for those that lose their taste when dried, such as fennel, dill, tarragon, chives, parsley, chervil and basil. Herbs can be frozen into ice cubes for use in 'wet' dishes such as soups – just rinse them, chop finely and place a tablespoon in each segment of an ice-cube tray, then top up with water and freeze. When the herbs are frozen, transfer them to a container and label them.

Drying herbs

If you grow your own herbs, drying them will provide a year-round supply of wonderful flavours. The best time to pick herbs for preserving is just before they are due to flower, as this is when they are at their most pungent. Choose a dry day and pick the herbs early in the morning after the dew has dried but before the sun is fully on them. Seeds, such as coriander, dill and fennel, can also be preserved and should be picked as soon as they have formed on the plants.

Drying leaves

Lay a piece of muslin on a large wire cooling rack and place it in a warm, dry, airy place, out of direct sunlight. Lay the herbs on the muslin, spacing them a little apart from each other. Cover with a second piece of muslin and leave for one to four days, until they are dry and brittle – don't leave them any longer

than necessary or they will lose their flavour. Crumble the leaves, or strip them from the stems and store in clean glass jars in a cool, dark cupboard. Label and date the jars.

Drying seeds

Keep the flower heads and stems intact and place on trays lined with kitchen paper. Cover with another layer of paper to keep off the dust. Leave in a warm, dry, airy place for 10 to 14 days, or until the seeds are dry. Shake the seeds from the flower heads onto the paper, then pour into clean, dry jars. Alternatively, tie the stems in bunches and place them, heads down, in paper bags and hang until dry. Shake the seeds into the bag, then store in dry jars. Label and date the jars.

Freezing vegetables

To preserve their colour, flavour and texture, always blanch vegetables before you freeze them. Allow 3 litres of boiling water and 2 teaspoons of salt for every 500g vegetables.

- First scrub, wash or peel the vegetables if necessary, then cut them into bite-sized pieces and place in a wire basket.
- Plunge the basket into the boiling salted water and bring the water back to the boil.
- Blanch for the times recommended below, then drain and plunge into iced water to stop the vegetables cooking further.
- Drain again and pack into bags or containers and freeze. (If you have young children who are still eating soft food, purée the vegetables in a food processor before freezing them.)
- Blanch root vegetables, asparagus, beans, broad beans, broccoli, brussels sprouts, cauliflower, celeriac, courgettes, leeks and

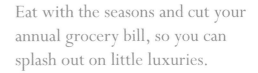

Eat with the seasons and cut your annual grocery bill, so you can splash out on little luxuries.

peas for about 2 minutes, depending on their size and thickness.
- Blanch spinach for 1 minute.
- Blanch small cobs of corn for 4 minutes and large corn cobs for 8 minutes.

Pickling vegetables

Pickles, relishes and chutneys rely on salt, sugar and vinegar to preserve the food and stop mould forming. Use a good-quality, well-flavoured vinegar such as red or white wine vinegar or cider vinegar; malt vinegar has a harsher taste. Pickles can be made from both ripe and unripe vegetables, but only fresh, sound produce should be used. Herbs and spices are often added to pickles for added flavour; the fresher the herbs and spices, the better the result. Use only plastic or plastic-coated lids for pickles, as the vinegar will corrode metal lids and cause spoilage. See 'Basics and techniques' (page 361) for pickle and chutney recipes and information on sterilising jars.

Freezing fruits

Most fruits don't freeze well, as the ice ruptures their cell walls and causes them to become mushy on thawing. Berries of all kinds are an exception. Frozen berries are particularly good for baking and don't need to be thawed before being added to batter.

To freeze your own berries, hull, rinse and dry perfect specimens of fruit, then freeze them in a single layer, uncovered, on a baking tray lined with baking parchment. When they are frozen, pack them into containers. Strawberries frozen in this way will be very soft when thawed and are best used in a coulis or purée rather than as whole fruits.

Bottling fruits

Boiling fruit in a sugar syrup is an excellent way of preserving it. The bottled fruits can be used in cooking, on top of breakfast cereal, or with ice cream, custard or cream for a quick and easy dessert. Bottled fruits require special preserving jars and lids. You'll need to sterilise the rubber bands and screw-on lids in boiling water (see 'Basics and techniques', page 360).

Preparing the fruit

Apples and pears Wash, then core, peel, halve or slice the fruit. Place in cold water with lemon juice to stop discolouration while preparing the rest.

Apricots, peaches and nectarines Remove the skins and leave whole, or halve and stone them.

Berries Remove the stems and hull them; wash the fruit only if necessary, draining well.

Mangoes Cut the flesh from the skin and stone.

Pineapple Remove the skin and all the brown 'eyes'. Slice and remove the central core. Leave in slices or cut into pieces.

Plums and cherries Remove the stalks, then wash the fruit but leave them whole.

Rhubarb Trim off leaves and wash the stalks, then cut into 2cm to 3cm lengths.

To sterilise clean jars for bottling, wash them in your dishwasher, using the rinse cycle and the hottest water temperature setting. Don't use any detergent.

Growing your own

You can grow your own fruit and vegetables even if you don't have a garden. Salad leaves, peppers, courgette flowers, tomatoes and strawberries can be grown in pots on a terrace or balcony. Use large pots and water often. If you're using terracotta pots, waterproof them first so the soil they hold won't dry out too quickly.

Other options for small spaces include using garden walls or fences to grow climbing vegetables such as tomatoes and peas, and installing pots of herbs on trellises. You can hang planter boxes off the outside, as well as the inside or on top of, a balcony railing. Or plant a range of herbs in the holes of a strawberry pot.

Preparing the sugar syrup

For a 500ml jar you'll need about 350g prepared fruit and 250ml of sugar syrup to cover the fruit. As a guide, 220g sugar and 500ml water will make about 750ml sugar syrup, so adjust the quantities according to how much fruit you would like to bottle.

To make the sugar syrup, combine the sugar and water in a saucepan over a low heat and stir until the sugar has completely dissolved. Bring to the boil and allow to boil for 1 minute, then remove from the heat.

The preserving process

- If using the hob method, fill a large saucepan or preserving saucepan halfway with water. Place a tea towel or wads of newspaper in the bottom of the pan. Place only enough bottles in the saucepan so they fit comfortably. Wrap cloths or newspapers around each bottle and secure with rubber bands, to protect them from touching other bottles, which could cause cracking. Cover with more water, to 2.5cm over the top of the jars. Bring to a fast boil, then turn down to a gentle boil and cover the pan. Use a timer for the different. Add more boiling water if necessary during cooking. When the jars have been preserved, carefully remove them from the pan, using thick rubber gloves, tongs or special jar-removing tongs.
- Only use the oven method with fruit that has a high acid content as it's less stable.
- Preheat oven to 150°C/gas 2, leaving only the centre shelf in place. Pack fruit into clean, warm jars (see page 360). Stand the jars in a heavy roasting tin lined with several layers of newspaper. Space the jars at least 5cm apart and, to ensure they heat through evenly, process one batch at a time.
- Bring the sugar syrup to the boil and pour into the filled jars to come within 3cm of the top. Screw lids on lightly. Place the jars in the oven and

---

Cooking times

Oven method

- For four jars of up to 1 litre of soft fruit, 35 to 40 minutes.
- For five to ten jars of up to 1.5 litres of soft fruit, 40 to 60 minutes.
- For up to four jars of stone and other fruits, 45 to 50 minutes; five or more, 50 to 70 minutes.

Water-bath hob method

- For 500ml to 1 litre jars, 20 to 25 minutes (apples, pears, cherries, plums, stone fruits).
- For 250ml to 500ml jars, 15 minutes (rhubarb).
- For 500ml to 1 litre jars, 15 to 20 minutes (berries).
- For 500ml to 1 litre jars, 15 to 20 minutes (pineapple).

---

cook for the recommended time (see box above), according to the type of fruit.
- Once the minimum time has been reached, check the oven frequently. As soon as bubbles rise regularly, remove the jars from the oven.
- Stand the processed jars on a wooden board. Wipe the tops with a damp cloth to remove any syrup. Tighten up the clips, screw on the sealing rings or tighten the screw-on lids. Leave the jars for 2 to 3 minutes, then tighten the lids again. Leave on the board until cold.
- When the jars are cold, test them to make sure they are vacuum sealed. Undo the clip or ring and carefully lift each jar a little by its lid – if the lid holds, a seal has been formed. Metal lids on screw-top jars become concave when a vacuum has been created. Use the contents of any unsealed jars immediately.
- Label, date and store the jars in a cool, dark place. Properly sealed, the contents will keep indefinitely. Once opened, they must be refrigerated and used within three to four days.

soups and starters

Grandmas all over the world knew the benefits of a really good soup – and how to start a meal with style. Here's a fine selection of classic soups, snacks and starters from Grandma's day, streamlined for the busy modern cook, but retaining their nourishing goodness and feel-good factor.

Express

Extra thrifty

Soup of pasta and beans

A favourite Italian peasant dish that traditionally is made with dried cannellini beans that need hours of soaking. Our version, which uses canned beans, is just as tasty but will be on the table in 20 minutes.

2 tablespoons extra virgin olive oil, plus more for drizzling
2 to 3 cloves garlic, crushed
2 x 400g cans cannellini beans
400g can chopped tomatoes
500ml beef stock (see Basics)
4 tablespoons fresh herbs, such as oregano, sage or basil leaves, plus extra to garnish
150g macaroni
grated or flaked Parmesan, to serve

Serves 4 (makes about 2 litres)
Preparation 5 minutes
Cooking 15 minutes

1 Heat the olive oil in a large saucepan over a low heat. Add the garlic and sauté for a few minutes. Add one can of beans (with their liquid) to the pan and mash until soft, using a potato masher.

2 Add the tomatoes, stock and half the herbs, then increase the heat and bring to the boil. Add the pasta and cook until it's just tender, stirring occasionally so it doesn't stick to the bottom of the pan, and adding some boiling water if the pasta is absorbing too much liquid.

3 Drain and rinse the remaining can of beans and add to the soup. Stir to warm through, then season with salt and freshly ground black pepper.

4 Ladle the soup into warm bowls and drizzle with a little olive oil. Top with grated or flaked Parmesan and more of the herb leaves, such as basil – shown here.

Money saver

Dried beans are more economical than canned beans. Soak and cook them in bulk and freeze until required. There's no need to thaw them before adding to a soup or stew.

Waste not, want not

To preserve fresh herbs, chop them, place in ice-cube trays with a little water, then freeze. Once frozen, store in a plastic bag in the freezer and use in soups and casseroles.

Quick   **Thrifty**

Vegetable soup with pesto

Grandma would have made this soup with any vegetables that were in season — such as peas, courgettes, mushrooms and sweet peppers. The fresh pesto topping is most delicious in summer when basil is at its peak.

2 tablespoons olive oil
1 small onion, finely chopped
2 cloves garlic, crushed
2 potatoes, peeled and diced
2 carrots, peeled and diced
2 celery stalks, finely diced
400g can chopped tomatoes
1.5 to 2 litres beef or chicken
    stock (see Basics)
2 tablespoons chopped fresh basil
150g small macaroni
125g green beans, chopped
400g can borlotti beans, drained
    and rinsed
400g can cannellini beans,
    drained and rinsed
grated Parmesan, to serve

PESTO
2 cloves garlic, peeled
100g fresh basil leaves
2 tablespoons pine nuts, toasted
80ml olive oil
35g grated Parmesan

Serves 6 (makes about 2.5 litres)
Preparation 20 minutes
Cooking 20 minutes

1 Heat the olive oil in a large saucepan over low heat. Sauté the onion and garlic for a few minutes, until they are lightly golden.

2 Add the potatoes, carrots and celery and stir for 1 minute. Add the tomatoes with all their juice, along with the stock and basil. Increase the heat and bring to the boil, then stir in the macaroni. Cook for 10 minutes or until the pasta is just tender.

3 Reduce the heat to medium, then add the green beans, borlotti beans and cannellini beans. Simmer for 2 to 3 minutes, then season well with salt and freshly ground black pepper.

4 Meanwhile, make the pesto. Put the garlic, basil and pine nuts in a food processor and blend until finely chopped. Work in the olive oil, then scoop the pesto into a bowl and stir the Parmesan through.

5 Ladle the soup into warm bowls and sprinkle with grated Parmesan. Allow diners to serve their own pesto.

Grandma's secret

If your soup is on the salty side, don't throw it away but simply add a raw peeled potato to the pot. The extra salt will be absorbed as if by magic.

Pumpkin soup

Pumpkins grow fast and plentifully over the warm summer months. This richly flavoured soup is superb in autumn, when this prolific crop is truly abundant.

1 tablespoon olive oil

1 large onion, finely chopped

1.5kg pumpkin, peeled, seeded and chopped into 2cm cubes

1 litre chicken stock (see Basics)

300ml double cream

60ml soured cream

2 tablespoons finely chopped fresh chives

Serves 4 (makes about 2 litres)
Preparation 5 minutes
Cooking 25 minutes

1 Heat the olive oil in a large, deep saucepan over a medium heat. Add the onion and sauté for 3 to 4 minutes, or until soft. Add the pumpkin and stock. Increase the heat to high and bring to the boil, then reduce the heat and simmer, uncovered, for 20 minutes, or until the pumpkin is soft.

2 Remove the saucepan from the heat. Using a hand-held blender or food processor, purée the pumpkin mixture until smooth. Gently reheat, then stir in the double cream and bring to a simmer over a medium heat.

3 Ladle into warm bowls or mugs. Top with a little sour cream, sprinkle with the chives and serve.

Kitchen wisdom

Pumpkin soup freezes well, so if you have a glut, it's worth making a large batch and freezing for later use.

Prepare and relax   **Thrifty**

Rich onion soup

When making onion soup, don't rush the cooking of the onions – slow and gentle caramelisation is essential for a sweetly mellow flavour.

1 tablespoon olive oil
1 tablespoon butter
1.25kg onions, halved and
    thinly sliced
2 teaspoons soft brown sugar
1 tablespoon plain flour
1 litre chicken or beef stock
    (see Basics)
1 baguette, cut into 12 slices
    each about 1.5cm thick
130g grated Gruyère cheese

Serves 4 (makes about 1.75 litres)
Preparation 10 minutes
Cooking 55 minutes

Waste not, want not

If you have some leftover white wine in the fridge, add it with the stock to enhance the final flavour.

1 Heat the olive oil and butter in a large, deep saucepan until the butter melts. Add the onions and cook over a medium-low heat for 15 minutes, stirring occasionally. Increase the heat to medium and cook for a further 20 minutes, or until golden brown. Stir in the sugar and flour, mixing well. Pour in the stock and 500ml water, stirring constantly until well combined. Bring to the boil, then reduce the heat and simmer for 15 minutes, or until the mixture is slightly thickened.

2 Just before serving, preheat the grill to high. Toast the slices of bread under the grill on both sides until they are lightly golden. Sprinkle with the cheese and briefly grill until it has melted fully.

3 Ladle the soup into warm bowls. Top each with three toasts and serve quickly before the bread goes soggy.

Prepare and relax

Thrifty

Scotch broth

Traditionally made with mutton, this modern version of a much-loved broth uses lamb leg chops, which are more easily available today. Simple to put together, it's the perfect antidote to a rainy weekend.

1 tablespoon olive oil
750g lamb leg chops
1 litre beef stock (see Basics)
100g pearl barley
2 carrots, peeled, cut in half
**   lengthways, then sliced**
2 swedes, peeled and cut into
**   2cm cubes**
15g chopped fresh parsley

Serves 4 to 6 (makes about
     2.75 litres)
Preparation 10 minutes
Cooking 1 hour 45 minutes

Grandma's secret

When buying lamb, check that the fat is a creamy white – a yellowish tinge may indicate that the meat is old.

1 Heat the olive oil in a large, heavy-based saucepan over a medium heat. Add the lamb chops and cook for 3 minutes on each side, or until browned. Pour the stock and 2 litres water over the chops and bring to the boil. Reduce the heat to low and gently simmer for 45 minutes, skimming the froth regularly.

2 Add the barley, carrots and swedes and partially cover the pan. Simmer gently for 45 minutes, or until the barley is tender but not mushy.

3 Remove the lamb chops from the soup. Strip off the meat, chop it roughly into small pieces and return to the soup, discarding the bones.

4 Season with salt and freshly ground black pepper, ladle into warm bowls and serve sprinkled with parsley.

Variations

Instead of lamb leg chops, use lamb shanks if you can find them at a good price. You can also use cabbage and leeks instead of root vegetables.

Potato and leek soup

Using starchy potatoes will give the soup a creamier texture. To impart a lovely green hue, blend the finished soup with some chopped fresh parsley.

60ml olive oil

3 slices bread, crusts removed and cut into 1cm cubes

1 onion, chopped

2 leeks, white part only, washed well and sliced

2 cloves garlic, crushed

4 large potatoes (750g), peeled and cut into 2cm cubes

1 litre chicken or vegetable stock (see Basics)

ground white pepper, to taste

Serves 4 to 6 (makes about 2.75 litres)

Preparation 10 minutes

Cooking 30 minutes

1 Preheat the oven to 200°C/gas 6. Line a baking tray with greaseproof paper or baking parchment. Pour half the olive oil into a bowl, add the bread cubes and toss until well coated. Spread the bread cubes over the baking tray and bake for 10 to 15 minutes, or until the croutons are light golden brown. Leave to cool.

2 Meanwhile, heat the remaining oil in a large saucepan over a medium heat. Sauté the onion and leeks for 4 to 5 minutes, or until soft. Add the garlic and cook for 1 minute, then add the potatoes, stock and 500ml water and bring to the boil. Reduce the heat to medium-low and simmer for 20 to 25 minutes, or until the vegetables are soft.

3 Using a hand-held blender or food processor, purée the soup until smooth – or leave some texture if you prefer. Season with salt and ground white pepper to taste, then ladle into warm bowls and top with the croutons.

Variations

Add chopped bacon to the soup when frying the onion and leek. Alternatively, fry or grill thin slices of prosciutto until crisp, then shred and serve on top of the soup. You can also replace the potatoes with sweet potatoes.

Kitchen wisdom

To prepare leeks, rinse well, then chop off the roots, green outer leaves and tops, leaving only the white stalk. Cut in half lengthways, hold the root end firmly, then fan the layers open and rinse under running water to release any sand or grit.

Quick

Thrifty

Lentil soup

A quick and nourishing soup that's ideal for a winter lunch or simple supper. Swiss chard is delicious in this soup as an alternative to spinach.

1 tablespoon olive oil
1 large onion, finely chopped
1 large carrot, peeled and diced
1 large potato, peeled and diced
2 celery stalks, diced
1 litre chicken or vegetable stock
  (see Basics)
2 x 400g cans lentils, drained
  and rinsed
60ml lemon juice
100g baby spinach leaves,
  shredded

Serves 4 to 6 (makes about
  2.75 litres)
Preparation 10 minutes
Cooking 30 minutes

1 Heat the olive oil in a large saucepan over a medium heat. Add the onion, carrot, potato and celery and sauté for 10 minutes, or until just tender.

2 Add the stock and 1 litre water. Bring to the boil, then reduce the heat to medium-low and simmer for 15 minutes, or until the vegetables are soft.

3 Stir in the lentils and lemon juice and cook for 3 to 4 minutes, or until the lentils are heated through. Stir in the spinach, ladle into warm bowls and serve.

Variations

For a super-thrifty soup, soak 200g dried green lentils in water overnight, then drain. Cook the soup as directed, but cook the lentils a little longer (25 to 30 minutes), until tender. Dried red lentils can also be used instead of green lentils; add them straight to the soup and cook for about 15 minutes.

Grandma's secret

One of Mother Nature's hidden treats, lentils are incredibly nutritious and extremely versatile. Even the most committed carnivores will enjoy the healing qualities of this sustaining soup – or you could humour them by adding a few cubes of ham or bacon.

Super quick   **Thrifty**

Chicken noodle soup

The ultimate remedy for winter sniffles, the healing properties of this magic soup have been backed up by science. Grandma would have used a stewing fowl, but you can use a barbecued bird or the remains of a roast chicken.

Half a large, shop-bought barbecued chicken or leftover cooked chicken
1 tablespoon olive oil
1 large onion, diced
2 carrots, peeled and diced
2 celery stalks, diced
1 litre chicken stock (see Basics)
2 x 85g packets quick noodles

Serves 4 (makes about 2 litres)
Preparation 15 minutes
Cooking 15 minutes

1 Remove the skin and meat from the chicken, then discard the skin and bones. Shred or chop the meat and set aside.

2 Heat the olive oil in a large, deep saucepan over a medium heat. Sauté the onion, carrots and celery for 5 to 7 minutes, or until the vegetables are tender. Add the stock and 1 litre of water and bring to the boil.

3 Break up the noodles while they're still in the packets, then add to the soup with the chicken meat. Cook for 2 minutes, or until the noodles are tender and the chicken is heated through. Serve immediately.

Variations

Instead of instant packet noodles, try using vermicelli, rice noodles or egg noodles in the soup and flavouring it with herbs and spices from South-east Asia, such as slices of fresh ginger, a little fresh chilli and a handful of coriander.

Grandma's secret

Whether it's the steam that helps to clear congestion, or the anti-inflammatory effect of its ingredients, scientific research has supported Grandma's belief in chicken noodle soup as a cold remedy.

Best-ever tomato soup

With canned tomatoes in your pantry you can enjoy this speedy soup at any time of year. In high summer, when flavourful ripe tomatoes abound, make the soup fresh from scratch.

1 tablespoon olive oil
1 tablespoon butter
1 large onion, finely chopped
2 cloves garlic, crushed
680g bottle tomato passata
400g can chopped tomatoes
1 litre chicken or vegetable stock
    (see Basics)
15g roughly chopped fresh basil
    (optional)
garlic bread, to serve

Serves 4 to 6 (makes about
    2.75 litres)
Preparation 5 minutes
Cooking 10 minutes

1 Heat the olive oil and butter in a large saucepan over a medium heat until the butter melts. Add the onion and sauté for 3 to 4 minutes, or until soft. Add the garlic and cook for a further minute.

2 Add the passata, tomatoes and stock and bring to the boil. Reduce the heat to medium-low and simmer gently for 5 minutes.

3 Using a hand-held blender or food processor, purée the soup until smooth. Season with salt and freshly ground black pepper, then ladle into warm bowls. Sprinkle with the basil, if using, and serve with garlic bread.

Variation

Instead of the passata use 2kg peeled, chopped tomatoes, 500ml water and 3 tablespoons of tomato purée. The finished soup will freeze for up to four months.

Minestrone

Italian grandmas had no rigid rules for what went in a minestrone — as long as the result was hearty, with plenty of vegetables, white beans and pasta or rice.

1 tablespoon olive oil
1 large onion, finely chopped
3 slices bacon, rind removed, chopped
680g bottle tomato passata
1 litre beef stock (see Basics)
150g macaroni
3 courgettes, diced
150g green beans, cut into thirds
400g can cannellini beans, drained and rinsed
4 tablespoons chopped fresh basil leaves (optional)
grated Parmesan, to serve
toasted ciabatta bread, to serve

Serves 4 to 6 (makes about 3 litres)
Preparation 10 minutes
Cooking 20 minutes

1 Heat the olive oil in a large saucepan over a medium heat. Add the onion and bacon and cook for 3 to 4 minutes, or until soft. Add the passata, stock and 750ml water. Increase the heat to high and bring to the boil.

2 Add the pasta and cook, stirring occasionally, for 8 minutes, or until almost tender. Add the courgettes, green beans and cannellini beans and stir until well combined. Cook for 2 to 3 minutes or until the vegetables are tender but not over-soft.

3 Ladle into warm bowls and top with the basil, if using, and Parmesan. Serve with slices of toasted ciabatta.

Variations

If you like, you can replace the bacon with spicy pancetta. You can also use any type of canned beans.

Time saver

To save time chopping vegetables, use a bag of mixed frozen vegetables.

Express

Thrifty

Pea soup with ham

When you've had a long, cold day outdoors, what you really want is hot, hearty soup — but without having to wait for it. This fresh take on one of Grandma's time-honoured classics will be ready in a flash.

1 tablespoon olive oil
1 onion, finely chopped
250g smoked ham, rind removed,
    chopped
1 litre chicken stock (see Basics)
500g frozen peas
10g fresh mint, roughly chopped

Serves 4 to 6 (makes about
    2.5 litres)
Preparation 5 minutes
Cooking 15 minutes

1 Heat the olive oil in a large saucepan over a medium heat. Add the onion and sauté for 3 to 4 minutes or until soft and light golden. Add most of the ham (reserving some as a garnish), stirring well.

2 Pour in the stock and 750ml water and bring to the boil. Add the peas and cook for 2 to 3 minutes or until they are heated through. Add the mint, reserving a little to garnish the soup.

3 Reserving some whole peas as a garnish, remove most of the soup to a bowl. Using a hand-held blender or food processor, purée until smooth. Return the purée to the saucepan and cook for 3 to 4 minutes to heat through.

4 Ladle into warm bowls and serve garnished with some reserved ham, peas and mint.

Grandma's secret

For a more traditional version of this soup, soak 200g green split peas in a bowl of water overnight and use a ham hock instead of the sliced ham. Cook the hock in the soup for about 1 hour, adding the drained peas in the last 30 minutes. Remove the hock, roughly chop the meat and return it to the soup. Heat through and serve.

Prepare and relax

Thrifty

Cream of chicken soup

Grandma knew how to extract every last bit of the goodness from a juicy bird. Slow, patient simmering will yield a rich, thick and flavoursome soup that's worlds away from canned versions in taste and satisfaction.

1.3kg whole chicken
3 tablespoons butter
1 tablespoon olive oil
1 onion, finely chopped
2 carrots, peeled and cut into
    1cm cubes
2 celery stalks, diced
50g plain flour
300ml double cream
150g frozen sweetcorn
10g fresh parsley

Serves 4 to 6 (makes about
    2.75 litres)
Preparation 10 minutes
Cooking 1 hour 15 minutes

Waste not, want not

The remaining chicken stock can be used in other soup recipes or in any dishes that require chicken stock.

1 Put the chicken in a large saucepan and cover with cold water (about 3 litres). Place over medium-high heat and bring to the boil, then reduce the heat to medium. Simmer, partially covered, for 45 minutes, or until the chicken is cooked through, skimming the froth regularly. (Don't allow the broth to boil or the chicken will be tough and tasteless.) Remove the pan from the heat.

2 Remove the chicken to a large plate. When it's cool enough to handle, remove the meat and shred or roughly chop into pieces, discarding the skin and carcass. Strain the stock into a large bowl.

3 Heat the butter and olive oil in a saucepan over a medium heat until the butter melts. Add the onion, carrots and celery and sauté for 8 minutes, or until the vegetables are tender.

4 Sprinkle the vegetables with the flour and stir in well. Remove the saucepan from the heat and slowly add 2 litres of the strained stock, stirring constantly. Return to the heat and bring the mixture to the boil.

5 Stir in the cream, shredded chicken and sweetcorn and simmer for 10 minutes to heat through. Season with salt and freshly ground black pepper.

6 Ladle the finished soup into warm bowls, sprinkle with a few leaves of parsley and serve.

Prepare and relax　　**Thrifty**

Salmon mousse

Smart and versatile, this luxurious mousse, accompanied by dainty melba toasts, makes a terrific light lunch or a superb starter at dinner.

6 slices white bread, crusts
　　removed
2 eggs, separated
2 tablespoons lemon juice
80g butter, melted
200g smoked salmon,
　　roughly chopped
80ml single cream
60g good-quality mayonnaise
1 teaspoon powdered gelatine
2 tablespoons finely chopped
　　fresh chives

Serves 4
Preparation 20 minutes
Cooking 30 minutes,
　　plus 2 hours to set

1 Preheat the oven to 150°C/gas 2.

2 Cut each slice of bread into four small triangles and place on two baking trays. Bake for 30 minutes, turning once, or until the toasts are lightly browned and crisp. Leave to cool, then store in an airtight container until required.

3 Meanwhile, put the egg yolks and lemon juice in a food processor and blend for 30 seconds, or until combined. With the motor running, slowly add the melted butter. Add the salmon, cream and mayonnaise, process until well combined, then transfer to a bowl.

4 In a small heatproof bowl, whisk the gelatine into 1 tablespoon of water. Stand for 2 minutes, or until the gelatine is soft, then place in a bowl of boiling water for 5 minutes, or until the gelatine has dissolved. Leave to cool for 5 minutes, then stir into the salmon mixture.

5 Beat the egg whites in a small bowl using an electric whisk until soft peaks form. Gently fold half the egg whites through the salmon mixture using a large metal spoon. Add the remaining egg whites and most of the chives and gently fold through. Spoon into a serving bowl, then cover and refrigerate for 2 hours, or until set.

6 Serve the mousse sprinkled with the remaining chives, with the melba toasts on the side.

Variations
You can replace half of the smoked salmon with cooked prawns. Alternatively, you can replace all of the smoked salmon with smoked trout.

Super quick   **Extra thrifty**

Cheese straws

Party snacks don't come much simpler than cheese straws. To add a twist, spread the pastry with tomato purée and sprinkle with crumbled feta and some finely shredded Parmesan.

2 sheets frozen puff pastry, thawed
1 egg white, whisked
125g grated Cheddar
25g finely shredded Parmesan

Makes 56 straws
Preparation 10 minutes
Cooking 15 minutes

1 Preheat the oven to 200°C/gas 6. Line two baking trays with greaseproof paper or baking parchment.

2 Lay the pastry sheets on a flat surface and cut in half. Brush with the egg white and sprinkle with the cheeses.

3 Using a sharp knife, cut the pastry into strips 1.5cm wide. Gently twist the strips into a decorative shape and place them on the baking trays.

4 Bake for 10 to 15 minutes, or until the pastry is golden and crisp. Serve warm or cold. The cheese straws will keep in an airtight container for up to five days.

Stuffed eggs

Fun and tasty, hard-boiled eggs halved, scooped out and re-filled with an olive and pickle stuffing make a starter with plenty of retro appeal.

6 hard-boiled eggs (see Basics)
2 tablespoons good-quality mayonnaise
1 teaspoon Dijon mustard
45g pimento-stuffed green olives, finely chopped
1 small gherkin, finely chopped
1 tablespoon finely chopped fresh flat-leaved parsley

Makes 12 halves
Preparation 10 minutes
Cooking 10 minutes

1 Peel each hard-boiled egg, taking care to keep the white intact, then cut in half lengthways. Carefully remove the egg yolks from the whites, using a teaspoon. Place the yolks in a small bowl and mash with a fork.

2 Add the remaining ingredients and season with salt and freshly ground black pepper. Mix well to get a creamy consistency.

3 Pipe or gently spoon a little of the mixture into the egg whites, mounding it slightly to resemble an egg. Refrigerate until ready to serve.

Grandma's secret

If you don't have a piping bag, improvise by using a clean plastic bag with a tiny hole cut in one corner.

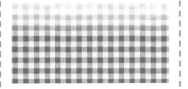

Quick **Thrifty**

Devilled crab

'Devilling' is a cooks' term for spiking a dish with spicy seasonings. Crab makes an elegant base, while the pepper, chilli and onion pack plenty of flavour.

2 tablespoons butter, plus
   1 tablespoon melted butter
1 small green pepper, finely diced
1 small onion, finely chopped
2 tablespoons plain flour
310ml milk
2 x 170g cans crabmeat, drained
2 hard-boiled eggs (see Basics),
   peeled and chopped
1 egg, beaten
2 tablespoons tomato sauce
¼ teaspoon chilli powder
80g fresh breadcrumbs (made
   from 2 slices of bread)
lemon wedges, to serve
toast fingers or crackers, to serve

Serves 4
Preparation 15 minutes
Cooking 25 minutes

1 Preheat the oven to 200°C/gas 6.

2 Melt 2 tablespoons of butter in a saucepan over a medium heat. Add the pepper and onion and sauté for 3 minutes, or until softened. Add the flour and stir until well combined. Cook for 1 minute, or until bubbly. Remove from the heat.

3 Slowly add the milk, stirring constantly until well combined. Return to the heat and stir constantly until the mixture comes to the boil. Reduce the heat to medium-low and simmer for 2 minutes, then remove from the heat.

4 Stir in the crabmeat, boiled eggs, beaten egg, tomato sauce and chilli powder. Spoon the mixture into four 185ml shallow, gratin-style dishes.

5 Combine the breadcrumbs and the extra tablespoon of melted butter and sprinkle over each dish. Bake for 15 minutes, or until the breadcrumbs are golden and crisp. Serve warm, along with lemon wedges and some toast fingers or crackers.

Waste not, want not

Never waste the ends of loaves of bread. Turn them into breadcrumbs and store them in the freezer where they'll always be ready to use. Breadcrumbs are often added to minced meat dishes, such as meat loaves or rissoles, to make them go further, and to lighten their texture.

Quick

Extra thrifty

Potato puffs

Snacks don't come much thriftier than this — you can make these light and fluffy puffs for hardly any money at all. Serve on their own as a starter, enjoy as a pick-me-up tummy filler or as a tasty side to a main meat dish.

500g mashing potatoes (such as King Edward or Maris Piper), peeled and chopped
80ml milk
knob of butter
1 egg, separated
2 tablespoons plain flour
1 small onion, finely chopped
3 tablespoons finely chopped fresh parsley
750ml vegetable oil, for deep-frying
1 to 2 tablespoons finely grated Parmesan

Makes 28
Preparation 20 minutes
Cooking 30 minutes

1 Put the potatoes in a saucepan and cover with cold water. Bring to the boil over a high heat, then reduce the heat and simmer for 15 to 20 minutes, or until soft. Drain the potatoes, return to the saucepan and cook for 1 to 2 minutes, or until dry.

2 Add the milk and butter and mash until smooth. Beat in the egg yolk and flour using a wooden spoon.

3 In a clean bowl, beat the egg white with a pinch of salt until stiff peaks form, using an electric mixer. Gently fold it into the mashed potatoes with the onion and parsley.

4 Heat the oil in a saucepan over a medium-high heat to 180°C/gas 4, or until a cube of bread dropped into the oil browns in 15 seconds. Drop tablespoons of the potato mixture into the oil and cook five or six potato puffs at a time for 1 to 2 minutes, or until golden. Turn and cook for a further minute. Transfer to a wire rack and season with salt and freshly ground black pepper. Sprinkle with the Parmesan and serve hot.

Variation

For a low-fat version, drop heaped tablespoons of the mixture onto two baking trays lined with greaseproof paper or baking parchment. Spray with olive oil cooking spray, season and sprinkle with Parmesan. Bake in a 200°C/gas 6 oven for 15 minutes, or until golden.

Blue cheese and walnut dip

Blue cheese and walnuts are a classy combination. If you have any of this delicious dip left over, try it as a gourmet topping for a chargrilled steak, chicken breast or pork chop.

250g light spreadable
  cream cheese
150g creamy blue cheese
½ small onion, grated
2 tablespoons milk
40g walnuts, finely chopped
crackers, to serve

Serves 6 (makes about 500g)
Preparation 10 minutes
Cooking nil

1 Put the cream cheese, blue cheese, onion and milk in a food processor and blend until smooth and well combined. Transfer to a bowl.

2 Reserving 2 teaspoons for garnishing, add the walnuts and stir until well combined. Spoon into a serving bowl and sprinkle with the reserved walnuts. Cover with plastic wrap and refrigerate until needed.

3 Serve with crackers. The dip will keep for up to three days refrigerated in an airtight container.

Variation
The blue cheese can be replaced with any other creamy soft cheese.

Super quick   **Extra thrifty**

Pâté pinwheels

These pinwheels are another simple yet versatile appetiser. Instead of pâté you could spread some pesto, chunky dip or even olive tapenade over the pastry and sprinkle with grated cheese.

2 sheets (425g) frozen puff pastry, thawed
170g shop-bought pâté of choice, at room temperature
1 egg, whisked

Makes 36
Preparation 10 minutes
Cooking 20 minutes

1 Preheat the oven to 200°C/gas 6. Line a large baking tray with baking parchment or greaseproof paper.

2 Place the pastry sheets on a flat surface and spread the pâté over the top. Roll each sheet into a long sausage shape, enclosing the pâté. Cut into slices 1cm thick.

3 Place the pinwheels on the baking tray and brush with the egg wash. Bake for 15 to 20 minutes, or until the pastry is golden and crisp. Serve warm.

Quick

Extra thrifty

Savoury scrolls

Flavoured with a cheesy-pepper filling, when you pull these yummy pastries out of the oven, you'll get plenty of appreciative comments. These scrolls are also excellent for packing in picnics and lunchboxes.

450g self-raising flour
3 tablespoons butter, chopped
310ml milk
60g tomato purée
1 small red pepper, finely chopped
1 small green pepper, finely chopped
110g grated Cheddar or mozzarella
100g ham, shredded
1 egg, beaten

Makes 16
Preparation 20 minutes
Cooking 20 minutes

1 Preheat the oven to 200°C/gas 6. Line a baking tray with baking parchment or greaseproof paper.

2 Sift the flour into a large bowl. Using your fingertips, rub in the butter until the mixture resembles fine breadcrumbs. Make a well in the centre and add the milk, then stir with a flat-edged knife until well combined.

3 Turn the dough onto a floured surface and lightly knead until smooth. Roll the dough out to a rectangle about 1cm thick, and about 38cm x 26cm in size.

4 Spread the tomato purée over the dough, then scatter the pepper, cheese and ham over the top. Carefully roll the dough over from the longest side of the rectangle, enclosing the filling. Cut into slices 2cm thick.

5 Place the scrolls on the baking tray and brush with beaten egg. Bake for 15 to 20 minutes, or until they are crisp and golden.

Variations

Try the following flavour partners with these scrolls: salami and cheese; a three-cheese combination using Stilton, Cheddar and Parmesan; or finely chopped seeded fresh tomato with chopped red onion, ham and chives.

Waste not, want not

The cooked scrolls can be frozen in an airtight container for up to three months.

eggs and dairy

Grandma really knew her eggs – and her cheese, cream
and milk. Using the simple goodness of dairy produce
you too can whip up a delectable array of appetising
dishes for breakfast, lunch and dinner.

Prepare and relax   **Extra thrifty**

Egg and bacon pie

Easier to make than a quiche, egg and bacon pie is perfect for a picnic; when travelling, wrap the whole pie dish in a clean tea towel to protect it.

melted butter, for brushing
2 sheets frozen puff pastry,
    thawed
5 slices bacon, rind removed, then
    chopped into large pieces
6 eggs
2 tablespoons roughly chopped
    fresh parsley or chives
1 egg yolk, beaten, or a little milk

Serves 4
Preparation 15 minutes,
    plus 20 minutes chilling
Cooking 35 minutes

1 Lightly brush the base and side of a shallow 20cm round pie dish with melted butter. Line the pie dish with one sheet of the pastry and refrigerate for 10 minutes.

2 Meanwhile, cook the bacon in a frying pan over a medium heat for 5 minutes, or until crisp. Place on kitchen paper to drain thoroughly.

3 Arrange half the bacon over the pastry base. Working one at a time, gently crack each egg into a small teacup, then tilt the teacup to slide the egg over the bacon, taking care not to break the yolks. Tilt the pie dish so that the whites of the eggs join together. Season with salt and freshly ground black pepper, then scatter the remaining bacon over. Top with the herbs.

4 Place the second sheet of pastry on top, press the edges together and trim. Brush the top of the pie with the egg yolk or some milk, then refrigerate for 10 minutes.

5 Meanwhile, preheat the oven to 200°C/gas 6. Bake the pie for 15 minutes, then bake at 180°C/gas 4 for a further 15 minutes, or until the pastry is golden. Serve warm or cold.

Kitchen wisdom

Thaw the frozen pastry slowly in the fridge if you have time – the pastry will puff more successfully.

Grandma's secret

Old-fashioned, shallow enamel pie dishes are ideal for cooking this pie. They conduct heat well, so you end up with a crisp puff pastry base, and they're the right depth for the pie. Brush first with melted butter to stop the pastry from sticking to the sides.

Express   **Extra thrifty**

Herb omelette

Omelettes are so quick and easy to prepare that you can have a satisfying meal for two, three or four on the table in moments.

2 eggs
2 teaspoons single cream
  or water
1 tablespoon chopped fresh herbs
  (try a mixture of chives, parsley
  and basil)
1 teaspoon butter
1 teaspoon olive oil

Serves 1
Preparation 5 minutes
Cooking 2 to 3 minutes

1 Crack the eggs into a bowl and add the cream, or water, and herbs. Season with salt and ground black pepper and then beat with a fork until the whites and yolks are just blended – but take care not to overbeat.

2 Heat a 20cm frying pan over a medium heat. Lift the pan from the heat, add the butter and olive oil and tilt the pan to coat the base and side. Return the pan to the heat, pour in the egg mixture, then tilt the pan so it evenly coats the base – it should begin to set immediately. Using a small spatula or spoon, draw the edges of the omelette into the centre. The liquid egg will flow into the space this creates; leave it for about 10 seconds – the egg will look slightly liquid and creamy.

3 Tilt the pan sideways, lift one side of the omelette off the pan and fold it over the other half. Gently slide the omelette from the pan onto a warm plate. Serve immediately with a green salad or grilled tomatoes.

Grandma's secret

The trick to a good omelette is to use eggs at room temperature and to cook it quickly over a heat that's brisk but not too fierce; if cooked too slowly it will turn out flat with an unpleasant rubbery texture.

Express   **Extra thrifty**

Welsh rarebit

A poor man's protein fix, Welsh rarebit is sometimes known as 'Welsh rabbit', even though no rabbit has ever been involved in its preparation.

knob of butter
2 teaspoons plain flour
80ml beer (or milk, but many believe that beer gives the best flavour)
80ml single cream
250g grated Cheddar
1 egg, lightly beaten
1 teaspoon mustard powder
pinch of cayenne pepper
4 slices of thick, hot, buttered toast, to serve

Serves 4
Preparation 10 minutes
Cooking 10 minutes

1 Melt the butter in a saucepan over a low heat. Stir in the flour until smooth, then cook, stirring, for 30 seconds, or until the flour is lightly golden.

2 Add the beer, or milk, and cream, stirring constantly. Stir in the cheese, making sure the mixture doesn't boil. Cook until the cheese has melted and the mixture is smooth.

3 Remove from the heat, then stir in the egg, mustard powder and cayenne pepper. Return to the heat and stir for about 2 minutes, or until the mixture has thickened.

4 Pour the mixture over hot, buttered toast and serve.

Variation

If you like, you can spread the mixture over the toast, then brown it under a hot grill.

Cheese soufflés

Soufflés can seem daunting but they don't have to be. To increase your chances of a well-risen dish, use room-temperature eggs and scrupulously clean utensils, plus don't overbeat the egg whites.

melted butter, for brushing
80g dry breadcrumbs
3 tablespoons butter
3 tablespoons plain flour
250ml milk
2 teaspoons Dijon mustard
125g grated Cheddar
3 large (60g) eggs

Serves 6
Preparation 20 minutes
Cooking 20 minutes

1 Lightly brush the base and side of six 250ml ramekins with melted butter. Refrigerate the ramekins to set the butter, then remove from the fridge and brush again with butter (double-greasing them will help the soufflés to rise). Sprinkle the base and sides with the breadcrumbs. Turn the ramekins upside down and tap them gently on the kitchen worktop to remove excess breadcrumbs. Place them on a large baking tray.

2 Melt the butter in a saucepan over a medium heat. Stir in the flour until smooth, then cook, stirring, for 30 seconds, or until the flour is lightly golden. Remove the saucepan from the heat.

3 Gradually stir in the milk, then the mustard. Return the saucepan to the heat and cook, stirring constantly, until the mixture boils and thickens. Reduce the heat to low and simmer for 1 minute. Remove from the heat, add the cheese and stir until it has melted. Transfer to a large bowl, cover the surface with cling film and allow to cool slightly.

4 Preheat the oven to 200°C/gas 6. Separate the egg whites and yolks, taking care that no yolk is in the egg whites. (If there is, use some eggshell to lift it out.) Whisk the egg yolks, then stir into the cheese mixture.

5 Beat the egg whites in a small clean bowl until soft peaks form, using an electric hand mixer. Take a spoonful of the egg whites and gently fold it into the cheese mixture to loosen it. Very gently fold the remaining egg whites into the rest of the mixture.

6 Working quickly, carefully spoon the soufflé mixture into the ramekins. Bake for 15 minutes, then remove from the oven and serve immediately.

Cheese and leek tart

It's easy to ring the changes with this super-tasty tart – if leeks aren't in season, you can use red onion instead – and try using Gruyère, Brie or a strong Cheddar instead of the Parmesan.

300g plain flour
½ teaspoon baking powder
125g chilled butter, chopped
1 to 2 tablespoons iced water
1 tablespoon olive oil
2 small leeks, white part only,
    finely sliced
3 eggs
250ml single cream
75g grated Parmesan

Serves 6
Preparation 10 minutes,
    plus 15 minutes chilling
Cooking 45 minutes

1 In a food processor, blend the flour, baking powder and butter until fine and crumbly. With the motor running, add 1 tablespoon of the iced water – the mixture should just begin to come together. Add the remaining water if needed to bind the pastry.

2 Turn the pastry out onto a lightly floured board and gently knead to form a ball. Pat out into a small round. Cover with cling film and refrigerate for 15 minutes.

3 Meanwhile, preheat the oven to 200°C/gas 6. Heat the olive oil in a small frying pan over a medium-low heat, add the leeks and sauté for 2 minutes, or until very soft but not browned. Remove from the heat and set aside.

4 Roll the pastry out until it's large enough to fit a shallow 11cm x 34cm flan tin. Gently ease the pastry into the tin and trim the edges. Prick the pastry case all over the base with a fork. In a bowl, lightly beat one of the eggs, then brush it lightly over the pastry base and side. You won't need to use all the egg (the pastry case should not be too wet). Set the remaining beaten egg aside.

5 Bake the pastry case for 10 to 15 minutes, or until golden. Remove from the oven and set aside to cool. Reduce the oven temperature to 180°C/gas 4.

6 Crack the remaining eggs into the bowl with the beaten egg. Add the cream and Parmesan, season well with salt and freshly ground black pepper and whisk until well combined.

7 Arrange the leeks in the pastry case, then carefully pour in the egg mixture. Bake for 30 minutes, or until the filling is set and the top is lightly golden. Remove from the oven and set aside to rest for 10 minutes. Serve warm.

Quick

Thrifty

Scotch eggs

Once you've made your own version of this picnic favourite, you'll never want the tasteless supermarket variety again. If you can't get sausage mince, just buy sausages and squeeze the meat from the casings.

500g sausage mince, or a mixture of pork and veal mince
1 teaspoon dried mixed herbs
1 small carrot, peeled and finely grated
75g plain flour
1 egg, lightly beaten
1 tablespoon milk
100g dry breadcrumbs
6 hard-boiled eggs, shelled
oil, for deep-frying

Serves 6
Preparation 30 minutes,
    plus 30 minutes chilling
Cooking 15 minutes

1 Place the mince, herbs and carrot in a large bowl. Season well with salt and freshly ground black pepper, then mix with your hands to bring the ingredients together. Divide the mince into six even portions.

2 Put the flour in a shallow bowl. In another bowl, whisk the egg and milk. Put the breadcrumbs on a plate.

3 Roll each egg in the flour, shaking off the excess. Reserve the remaining flour. Take a portion of the mince and shape it around an egg to coat it evenly. Pat it into a neat egg shape, then repeat with the remaining eggs.

4 Gently roll each egg in the flour again and carefully shake or brush off the excess. Dip the eggs, one at a time, in the beaten egg mixture, and then into the breadcrumbs. Press the breadcrumbs gently around the eggs so they adhere well. Place the eggs on a tray and refrigerate for 20 to 30 minutes (this will help the crumbs to stay on during cooking).

5 To cook the eggs, half-fill a medium-sized saucepan with oil and place over a medium heat. When the oil is hot, deep-fry the eggs in two batches – they will take about 5 to 6 minutes per batch to cook. Drain the eggs on kitchen paper. Reheat the oil between each batch, but it's important that the oil is not too hot, or the eggs will brown too quickly and the mince won't be cooked. Serve warm or cold with your favourite salad.

Grandma's secret

To test whether the oil is hot enough, place a wooden spoon handle in the oil – when the temperature is correct, bubbles should form all around it.

Eggs en cocotte

Eggs 'en cocotte' sounds sophisticated, but the French word 'cocotte' refers simply to the small dishes that the eggs are cooked in. We'd call them ramekins, but you can even use heatproof teacups.

melted butter, for brushing
6 eggs
3 tablespoons softened butter
ground white pepper, to taste
6 tablespoons single cream
   (about 125ml)

Serves 6
Preparation 5 minutes
Cooking 15 minutes

1 Preheat the oven to 180°C/gas 4. Brush the base and side of six 125ml ramekins with melted butter.

2 Carefully crack an egg into each ramekin. Dot each one with ½ tablespoon of the butter, then season with salt and a little ground white pepper.

3 Place in a large baking dish and spoon 1 tablespoon of cream over each egg. Carefully pour enough hot water into the baking dish so that it comes halfway up the sides of the ramekins.

4 Bake for 12 to 15 minutes, or until the eggs are just set, with the yolks a little runny. Serve immediately, as the eggs will continue to cook in the dishes.

Variations

For an extra-special brunch dish, sprinkle with finely chopped fresh chives, some smoked trout, ham or cooked asparagus tips.

Express   **Extra thrifty**

Best-ever scrambled eggs

For soft, creamy scrambled eggs, heat the butter until it's hot and frothy but not browned, then keep an eye on the heat: it shouldn't be too high or too low.

5 eggs
2 tablespoons water, milk
**   or single cream**
knob of butter
thick, hot, buttered toast, to serve

Serves 2
Preparation 3 minutes
Cooking 5 minutes

Grandma's secret

Using water gives light scrambled eggs; milk or cream makes them denser, but creamier. For extra 'lift', add a splash of sherry before cooking.

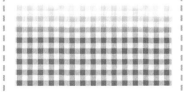

1 Crack the eggs into a bowl and add the water, milk or cream. Season well with salt and freshly ground black pepper and whisk with a fork until just combined.

2 Melt the butter in a heavy-based saucepan or small frying pan over a medium heat until it foams or is frothy. Pour in the eggs. Using a wooden spoon, stir the eggs as they cook, starting with a brisk backwards and forwards movement, then more gently as the eggs just begin to set.

3 Immediately remove from the heat and serve on toast.

Variations

Scrambled eggs are superb with fresh herbs – try chives, parsley, chervil or tarragon.

Prepare and relax   Extra thrifty

Ham quiche

Great served warm or cold for a picnic, light lunch or high tea. Old recipes for this French classic call for unsmoked bacon. We've used good-quality cooked ham, but you can also use chopped, pan-fried rindless bacon.

**300g plain flour for the pastry,
    plus 1 extra tablespoon
    for the filling**
½ teaspoon baking powder
125g chilled butter, chopped
2 to 3 tablespoons chilled water
5 eggs
500ml single cream
¼ teaspoon grated nutmeg
**200g sliced cooked ham, cut into
    small pieces**
100g Gruyère, diced

Serves 6
Preparation 20 minutes,
    plus 15 minutes chilling
Cooking 50 minutes

1 Put the flour for the pastry in a food processor with the baking powder and butter, and blend until fine and crumbly. With the motor running, add 1 tablespoon of the chilled water – the mixture should just begin to come together. Add the remaining water if needed. Turn the pastry out onto a lightly floured board and gently knead to form a ball. Pat out into a small round, cover with cling film and refrigerate for 15 minutes to rest the pastry.

2 Meanwhile, preheat the oven to 200°C/gas 6. Roll the pastry out into a circle large enough to fit a 23cm round flan tin. Gently ease the pastry into the tin and trim the edges. Prick the pastry case all over the base with a fork. In a bowl, lightly beat one of the eggs, then brush it over the pastry base and side to seal the pastry. You won't need to use all the egg (you don't want to make the pastry case too wet). Set the remaining beaten egg aside.

3 Bake the pastry case for 10 minutes, or until lightly golden. Remove from the oven and set aside to cool. Reduce the oven temperature to 180°C/gas 4.

4 Crack the remaining eggs into the bowl with the beaten egg. Add the cream, nutmeg and extra flour. Season well with salt and freshly ground black pepper and whisk until combined.

5 Arrange the ham and cheese in the pastry case, then carefully pour in the egg mixture. Bake for 30 to 35 minutes, or until the filling is set and the top is lightly golden. Remove from the oven and set aside to rest for 10 to 15 minutes. Serve warm.

Super quick   **Extra thrifty**

Savoury frittata cake

Layers of omelette filled with chargrilled peppers and aubergine make this a special dish for a smart brunch or light supper – and it's much easier to prepare than you'd think.

6 eggs
1 teaspoon softened butter
1 teaspoon olive oil
75g grated Parmesan
270g jar chargrilled red pepper, drained and sliced (or prepare your own by blackening the skins under the grill and then removing)
270g jar chargrilled aubergine, drained and sliced
fresh parsley leaves, to serve

Serves 6
Preparation 15 minutes
Cooking 15 minutes

1 Preheat the oven to 180°C/gas 4. Crack the eggs into a bowl. Add 2 tablespoons of water and season well with salt and freshly ground black pepper. Beat quickly with a fork until the whites and yolks are just blended – don't overbeat.

2 Heat a 23cm non-stick frying pan with a heatproof handle over a medium-high heat. Remove the pan from the heat and add a little butter and a little olive oil to the pan – the pan should be hot enough to melt the butter immediately. Tilt the pan so the butter and oil coat the base and the side.

3 Reduce the heat to medium and return the pan to the heat. Pour in about one-third of the egg mixture and tilt the pan so the egg mixture coats the base evenly. It should begin to set immediately.

4 Using a small spatula, draw the edges of the omelette into the centre of the pan; the liquid egg will flow in the space this creates. Leave it for about 20 seconds to cook, then slide the omelette onto a plate. Reheat the pan and cook another one-third of the egg mixture into an omelette, then slide onto a separate plate.

5 Cook a third omelette in the same way. Remove the pan from the heat, sprinkle half the Parmesan over the omelette and top with the peppers. Slide one of the other omelettes over the peppers, then sprinkle with the remaining Parmesan. Top with the aubergine and then the remaining omelette.

6 Transfer the frying pan to the oven and cook the frittata for 10 minutes, or until hot. Slide the frittata onto a serving plate, sprinkle with parsley and a little grated Parmesan and serve.

Quick

Extra thrifty

Cheese pasties

Most nations have their own version of the humble cheese pasty; this one hails from France, where it's called a 'corniotte' or 'cheese pocket'.

300g plain flour
1 teaspoon baking powder
125g chilled butter, chopped
1 egg, lightly beaten
1 to 2 tablespoons chilled water
300g ricotta
**200g grated Gruyère or
    Emmenthal**
¼ teaspoon ground nutmeg
60ml single cream
milk, for glazing

Makes 16
Preparation 30 minutes,
    plus 15 minutes chilling
Cooking 12 minutes

1 In a food processor, blend the flour, baking powder and butter until fine and crumbly. Beat the egg with a tablespoon of the chilled water. With the motor running, add the egg to the processor – the mixture should just start to come together. Only add the remaining water if needed to bring the mixture together.

2 Turn the pastry out onto a lightly floured board and gently knead to form a ball. Divide the pastry into 16 smooth balls, place on a tray and refrigerate for 15 minutes.

3 Meanwhile, preheat the oven to 200°C/gas 6 and line two baking trays with greaseproof paper or baking parchment. Place the ricotta, Gruyère, nutmeg and cream in a bowl and mash together with a fork. Season with a little salt and freshly ground black pepper.

4 Roll each ball of pastry out to a 14cm circle. Place a tablespoon of the cheese mixture in the centre of each round. Brush the edges lightly with water, then fold over into a semicircle and press the edges together with a fork to seal. Brush with milk to glaze.

5 Place on the baking trays and bake for 10 to 12 minutes, or until the pasties are golden. Serve warm.

Time saver

Ready-rolled shortcrust pastry sheets can be used in place of homemade pastry. The casing for the pasties will be slightly thicker and they will take just a little longer to cook.

Prepare and relax   **Extra thrifty**

Macaroni cheese

Homely and so easy to eat, macaroni cheese is a favourite comfort dish – here made extra tasty with nutmeg and given crunch with breadcrumbs.

melted butter, for brushing
100g butter
75g plain flour
750ml milk
250ml single cream
¼ teaspoon ground nutmeg
185g grated Cheddar
50g grated Parmesan, plus an
    extra 25g for sprinkling
    (or use a strong Cheddar)
500g macaroni, cooked
    and drained
1 tablespoon dry breadcrumbs

Serves 4
Preparation 15 minutes
Cooking 50 minutes

1 Preheat the oven to 180°C/gas 4. Meanwhile, lightly brush the base and sides of a deep, rectangular baking dish with melted butter.

2 Melt the 100g of butter in a saucepan over a medium heat. Stir in the flour until smooth, then stir for 30 seconds, or until light golden. Remove from the heat and slowly stir in the milk and cream. Add the nutmeg, return to the heat and stir constantly until the sauce boils and thickens. Simmer over a low heat for 1 minute.

3 Remove from the heat, add the Cheddar and the 50g of Parmesan and stir until melted. Spread the macaroni in the baking dish, then pour the cheese sauce over and mix well. Combine the breadcrumbs and extra Parmesan and sprinkle over the macaroni. Bake, uncovered, for 30 to 40 minutes, or until the macaroni is thoroughly hot and the top is golden and the breadcrumbs are crunchy.

Grandma's secret

Take a tip from Italian grandmas: before you drain the cooked pasta, save about 125ml of the cooking water and use it to moisten the pasta if it begins to stick as it cools.

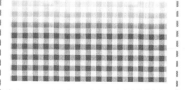

Gratin of ham, cabbage and cheese

Savoy cabbage is a good choice for this recipe. Its mild flavour and soft texture complement the cream and cheese, whereas other varieties of cabbage tend to overpower them. The ham adds a wonderful smokiness to this simple dish.

melted butter, for brushing

½ small savoy cabbage, finely shredded

2 teaspoons salt

1 tablespoon olive oil

1 red onion, halved, then sliced

200g sliced ham, shredded

125g grated Gruyère or mild Cheddar

250ml single cream

Serves 4
Preparation 10 minutes,
    plus 10 minutes standing
Cooking 25 minutes

1 Preheat the oven to 180°C/gas 4. Lightly brush a shallow baking dish with melted butter.

2 Put the cabbage in a colander and mix the salt through with your hands. Leave to stand for 10 minutes, then rinse the cabbage under cold water and drain well. Squeeze dry in a clean tea towel.

3 Meanwhile, heat the olive oil in a medium frying pan over a medium heat. Sauté the onion for 3 minutes, or until soft and lightly golden.

4 Spread the cabbage in the baking dish, then add the onion and the ham. Sprinkle the cheese over the top, then pour the cream over. Bake, uncovered, for 20 minutes, or until the mixture is thoroughly hot and the top is golden.

Quick   **Extra thrifty**

Baked tomatoes and eggs

Prepare this dish when vine-ripened tomatoes are at the peak of their flavour in summer. These are so delicious that you should really cook a few extras.

2 tablespoons olive oil, plus extra for brushing
6 large vine-ripened tomatoes
1 small clove garlic, crushed
1 teaspoon dried oregano
6 eggs
small fresh basil or flat-leaved parsley, to serve

Serves 6
Preparation 10 minutes
Cooking 30 minutes

1 Preheat the oven to 180°C/gas 4. Lightly brush a large baking dish with olive oil.

2 Using a small sharp knife, remove the core of each tomato by cutting a large cone-shaped piece out of the top. Using a teaspoon, carefully scoop out the seeds and flesh. Slice a very thin layer off the base of each tomato so the tomatoes will sit flat.

3 Place the tomatoes in the baking dish and season with a little salt and freshly ground pepper. Mix together the olive oil, garlic and oregano, and drizzle some of the dressing into each tomato.

4 Bake for about 8 minutes, or until the tomatoes begin to soften but still hold their shape. Remove the tomatoes from the oven. Crack an egg into a small teacup and gently tilt the teacup to slide the egg into a tomato. Repeat with the remaining eggs.

5 Return the tomatoes to the oven and bake for a further 15 to 20 minutes, or until the eggs are just set. Scatter with basil or parsley leaves and serve.

Kitchen wisdom

In summer, bag a bargain and buy a box of tomatoes late in the day at a farmers' market. Purée the tomatoes with some fresh home-grown herbs (such as basil or parsley) to make your own super-tasty tomato passata to use in soups, stews or tomato-based sauces.

Super quick   **Extra thrifty**

Courgette and pepper frittata

A frittata is a great option for a no-fuss lunch, light supper or picnic offering. Any leftover slices make a welcome lunchbox treat the following day.

8 eggs
185ml milk
100g grated Parmesan or
    other strong cheese
2 tablespoons olive oil
3 small courgettes, cut
    lengthways into strips
    5mm thick
1 large red pepper, cut
    lengthways into strips 1cm
    thick
2 cloves garlic, crushed
fresh basil leaves, to serve

Serves 4
Preparation 10 minutes
Cooking 20 minutes

1 Preheat the oven to 180°C/gas 4. Crack the eggs into a large bowl, add the milk and Parmesan and season with salt and freshly ground black pepper. Whisk together and set aside.

2 Heat half the olive oil in a large (about 27cm diameter) non-stick frying pan with a heatproof handle over a medium heat. Add the courgette and pepper and cook for 2 to 3 minutes, or until tender. Add the remaining oil and garlic and cook for 30 seconds.

3 Pour the egg mixture into the pan. Using a spatula, lift the courgette and pepper strips a little so the egg can settle around them. Reduce the heat to medium-low and cook for 6 to 8 minutes, or until the frittata is cooked and golden underneath.

4 Transfer the frying pan to the oven and bake for a further 6 to 8 minutes, or until the frittata is cooked through.

5 To serve, turn the frittata out onto a baking tray. Place a serving plate over the frittata and invert again. Scatter with basil leaves and serve.

Grandma's secret

If your frying pan doesn't have a heatproof handle, cook the frittata for a little longer on the hob over a lower heat, then brown the top under a hot grill. Or, carefully invert the frittata onto a plate, then slide it back into the pan and place back over the heat to cook the other side.

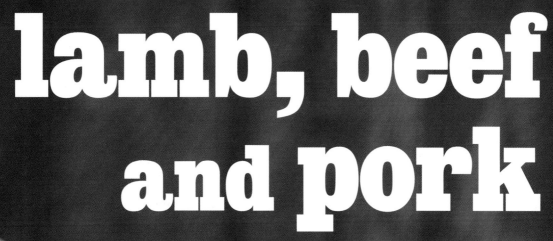

lamb, beef and pork

For many of us, meat is still the centrepiece of a memorable meal. Here are a host of nostalgic and delicious dishes that showcase Grandma's many marvellous ways with meat in all its incarnations. And as in Grandma's day, these recipes will fill up the hungriest diners without breaking the budget.

Prepare and relax   **Thrifty**

Roast shoulder of lamb with fruity stuffing

A sweet and succulent shoulder of lamb makes a tasty but inexpensive family roast. We've modernised the recipe so that the lamb is cooked a little less than in Grandma's day, so that it stays juicy and pink.

FRUIT STUFFING
80g fresh breadcrumbs
100g chopped dried apricots
35g currants
3 tablespoons chopped
    fresh parsley
2 tablespoons butter,
    melted

LAMB SHOULDER
1.5kg shoulder of lamb, boned
    (ask your butcher to do this
    for you, although boned
    shoulder is often available
    in supermarkets)
olive oil, for brushing
60g ready-made mint jelly,
    warmed
500ml beef stock (see Basics)

Serves 6
Preparation 15 minutes
Cooking 1 hour,
    plus 15 to 20 minutes resting

1 Preheat the oven to 180°C/gas 4. Put all the fruit stuffing ingredients in a bowl and mix together well.

2 Lay the lamb out flat, cut side up. Press the fruit stuffing onto the lamb. Compress the meat into a neat shape, then roll it up to secure the stuffing, tucking in any loose bits of meat. Using kitchen string, tie the lamb at 4cm intervals to hold its shape. Rub with olive oil and season well with salt and freshly ground black pepper.

3 Place the lamb in a roasting tin and roast for 50 minutes. Mix the mint jelly with 60ml hot water, then pour over the lamb. Reduce the oven temperature to 160°C/gas 3, cover the dish with foil and roast for a further 40 minutes.

4 Remove the lamb from the roasting tin, loosely cover with foil and allow to rest for 15 to 20 minutes before carving.

5 While the lamb is resting, make the gravy. Place the roasting tin on the hob and pour in the stock, stirring well to scrape up any stuck-on bits. Bring to the boil, then reduce the heat and simmer for 5 minutes, or until the liquid has reduced. Strain.

6 Remove the foil from the lamb, then snip the string with scissors. Slice the lamb and serve with the pan gravy, some roasted vegetables and steamed green beans.

Prepare and relax

Luxury on a budget

French-style lamb stew

Slow, gentle simmering renders lamb shoulder meltingly tender in this sumptuous stew with herbs, peppers and courgettes. Just make sure the liquid isn't allowed to boil, or the lamb will become tough.

1 large aubergine, cut into
 large cubes
1kg boneless lamb shoulder,
 trimmed and cut into
 3cm cubes
125ml red wine
3 tablespoons olive oil
4 to 6 sprigs fresh thyme
2 cloves garlic, sliced
1 large red pepper, cut into
 large chunks
1 large green pepper, cut into
 large chunks
2 courgettes, cut into
 thick rounds
1 onion, chopped
3 tomatoes, chopped
250ml beef stock (see Basics)

Serves 4
Preparation 20 minutes,
 plus 10 minutes standing
Cooking 1 hour 10 minutes

1 Put the aubergine in a colander, sprinkle generously with salt and leave to stand for 10 minutes.

2 Meanwhile, place the lamb in a large bowl, add the wine, thyme and garlic, and 1 tablespoon of olive oil, and toss well to coat.

3 Rinse the aubergine and pat dry with a tea towel. Heat 1 tablespoon of olive oil in a large frying pan over a medium heat. Cook the aubergine until it browns, then remove to a plate. Heat another tablespoon of the oil in the pan. Add the peppers and sauté for 2 minutes, then remove. Add the courgette and onion to the pan, sauté for 2 minutes, then remove from the heat.

4 Tip the lamb and its marinade into a large, heavy-based saucepan. Season with salt and freshly ground black pepper. Add the sautéed vegetables, tomatoes and stock and slowly bring to the boil. Reduce the heat to medium-low, cover and simmer for 50 minutes, or until the lamb is just tender, stirring occasionally and adding a little more stock or water to keep the lamb and vegetables just covered.

5 Remove the lid and simmer for a further 10 minutes, or until the liquid has reduced slightly. Serve hot.

Time saver

This is a great dish to make ahead and reheat. As soon as it has cooled completely, transfer the cooked stew to a casserole dish, cover and refrigerate for up to three days. Scrape off any solidified fat, then reheat, covered, in a 160°C/gas 3 oven for 30 minutes, or until heated through.

Lamb rissoles and onion gravy

Rissoles may sound old-fashioned, but they are so delicious that they are bound to be a hit with everyone, both young and old. Serve with perfect mashed potatoes, buttered green beans or peas and our terrific onion gravy.

50g plain flour
500g lamb mince
1 small onion, finely chopped
1 teaspoon dried mixed herbs
2 tablespoons tomato sauce
vegetable oil, for pan-frying

ONION GRAVY
2 teaspoons olive oil or
    softened butter
1 large onion, halved and sliced
1 tablespoon plain flour
250ml beef stock (see Basics)
1 tablespoon Worcestershire
    sauce
1 tablespoon tomato sauce

Serves 4
Preparation 10 minutes
Cooking 20 minutes

1 Put the flour in a shallow bowl. Have a bowl of water on the worktop so that you can wet your hands while shaping the rissoles. Put the mince into a large bowl with the onion, herbs and tomato sauce. Season well with salt and freshly ground black pepper, then mix well to bring the ingredients together.

2 With moistened hands, shape the mixture into 12 even rounds. Roll each rissole in the flour and shake off the excess.

3 Heat some oil in a large frying pan over a medium heat. Cook the rissoles in two batches for 3 to 4 minutes on each side, or until cooked through, adding more oil to the pan as needed. Drain on kitchen paper and keep warm.

4 Meanwhile, make the onion gravy. Heat the olive oil or butter in a small frying pan or saucepan over a medium heat. Add the onion to the pan and sauté for 3 minutes, or until softened. Add the flour and stir for a minute, then gradually stir in the stock, stirring constantly until the mixture thickens. Add the Worcestershire sauce and tomato sauce, then reduce the heat and let it simmer for 2 minutes.

5 Serve the rissoles hot, with the onion gravy and simple vegetables such as mashed potatoes and green beans.

Time saver

Buy mince in bulk and keep a quantity of uncooked rissoles in the freezer. Thaw overnight in the fridge, pat dry, lightly flour, then fry up for a speedy meal.

Prepare and relax   Thrifty

Quintessential shepherd's pie

Traditionally, this pie was a way of using up leftover lamb from a roast dinner. If you want to make a 'cottage' pie, use beef mince instead of lamb. If you're feeling adventurous you can try sweet potato for the topping.

2 teaspoons olive oil
500g lamb mince
1 small onion, finely chopped
400g can chopped tomatoes
125ml beef stock (see Basics)
1 tablespoon Worcestershire
    sauce
400g frozen peas and carrot mix
2 tablespoons chopped
    fresh parsley

POTATO MASH TOPPING
4 large potatoes (about 600g),
    peeled and chopped
2 tablespoons butter
60ml milk
60g grated Cheddar

Serves 4
Preparation 15 minutes
Cooking 45 minutes

1 Preheat the oven to 180°C/gas 4.

2 To make the potato mash topping, cook the potatoes in a saucepan of salted boiling water for 15 minutes, or until tender. Drain, return to the saucepan and mash well. Stir in the butter, milk and cheese. Season with salt and freshly ground black pepper and beat with a wooden spoon until the texture is creamy.

3 Meanwhile, heat the olive oil in a large non-stick frying pan over a medium heat. Add the mince and cook for 5 minutes, breaking up any lumps with a fork or wooden spoon. (If you don't have a large frying pan, brown the mince in two batches. Tilt the pan and spoon away any excess fat or liquid as the mince cooks – this ensures it browns well.) Add the onion and cook for a further 3 minutes, or until the onion is soft. Add the tomatoes, stock, Worcestershire sauce and frozen vegetables, then reduce the heat and simmer, uncovered, for 5 minutes. Stir in the parsley.

4 Spoon the lamb mixture into a baking dish. Spoon the mash topping over the lamb, and spread so that it covers the meat evenly. Bake, uncovered, for 30 minutes, or until the topping is lightly browned and the dish is heated through.

Grandma's secret

Grandma made her own mince by grinding meat in an old-fashioned mincer. To make your own mince, buy lean cuts of meat and process them in short bursts in a food processor. Don't over-process or the meat will turn into a paste.

Braised lamb shanks

Long, slow cooking will ensure that the meat on these lamb shanks literally slips from the bone. Serve the shanks and their rich tomato sauce with mash or creamy polenta and with fresh greens such as spinach or baby green beans.

4 lamb shanks, trimmed of
 excess fat and with the
 knuckle joint removed
1 tablespoon plain flour
2 tablespoons olive oil
1 small onion, finely diced
2 x 400g cans chopped tomatoes
375ml beef stock (see Basics)
125ml red wine
3 tablespoons chopped
 fresh parsley

Serves 4
Preparation 10 minutes
Cooking 2 hours 15 minutes

1 Season the shanks with salt and freshly ground black pepper, then dust with the flour.

2 Heat the olive oil in a large frying pan over a medium heat. Add the shanks and brown well on all sides, then remove and set aside. Add the onion to the pan and sauté for 5 minutes, or until softened.

3 Pour the tomatoes, stock and wine into a large deep saucepan. Bring to the boil, then reduce the heat to low. Add the shanks, sautéed onion and parsley and cook, uncovered, for 2 hours, or until the lamb is very tender, stirring now and then and adding a little more stock or water if needed to keep the shanks just covered. Serve hot.

Variations
Build on the classic flavour base of this recipe by adding black olives, a strip of orange zest and a few bay leaves. Rosemary or thyme work well too, as do chopped red or green peppers, carrot and celery.

Kitchen wisdom

Trimming lamb shanks of tendons and excess fat is sometimes known as 'Frenching'. The knuckle joint from each end is also removed so that the shanks are neater — and fit more easily into baking dishes.

Scrumpy lamb shanks

The scrumpy cider used in this recipe is quite cloudy and lacking in fizz and is sometimes called 'rough' or 'farmhouse' cider. You can use apple juice as an alternative.

8 lamb shanks, trimmed of
    excess fat and with the
    knuckle joint removed
1 tablespoon plain flour
3 tablespoons olive oil
1 onion, finely diced
1 small carrot, peeled and
    finely diced
2 stalks celery, finely diced
250ml beef stock (see Basics)
750ml apple cider or apple juice
2 large green apples, peeled,
    cored and cut into large chunks
1 bay leaf

Serves 4
Preparation 15 minutes
Cooking 2 hours 15 minutes

1 Preheat the oven to 180°C/gas 4. Season the shanks with salt and freshly ground black pepper and dust with the flour.

2 Heat 2 tablespoons of the olive oil in a large frying pan over a medium heat. Brown the shanks well on all sides and place in a large baking or casserole dish.

3 Heat the remaining oil in the frying pan, then add the onion, carrot and celery. Sauté for 3 minutes, or until the onion is soft. Add the stock and stir to mix. Pour the mixture over the shanks; add the cider, apples and bay leaf.

4 Cover and bake for 2 hours, or until the lamb is very tender, turning the shanks from time to time, and adding a little more stock or water if needed to keep them just covered with liquid. Serve hot.

Legendary Irish stew

Serve this beloved one-pot wonder with hunks of crusty white bread or – even better – Irish soda bread to ensure that you mop up every last drop of the juices.

2 large onions, thickly sliced
6 large potatoes (about 800g), peeled
1kg lamb neck chops, trimmed of excess fat
3 carrots, peeled and cut into chunks
1 small swede, peeled and cut into chunks
½ bunch fresh thyme or 2 tablespoons chopped fresh parsley, plus extra, to serve
500ml beef stock (see Basics)

Serves 6
Preparation 10 minutes
Cooking 2 hours

1 Preheat the oven to 160°C/gas 3. Spread the onions in a large baking or casserole dish. Slice four of the potatoes and cut the others into large chunks. Place half the sliced potatoes over the onions, then all the chops. Add the carrots, swede and chopped potatoes. Season well with salt and freshly ground black pepper and add the thyme or parsley.

2 Top with the remaining sliced potatoes, then gently pour the stock over – it should cover the vegetables by about 3cm, so add a little more if needed. Cover the dish with a sheet of foil, then the lid (or another sheet of foil if it doesn't have one).

3 Bake for 2 hours, or until the lamb is really tender. Carefully lift the lid and foil from time to time during cooking to check that the liquid hasn't evaporated and the onions aren't catching on the bottom of the dish – add just a little stock or water if needed. Serve sprinkled with fresh thyme or parsley.

Prepare and relax   **Thrifty**

Roast leg of lamb with mint sauce

A leg of lamb is always impressive, yet it's one of the easiest dishes to cook perfectly. Any leftovers are delicious in sandwiches, wraps and salads – or stir fry with pre-cooked rice for a quick supper.

1.5kg leg of lamb
olive oil, for brushing
2 tablespoons chopped fresh
rosemary or thyme (optional)

MINT SAUCE
250ml vinegar
90g caster sugar
50g roughly chopped fresh mint

Serves 6
Preparation 15 minutes
Cooking 1 to 1½ hours,
    plus 15 minutes resting

1 Preheat the oven to 180°C/gas 4. Place the lamb in a roasting tin that's close to it in size. Brush the lamb with olive oil and season well with salt and freshly ground black pepper. Rub the chopped herbs over the lamb, if using.

2 Roast the lamb for about 60 minutes for rare, 75 minutes for medium or 90 minutes for well done.

3 Remove the lamb from the oven, cover loosely with foil and leave to rest for 15 minutes before carving.

4 While the lamb is resting, make the mint sauce. Put the vinegar and sugar in a small saucepan with 125ml water. Stir well to dissolve the sugar, then bring to the boil over a medium-high heat. Reduce the heat and simmer for 3 minutes, then remove from the heat. Add the mint and allow it to infuse for 10 minutes before serving.

5 Carve the lamb by slicing across the width of the leg, using a sharp knife. Serve with the mint sauce.

Time saver

For a super-quick mint sauce, chop 20g mint leaves and place in a microwave-proof glass bowl with a 300g jar of mint jelly and 1 tablespoon of vinegar. Cover with cling film and microwave on high for 1 minute. Stir and serve.

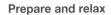

Prepare and relax   **Thrifty**

Lancashire hotpot

Northern grandmas knew a thing or two about the perfect hotpot. They would have used mutton chops and might even have slipped a few oysters under the top layer of potatoes. Any grandma would be proud of this heart-warming version.

800g neck fillet of lamb, cubed or cutlets, trimmed of fat
plain flour, for coating meat
1 tablespoon vegetable oil
3 onions (about 350g), peeled and sliced
400g carrots, peeled and sliced
2 sticks celery, thinly sliced
1 leek, thinly sliced
2 tablespoons chopped fresh herbs (parsley, thyme, sage)
800g potatoes, peeled and thinly sliced
900ml chicken or lamb stock (see Basics)
olive oil, for basting

Serves 4 to 6
Preparation 20 minutes
Cooking 2 hours to 2 hours
    30 minutes

1 Preheat the oven to 180°C/gas 4. Roll the lamb in seasoned flour in a large bowl. Heat the oil in a frying pan, fry the pieces of lamb until browned and then set to one side.

2 Place half of the potatoes in overlapping layers in the base of a large heatproof casserole dish. Add a layer of lamb, then a layer of vegetables and season with the herbs and salt and freshly ground black pepper. Add a second layer of meat and vegetables and season again. Place the remaining potatoes in neatly overlapping layers on the top.

3 Pour the stock into the casserole dish until it just reaches the top layer of potatoes. Cover with a layer of buttered greaseproof paper and a lid. Place the dish in the hot oven and cook for 2 hours.

4 About 30 minutes before serving, remove the casserole lid and buttered paper and brush the top of the potatoes with a little olive oil. Increase the oven temperature to 220°C/gas 7 and cook, uncovered, for another 25 to 30 minutes or until the potatoes are crisp and golden.

5 Serve immediately either on its own or with an accompaniment of green cabbage or pickled red cabbage.

Quick

Extra thrifty

Mediterranean lamb pilaf

As well as being a fabulous family meal, this tasty and attractive dish is also perfect as part of a warm buffet selection when you have a crowd to feed.

LAMB MEATBALLS
500g lamb mince
1 teaspoon ground coriander
1 teaspoon ground cinnamon
1 tablespoon olive oil

PILAF
1½ tablespoons butter
1 tablespoon olive oil
1 small onion, finely chopped
2 cloves garlic, crushed
1 teaspoon ground coriander
1 teaspoon ground cumin
½ teaspoon salt
300g long-grain white rice
500ml beef stock (see Basics)
2 tablespoons currants
2 tablespoons pine nuts
3 tablespoons fresh coriander
    or parsley

Serves 4
Preparation 15 minutes
Cooking 20 minutes

1 To make the meatballs, put the mince, coriander and cinnamon in a bowl. Season well with salt and freshly ground black pepper and mix using your hands to bring the ingredients together. Shape into 24 small meatballs, each about the size of a walnut, and set aside.

2 To make the pilaf, heat the butter and olive oil in a large frying pan over a medium heat. Add the onion and garlic and sauté for 1 minute. Add the spices, salt and rice, then cook, stirring often, for 2 minutes, or until the rice just begins to colour to a light golden brown – take care that it doesn't darken too much, or burn.

3 Stir in the stock and bring to the boil, then reduce the heat to low and cover with a lid. Cook for 12 minutes, or until the rice is just tender, adding a little more water or stock if the rice starts to dry out. Sprinkle the currants over the rice during the last 2 minutes or so of cooking.

4 Meanwhile, heat the remaining tablespoon of olive oil in a frying pan over a medium heat. Cook the meatballs in two or three batches for 3 to 5 minutes at a time, or until cooked through, shaking the pan from time to time so they cook evenly. Keep warm.

5 Fluff up the rice grains with a fork. Fold the meatballs, pine nuts and coriander or parsley through the rice and serve with sliced tomatoes and salad leaves on the side.

Time saver

The meatballs can be shaped and cooked a day ahead. Place the cooked meatballs on a baking tray lined with baking parchment or greaseproof paper and reheat them in a 180°C/gas 4 oven while cooking the rice.

Quick

Extra thrifty

Spaghetti with meatballs

Bread that has been soaked in milk enriches the beef meatballs, and helps to keep them moist – a touch of Parmesan in the mix and cooking in a herby tomato sauce infuses them with extra flavour.

3 slices thick white Italian-style
  bread, such as focaccia,
  crusts removed
125ml milk
500g lean beef mince
100g grated Parmesan
3 tablespoons chopped fresh
  flat-leaved parsley
1 clove garlic, crushed
60ml olive oil
1 small onion, finely chopped
680g bottle tomato passata
3 tablespoons chopped fresh
  basil, plus extra small leaves,
  to garnish
500g spaghetti

Serves 6
Preparation 20 minutes
Cooking 20 minutes

1 Tear the bread into small pieces and place in a bowl. Pour the milk over, then set aside for 10 minutes, or until the bread has absorbed most of the liquid. Mix with a fork until smooth.

2 Put the mince, Parmesan and parsley in a large bowl and season with freshly ground black pepper. Add the bread mixture and garlic. Using your hands, knead lightly until just combined. Moisten your hands and gently shape tablespoonfuls of the mixture into balls, keeping the size consistent. Place on a tray and refrigerate while making the tomato sauce.

3 Heat the olive oil in a large, deep heavy-based saucepan. Add the onion and sauté over a medium-low heat for 3 minutes, or until soft but not coloured. Stir in the passata, about 375ml water and the basil. Cook, uncovered, over a medium heat for about 5 minutes, stirring occasionally. Keep the sauce at simmering point – no higher or the meatballs may break apart when added.

4 Carefully spoon the meatballs into the sauce and simmer, uncovered, for 12 minutes, or until just cooked, gently turning them during cooking if necessary to help them to cook through.

5 Meanwhile, cook the spaghetti in a large saucepan of boiling salted water for 10 minutes, or until al dente (check the packet instructions). Drain well. Serve onto plates or shallow bowls, then add the tomato sauce and meatballs, scattering some basil leaves over the top.

Prepare and relax   Thrifty

Meatloaf with chutney glaze

One of the tastiest ways to use beef, this is just the kind of meatloaf that Grandma used to make, in this case with a super-easy but delicious chutney glaze. It tastes just as good cold for a picnic or served with salad.

MEATLOAF
1kg beef mince
120g fresh white breadcrumbs
250ml evaporated milk
1 small onion, finely chopped
60ml tomato sauce
**good dash of Worcestershire
  sauce**
30g chopped fresh parsley
1 teaspoon salt
**1 teaspoon freshly ground
  black pepper**

CHUTNEY GLAZE
210g fruit chutney
60ml tomato sauce
45g soft brown sugar
2 tablespoons balsamic vinegar

Serves 6
Preparation 20 minutes
Cooking 40 minutes

1 Preheat the oven to 180°C/gas 4. Cut out two sheets of foil and two sheets of baking parchment or greaseproof paper, making each sheet about 45cm long. Lay each sheet of parchment or paper on a sheet of foil.

2 Combine the meatloaf ingredients in a large bowl and mix well. Divide into two portions and place each on a sheet of baking parchment or greaseproof paper. Shape each portion into an oval, then wrap the foil securely around each meatloaf. Carefully place the meatloaves on a baking tray and bake for 25 minutes.

3 In a bowl, mix together the chutney glaze ingredients. Turn the oven up to 210°C/gas 6½. Remove the meatloaves from the oven and carefully undo the foil (the steam will be very hot). Drain away the excess liquid, then spoon the chutney glaze over each meatloaf.

4 Bake the meatloaves, uncovered, for a final 10 to 15 minutes. Remove from the oven and allow to cool slightly. Cut into thick slices and serve with any glaze left in the foil spooned over.

Kitchen wisdom

Instead of baking the meatloaf in parchment or paper and foil, you could cook it in a well-greased loaf tin and cover it with foil.

Prepare and relax   **Luxury on a budget**

Beef and Guinness pie

The hearty filling for this fabulous, richly flavoured pie can also be served on its own as a beef casserole, along with plenty of creamy mashed potato and green beans – or, if you prefer – a green salad.

1kg beef braising steak
olive oil, for pan-frying
1 large onion, halved, then sliced
200g button mushrooms, quartered
2 slices rindless bacon, chopped
2 tablespoons plain flour
625ml beef stock (see Basics)
2 tablespoons tomato purée
1 tablespoon soft brown sugar
1 tablespoon Worcestershire sauce
440ml can Guinness (or other beer, if you prefer)
2 sheets frozen puff pastry, thawed
1 egg, lightly beaten

Serves 6
Preparation 20 minutes
Cooking 2 hours 50 minutes

1 Preheat the oven to 180°C/gas 4. Cut the beef into 3cm cubes, then season well with salt and freshly ground black pepper. Heat the olive oil in a large, deep frying pan over a medium heat. Brown the beef in batches, then remove to a baking or casserole dish.

2 Reduce the heat to low and sauté the onion, mushrooms and bacon in the pan for 2 minutes. Sprinkle the flour over the top and stir for 1 to 2 minutes, or until smooth. Add the stock, tomato purée, sugar and Worcestershire sauce, scraping up the residue from the bottom of the pan. Stir constantly until the mixture boils. Pour in the Guinness and mix well, then carefully transfer to the casserole dish. Cover tightly and bake for 2 hours, or until the beef is tender, stirring occasionally and adding a little water if needed to keep it covered.

3 Cool the beef mixture completely if time allows, or at least until the steam has evaporated. (This helps the pastry puff to become crisp and brown when baked.)

4 Heat the oven to 200°C/gas 6. Cut the pastry into wide strips and criss-cross these in a lattice pattern over the filling. Brush the top of the pastry (but not the edges) with the egg. Bake for 10 minutes, then reduce the oven temperature to 180°C/gas 4 and bake for a final 15 to 20 minutes, or until the pastry is puffed and golden.

Prepare and relax   **Extra thrifty**

Beef pot roast

A great way to use an inexpensive cut of beef, a pot roast needs an attentive eye as it simmers, so that it doesn't boil dry or stick. Don't add too much liquid, though, or it will have little flavour.

2 tablespoons plain flour
2 teaspoons mustard powder
1.2kg beef shoulder or topside, trimmed of excess fat
1 tablespoon olive oil
1 onion, diced
1 carrot, peeled and diced
2 stalks celery, diced
2 slices rindless bacon, finely chopped
2 bay leaves
250ml beef stock (see Basics), plus extra as needed

Serves 6
Preparation 15 minutes
Cooking 2 hours 20 minutes, plus 15 minutes resting

1 Mix the flour and mustard powder and season with salt and freshly ground black pepper. Rub the mixture over the beef ensuring that it's thoroughly covered.

2 Heat the olive oil in large heavy-based pot or saucepan over a medium heat. Brown the beef on all sides, making sure the flour doesn't burn. Remove the beef and set aside.

3 Add the onion, carrot, celery and bacon to the pan and sauté for 4 minutes, or until the onion is soft. Add the bay leaves and stock and bring to the boil, then reduce the heat to low so the mixture is just simmering.

4 Place the beef over the vegetables. Cover and simmer for 2 hours, or until the beef is tender – a fork should easily penetrate the centre. Turn the beef occasionally during cooking, adding just a little extra stock – about 80ml at a time – as needed. It's important to keep the heat low during cooking, so check and adjust the heat and the liquid often.

5 Remove the beef to a warm serving plate and cover loosely with foil. Allow to rest for 15 minutes.

6 To serve, carve the beef into thin slices and spoon the warm vegetables and their liquid over.

Grandma's secret

Beef shoulder is a good choice for this dish – it's a really economical cut, it will cook beautifully and become quite tender after slow simmering, and it's easy to carve. As an alternative you could also use a piece of rolled beef brisket.

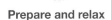

Prepare and relax   **Extra thrifty**

Magnificent meat pie

Many of us have fond memories of Grandma's lovingly prepared meat pies. As it's made in three stages, this old-fashioned pie takes a little time to put together, but actually requires minimal effort from the cook.

PIE FILLING
1 tablespoon olive oil
600g beef mince
1 onion, finely chopped
350g jar tomato pasta sauce
185ml beef stock (see Basics)
1 tablespoon Worcestershire
    sauce
2 teaspoons dried mixed herbs

PASTRY BASE
110g plain flour
50g self-raising flour
90g chilled butter, chopped
1 to 2 tablespoons chilled water

PASTRY TOP
2 sheets frozen puff pastry,
    thawed
1 egg, lightly beaten

Serves 6
Preparation 20 minutes,
    plus 30 minutes resting
Cooking 55 minutes

1 Start by making the filling. Heat a large non-stick frying pan over a medium heat. Add the olive oil and mince and cook for 5 minutes, breaking up the lumps with a wooden spoon. Add the onion and sauté for 3 minutes, or until the onion is soft. Add the pasta sauce, stock, Worcestershire sauce and mixed herbs. Reduce the heat to medium-low and simmer, uncovered, for 8 minutes, or until almost all the liquid has evaporated. Set aside and allow the filling to cool completely.

2 Meanwhile, make the pastry base. In a food processor, blend the flours and butter until fine and crumbly. With the motor running, add 1 tablespoon of the chilled water – the mixture should just begin to come together; add the remaining water if needed. Turn the pastry out onto a lightly floured board and gently knead together to form a ball. Cover with cling film and refrigerate for 30 minutes.

3 Preheat the oven to 200°C/gas 6. Roll the pastry base out to fit a deep, 23cm round pie dish or flan tin (use a metal tin if you like a crisp pie base, and sit it on a preheated baking tray when you place it in the oven). Gently ease the pastry into the pie dish and trim. Spoon the beef mixture into the pastry, then brush the edge of the pastry with a little beaten egg.

4 Overlap the puff pastry sheets so they fit to a size that will cover the pie. Carefully place the pastry over the pie. Trim any overhang, holding the knife upright as you trim so you don't drag the edge of the pastry (this helps to ensure that the pastry puffs).

5 Brush the pastry top (but not the edges) with beaten egg, then make two or three cuts in the top for the steam to escape. Bake for 15 minutes, then reduce the oven to 180°C/gas 4 and bake for a further 20 minutes, or until the pastry top is puffed and golden. Serve hot.

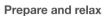

Prepare and relax   **Luxury on a budget**

Roast beef with Yorkshire puddings

Nothing beats a just-right joint of roast beef with plenty of gravy and Yorkshire pudding. Our mini puddings are easier and a little healthier than Grandma's traditional versions – they're cooked in olive oil rather than lard, and made in a muffin tin.

1.5kg beef topside
olive oil, for brushing
2 tablespoons fresh thyme
beef stock (see Basics), for
    basting (optional)

YORKSHIRE PUDDINGS
300g plain flour
1 teaspoon salt
4 eggs
250ml milk
60ml olive oil

Serves 6
Preparation 10 minutes
Cooking 1 to 1½ hours,
    plus 25 minutes resting

1 Preheat the oven to 200°C/gas 6. Heat a large frying pan over a medium-high heat. Brush the beef all over with a little olive oil and brown on all sides. Remove from the pan, season the beef with salt and freshly ground black pepper and rub with the thyme.

2 Place the beef in a roasting tin. Make sure the tin isn't too big – if you put a small roast in a large roasting tin, the pan juices will burn over the large surface area, giving the meat a charred flavour. Roast for 45 minutes for rare, 60 minutes for medium and 75 minutes for well done, basting the beef two or three times with the pan juices (or beef stock) during cooking.

3 While the beef is roasting, make the Yorkshire pudding batter. Sift the flour and salt into a bowl. Crack the eggs into another bowl, add the milk and 185ml water and whisk until smooth. Add to the flour mixture and mix to a smooth batter. Set aside for at least 30 minutes.

4 When the beef is done to your liking, remove from the oven, cover loosely with foil and rest for 25 minutes before carving.

5 While the beef is resting, bake the Yorkshire puddings. Pour 1 teaspoon of the olive oil into each hole of a 12-hole muffin tin (you'll need one with 125ml holes). Place the tin in the oven for 3 minutes to heat the oil. Remove from the oven and carefully pour the batter into each muffin hole. Bake for 20 minutes, or until the puddings are puffed up and cooked. Serve immediately with the roast beef.

Prepare and relax   **Luxury on a budget**

Hungarian-style veal goulash

The signature taste and colour of goulash comes mainly from the warmly flavoured sweet paprika. A little hot paprika adds more spice to the mix.

1kg boneless veal shoulder

2 tablespoons olive oil

1½ tablespoons butter

2 large onions, halved and
thinly sliced

2 cloves garlic, chopped

2 large red peppers, cut
into chunks

2 tablespoons sweet paprika

2 teaspoons hot paprika
(optional)

1 tablespoon caraway seeds

1 tablespoon plain flour

500ml tomato passata

250ml beef stock (see Basics),
plus extra as needed

1 teaspoon dried sweet marjoram
or oregano, plus a few fresh
leaves, to garnish if desired

Serves 4
Preparation 20 minutes
Cooking 1 hour 50 minutes

1 Trim the veal of any fat or sinew, cut into 3cm cubes and season with salt and freshly ground black pepper. Heat the olive oil in a large frying pan over a medium heat, then brown the veal in batches and set aside.

2 Melt the butter in a large deep saucepan over a medium-low heat. Add the onions, garlic and peppers and cook for 2 minutes, or until the onion is soft, stirring occasionally. Add the sweet paprika, hot paprika (if using) and the caraway seeds. Stir for 30 seconds, then add the flour and stir constantly for 1 minute.

3 Stir in the passata, stock and marjoram or oregano. Bring to the boil, then reduce the heat to low. Add the veal and simmer, uncovered, for 1½ hours, or until the veal is tender, stirring occasionally and adding a little more stock or water if needed during cooking to keep the veal covered.

4 Serve with noodles or mashed potato. A dollop of sour cream on the side, while not traditional, adds a little richness.

Variation

For a truly speedy and even more economical goulash, use pieces of chicken instead of the veal. They will reduce the cooking time and the cost.

Kitchen wisdom

The shoulder is usually cheaper than other cuts of veal and gives a very tender result when slowly cooked. Diced veal is another good option. You could also use beef braising steak.

Salt beef and creamy onion sauce

Salt beef is traditionally used in Jewish cookery. Although not always readily available in the UK, it's worth seeking it out for its unique flavour. Serve with mashed potato and baby carrots that have been simmered with the beef in the last 20 minutes of cooking.

1kg salt beef
60ml vinegar
45g soft brown sugar
5 to 8 cloves
1 bay leaf

CREAMY ONION SAUCE
1 large onion, chopped
250ml chicken stock
1½ tablespoons butter
2 tablespoons plain flour
185ml milk
125ml single cream
2 tablespoons chopped fresh
   parsley (optional)

Serves 6
Preparation 10 minutes
Cooking 1 hour 20 minutes,
   plus 15 minutes resting

1 Rinse the salt beef in cold water to remove any surface brine. Place in a large pot, cover with cold water and bring slowly to the boil over a medium heat. Use a large spoon to skim any froth from the surface, then reduce the heat to low – the liquid should be barely simmering and should cover the beef by about 6cm; add a little more water if needed to keep the meat covered.

2 Add the vinegar, sugar, cloves and bay leaf. Keeping the heat at simmering point, cook the beef for between 1 hour and 1 hour 10 minutes, or until it's tender when tested with a fork – the fork should easily penetrate the centre of the meat. Remove the beef to a carving board, cover loosely with foil and rest for 15 minutes.

3 While the beef is resting, make the onion sauce. Put the onion and stock in a small saucepan and cook over a medium heat for 3 minutes, or until the onion is tender. Drain, reserving the stock and the onion separately. Melt the butter in a small saucepan over a medium heat, then add the flour and stir for 1 minute, or until the flour is a light golden colour. Remove from the heat and gradually add the milk and the reserved stock. Return to the heat and cook, stirring constantly, until the mixture boils and thickens. Stir in the cream, cooked onion and parsley, if using.

4 Carve the beef and serve with the onion sauce.

Grandma's secret

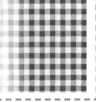

If you want to draw some of the salt from the beef, soak it in a bowl of cold water overnight in the fridge.

Prepare and relax

Luxury on a budget

Braised oxtail with red wine

Refrigerating the cooked oxtail and sauce separately overnight allows you to skim the excess fat from the rich oxtail and deepens the flavour.

1.3kg beef oxtail
1 tablespoon olive oil
2 cloves garlic, sliced
1 small onion, finely diced
400g can chopped tomatoes
500ml beef stock (see Basics),
   plus extra if needed
250ml red wine
2 bay leaves
1 teaspoon sugar
1 teaspoon salt
cooked pasta, such as
   pappardelle, to serve

Serves 4
Preparation 15 minutes
Cooking 2 hours 20 minutes,
   plus overnight refrigeration

1 Using a small sharp knife, cut and scrape away the outside fat sections from the larger pieces of oxtail. Season the meat with salt and freshly ground black pepper.

2 Heat a large frying pan over a medium heat. Add the oxtail pieces and brown each piece well on both sides (you won't need to oil the pan). Set aside.

3 Heat the olive oil in a large deep saucepan over a medium heat. Add the garlic and onion and sauté for 2 minutes, or until the onion is soft. Add the remaining ingredients and a little black pepper and bring to the boil. Reduce the heat to low and add the oxtail pieces. Simmer, uncovered, stirring occasionally, for 2 hours, or until the oxtail is very tender – the meat should be nearly falling off the bone. Add a little more stock or water if needed during cooking to keep the oxtail just covered.

4 Remove the oxtail pieces from the sauce. Pour the sauce into a bowl and cover with cling film. Use a fork to remove the meat from the oxtails, then lightly shred the meat with the fork. Discard the bones. Place the oxtail meat in a small bowl and cover. When the sauce and meat have cooled, put them in the fridge overnight.

5 When you're ready to serve, carefully remove the layer of solidified fat from the top of the sauce. Spoon the sauce into a saucepan and bring to the boil, then reduce the heat to low and simmer for 3 minutes. Add the oxtail meat and simmer, uncovered, for 5 minutes, or until both the meat and the sauce are heated through. Serve hot, spooned over cooked pasta or, if you prefer, with boiled potatoes and a selection of vegetables.

Kitchen wisdom

You could substitute osso buco (veal shin) pieces for the oxtail. Osso buco is not quite as fatty as oxtail, but it also produces a rich, flavoursome sauce.

Curried sausages and rice

Golden curried beef sausages are simply lovely served with fluffy rice and green peas. Adjust the quantity of curry powder to suit your taste.

1kg thick beef sausages
2 tablespoons vinegar
1½ tablespoons butter
1 large onion, halved, then sliced
1 tablespoon mild curry powder
1 small apple, peeled and
   finely chopped
1 tablespoon sultanas (optional)
185ml beef stock (see Basics)
2 teaspoons cornflour, mixed to
   a smooth paste with
   1 tablespoon water

Serves 4
Preparation 10 minutes
Cooking 20 minutes

Kitchen wisdom

To take the 'edge' off the curry powder, some old recipes advise you to add a tablespoon of plum jam near the end of cooking.

1 Place the sausages in a large saucepan, cover with cold water and add the vinegar. Place over a medium heat and bring slowly to the boil. Reduce the heat to low, simmer for 5 minutes, then drain.

2 Heat a large frying pan over a medium heat. Add the butter and melt until foamy, then add the sausages and fry for 2 minutes, or until golden, turning often.

3 Push the sausages to one side of the pan. Add the onion, curry powder, apple and sultanas, if using, and sauté for 1 to 2 minutes, or until the onion is soft. Add the stock and bring to the boil, then gently stir the sausages to coat with the sauce. Stir the cornflour paste through the sauce and cook for 3 minutes, or until it boils and thickens. Serve hot, with steamed white rice.

Variation

Pork and lamb sausages also work well with these flavours.

Pan-fried liver and bacon

The secret of the best pan-fried liver is to cook the liver quickly, until it is only just done (many like it still a little pink in the middle).

600g calf's liver, with the fine
  membrane peeled away
2 tablespoons plain flour,
  seasoned well with salt and
  freshly ground black pepper
1 tablespoon olive oil
1 large onion, finely sliced
3 slices rindless bacon,
  finely chopped
3 tablespoons butter
2 to 3 teaspoons gravy powder
250ml beef stock (see Basics)

Serves 4
Preparation 15 minutes
Cooking 15 minutes

1 Rinse the liver with cold water and pat dry with kitchen paper; thinly slice and set aside. Put the flour in a shallow bowl.

2 Heat the olive oil in large frying pan over a medium heat. Sauté the onion and bacon for 2 minutes. Remove the pan from the heat, and place the onion and bacon on a plate.

3 Toss the liver slices in the flour. Reheat the frying pan to medium-high, then add the butter. When the butter foams, cook the liver in two or three batches for 2 minutes on each side, turning once. Remove to warm serving plates.

4 Reduce the heat to low and add the gravy powder to the pan, scraping up any residue. Pour in the stock and stir until the mixture boils and thickens. Stir in the sautéed onion and bacon to combine. Pour the gravy over the liver and serve with seasonal green vegetables.

Variation
You can also leave the bacon slices whole, grill until crisp, and serve on top of the liver and gravy.

Kitchen wisdom

For a slightly milder taste, soak the liver in cold milk (or water with a dash of vinegar) for an hour, or even overnight.

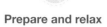

Steak and kidney pie

Possibly the ultimate in comfort food. Here are instructions for a home-made pastry top, but to save time use frozen puff pastry (follow the Beef and Guinness pie recipe on page 121).

PIE FILLING

300g ox kidneys, cut in half lengthwaya and with the hard core removed

2 tablespoons plain flour

½ teaspoon ground nutmeg

1kg beef braising steak, cut into 3cm cubes

2 tablespoons olive oil

1 large onion, chopped

750ml beef stock (see Basics)

1 tablespoon Worcestershire sauce

1 tablespoon soy sauce

1 egg, lightly beaten

PASTRY CRUST

125g plain flour

1 teaspoon baking powder

½ teaspoon salt

60g cold butter, chopped into small cubes (or 3 tablespoons grated suet)

80ml iced water

Serves 6
Preparation 20 minutes,
   plus 30 minutes resting
Cooking 2 hours 45 minutes

1 Preheat the oven to 180°C/gas 4. Wash the kidneys and pat dry with kitchen paper, then cut into small dice. Put the flour and nutmeg in a shallow bowl and season well with salt and freshly ground black pepper. Toss the beef and kidneys in the flour mixture to coat.

2 Heat the olive oil in large frying pan over a medium heat. Working in batches, brown the beef and then the kidneys, removing each batch to a casserole dish. Reduce the heat to low and add the onion to the pan. Sauté for 2 minutes, then add the stock, Worcestershire sauce and soy sauce, scraping up the residue from the bottom of the pan. Cook, stirring constantly, until the mixture boils. Pour the mixture into the casserole dish.

3 Cover tightly with foil, transfer to the oven and bake for 2 hours, or until the beef is very tender, stirring occasionally and adding a little water to keep the beef just covered. Remove from the oven and let the casserole stand for 10 minutes, so all the steam has evaporated.

4 While the beef is in the oven, make the pastry. Mix the flour, baking powder and salt in a bowl. Rub in the butter with your fingertips, then add the iced water and mix using a flat-bladed knife until just combined. Turn out onto a lightly floured surface and gently knead until just smooth. Wrap in cling film and refrigerate for 30 minutes.

5 Turn the pastry out onto a lightly floured surface and gently roll it out to fit the top of the casserole. Place an eggcup upside down in the centre of the casserole dish to support the pastry top. Brush the rim of the casserole dish with a little water. Carefully lift the pastry over the dish, pushing it down gently and crimping the edges against the rim. Brush the top of the pastry with the beaten egg, cut two or three slits in the top and bake for 20 to 25 minutes, or until the pastry is golden. Serve hot.

Prepare and relax   **Luxury on a budget**

Pot-au-feu

Beef brisket is stuffed with a herb and garlic mixture and simmered with beef ribs for two hours to bring out its full flavour. The French often serve the broth from this dish as a clear soup. Try it with a little Dijon mustard on the side.

2kg rolled beef brisket

30g roughly chopped fresh parsley

2 cloves garlic, crushed

500g beef thin ribs, trimmed of excess fat

2 litres beef stock (see Basics)

2 bay leaves

4 sprigs fresh thyme

6 to 8 black peppercorns

3 carrots, peeled and cut into 6cm lengths

2 leeks, white part only, washed and cut into 6cm lengths

4 whole baby turnips, peeled (or 1 large turnip, cut into 6 pieces)

6 waxy potatoes, washed and cut in half lengthways

Serves 6
Preparation 15 minutes
Cooking 2 hours 30 minutes,
   plus 15 minutes resting

1 Unroll the brisket; if it has been rolled and tied by your butcher, you'll need to cut off the string. In a small bowl, combine the parsley, garlic and a little salt and freshly ground black pepper. Spread the mixture over the inside of the brisket, then roll the brisket up again and tie in three or four places with kitchen string.

2 Put the brisket and ribs into a large pot, pour in the stock and bring slowly to the boil over a medium heat. Use a large spoon to skim any froth from the surface, then reduce the heat to low – the liquid should be barely simmering and should cover the beef by about 6cm, so add a little water if needed.

3 Add the bay leaves, thyme and peppercorns. Keeping the liquid just at simmering point, cook the beef for 1¾ hours. Add the carrots, leeks, turnips and potatoes and simmer for a further 30 minutes, or until the vegetables are tender and the beef is also tender when tested with a fork – the fork should easily penetrate the centre of the meat.

4 Carefully remove the vegetables, brisket and ribs from the broth and place on a warm serving plate. Cover loosely with foil and allow the beef to rest for at least 15 minutes before carving.

5 Strain the liquid and serve as a broth, or ladle some of the broth over the sliced brisket, ribs and the vegetables.

Super quick **Luxury on a budget**

Beef stroganoff

Although it's already one of the easiest dishes to make in a hurry, buying ready-cut beef stir-fry strips makes the stroganoff even quicker to prepare. Serve with fresh egg noodles and lightly steamed asparagus.

600g rump steak, sliced into
    thin strips across the diagonal
2½ tablespoons olive oil
1½ tablespoons butter
1 small onion, finely chopped
2 cloves garlic, crushed
250g mushrooms, thinly sliced
2 teaspoons sweet paprika
185ml beef stock (see Basics)
2 tablespoons tomato purée
2 teaspoons cornflour
250ml sour cream
2 tablespoons finely chopped
    fresh chives or parsley

Serves 4
Preparation 10 minutes
Cooking 20 minutes

1 Place the beef strips in a bowl, add 2 tablespoons of the olive oil and mix well.

2 Heat a large heavy-based frying pan over a high heat. Cook the beef in two batches for about 2 minutes each time, or until just done, removing each batch to a plate.

3 Heat the butter and remaining oil in the pan. Add the onion and sauté for 2 minutes, or until soft. Add the garlic and mushrooms and sauté for 3 minutes, or until the mushrooms are tender. Stir in the paprika.

4 Stir in the stock and tomato purée and bring to the boil, then reduce the heat to low and simmer for 5 minutes.

5 Mix the cornflour through the sour cream, then add to the mushroom mixture and stir until well combined. Simmer for 1 minute, then season to taste with salt and freshly ground black pepper.

6 Return the beef to the pan and simmer for 2 minutes to heat through. Stir in the chives or parsley and serve.

Prepare and relax **Thrifty**

Beef miroton

Here's a delicious way to use up any leftover roast beef or pot roast – cut into slices and just bake it anew interleaved with layers of sliced potatoes, onions, gravy and topped with a crust of buttery breadcrumbs.

**3 tablespoons butter, plus melted
   butter for brushing**
2 large onions, halved, then sliced
1 tablespoon plain flour
250ml beef stock (see Basics)
5 cooked potatoes, thickly sliced
**10 to 12 slices leftover
   cooked beef**
80g fresh breadcrumbs
**1 tablespoon chopped
   fresh parsley**
60g grated Cheddar (optional)

Serves 4
Preparation 15 minutes
Cooking 50 minutes

1 Preheat the oven to 180°C/gas 4.

2 Melt half the butter in a small frying pan or saucepan over a medium heat. Add the onions and sauté for 4 minutes, or until soft. Add the flour and stir for 1 minute, then gradually add the stock, stirring constantly until the mixture thickens to a gravy. Reduce the heat to low and simmer for 1 minute.

3 Lightly brush a shallow baking dish with melted butter. Arrange the potato slices in the dish, then lay the beef slices over the potato. Pour the onion gravy over the top.

4 In a bowl, mix together the breadcrumbs, remaining butter and parsley. Sprinkle the mixture over the gravy and sprinkle with the cheese, if using. Bake, uncovered, for 20 to 25 minutes, or until the dish is heated through and the breadcrumbs are golden brown.

Variations
You can also use leftover roast potatoes here, or other roasted vegetables such as carrot or parsnip – slice and layer them in the dish before adding the beef. Instead of sliced potatoes, mashed potato is sometimes used as a topping. Sliced tomatoes can also be added – place them on top of the beef before adding the mashed potato.

Quick

Luxury on a budget

Sweet and sour pork

A popular fixture on many Chinese restaurant menus, this dish is so easy to make at home – and tastes infinitely better than a takeaway. Eat with chopsticks and plenty of steamed rice.

750g pork neck
2 tablespoons soy sauce
2 tablespoons dry sherry
2 teaspoons grated fresh ginger
vegetable oil, for deep-frying
60g cornflour
1 spring onion, shredded

SWEET AND SOUR SAUCE
1 tablespoon vegetable oil
1 onion, cut into wedges
1 red pepper, cut into chunks
1 green pepper, cut into chunks
1 carrot, peeled and cut into
  fine matchsticks
450g can pineapple pieces in
  natural juice, drained,
  reserving the juice
60ml tomato sauce
45g soft brown sugar
60ml white or malt vinegar
1 tablespoon cornflour
1 teaspoon sesame oil

Serves 4
Preparation 20 minutes,
   plus 10 minutes marinating
Cooking 20 minutes

1 Thinly slice the pork on the diagonal. (To make this easier, partially freeze the meat first.) Toss the pork in a bowl with the soy sauce, sherry and ginger, then set aside to marinate for 5 to 10 minutes.

2 Half-fill a saucepan with oil and place over a medium heat. Put the cornflour in a shallow bowl and dust the pork slices with the cornflour, shaking off any excess. When the oil is hot, deep-fry the pork in batches and drain on kitchen paper. Keep the pork warm while making the sweet and sour sauce.

3 Heat the oil in a wok until hot. Add the onion, peppers and carrot and stir-fry for 3 minutes, or until the onion is just soft and the pepper brightly coloured. Add the pineapple pieces and stir-fry for 1 minute.

4 In a bowl, mix together the reserved pineapple juice, tomato sauce, sugar, vinegar and cornflour until smooth. Pour into the wok and stir constantly for 1 to 2 minutes, or until the mixture boils and thickens slightly. Stir in the sesame oil.

5 Divide the pork among warm serving plates and spoon the sauce over. Sprinkle with the spring onion and serve with a bowl of steamed rice on the side.

Money saver

Buying a piece of pork neck and trimming it yourself is an economical way to prepare this dish. Cut it across the grain into thin strips. Pork neck has a little fat so it keeps the pork moist.

Crackling roast pork with fresh apple sauce

One of the nicest ways to eat pork is as a succulent roast joint. Serve with homemade apple sauce as its perfect complement. To get a really crisp crackling, don't baste the pork rind during roasting.

**1.5kg pork leg, with rind on
a little vinegar or lemon juice
cooking salt**

APPLE SAUCE
**3 dessert apples, peeled, cored
    and thinly sliced**
2 teaspoons sugar
2 teaspoons lemon juice
**1 small cinnamon stick,
    broken in half (optional)**

Serves 6
Preparation 10 minutes
Cooking 1 hour 30 minutes,
    plus 20 minutes resting

1 Preheat the oven to 220°C/gas 7. Rub the pork rind with a little vinegar or lemon juice, then rub generously with cooking salt.

2 Place the pork in a roasting tin. Roast for 20 minutes to crisp the crackling, then reduce the oven temperature to 180°C/gas 4 and roast for a further 1 hour 10 minutes.

3 Meanwhile, make the apple sauce. Place the apples, sugar, lemon juice and 60ml water in a small saucepan with the cinnamon stick, if using. Cook over a low heat, stirring often, for 10 minutes or until the apples are really soft. Remove the cinnamon stick and beat the mixture with a wooden spoon until smooth. Set aside until required.

4 When the pork is done, remove it from the oven and gently remove the crackling (this will keep it crisp). Cover the pork loosely with foil and allow to rest for 20 minutes before carving. Serve with the apple sauce.

Waste not, want not

Any leftover roast pork is perfect in our Pork hash recipe on page 161.

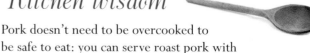

Kitchen wisdom

Pork doesn't need to be overcooked to be safe to eat: you can serve roast pork with a faint hint of pink in the centre.

Prepare and relax **Thrifty**

Braised pork sausages with onion and apple

There are fabulous varieties of sausage available today, many with added ingredients, including apple, tomatoes, cheese and herb mixes. Italian-style pork sausages with fennel, sage or rosemary are superb in this dish.

2 teaspoons vegetable oil

1kg small pork sausages or
   pork chipolatas

2 slices bacon, rind removed,
   chopped

1 stalk celery, finely diced

1 large onion, halved, then cut
   into thick wedges

2 apples, peeled, cored and cut
   into thick wedges

250ml apple juice

375ml beef stock (see Basics)

2 to 3 sprigs fresh thyme

1 tablespoon cornflour

Serves 4
Preparation 15 minutes
Cooking 45 minutes

1 Preheat the oven to 180°C/gas 4. Heat the oil in a large frying pan over a medium heat. Add the sausages and cook, turning often, so they brown evenly. Remove the sausages to a casserole dish.

2 Add the bacon, celery, onion and apples to the frying pan and sauté for 1 to 2 minutes, or until the onion is just soft. Add the mixture to the casserole dish.

3 Pour in the apple juice and stock, then add the thyme sprigs. Blend the cornflour with a tablespoon of water, pour over the sausages and stir to mix.

4 Cover and bake for 30 minutes, or until the sausages are cooked through and the mixture is hot and slightly thickened. Serve hot.

Variation

For a change try chicken or lamb sausages, which also taste good with this combination of flavours.

Kitchen wisdom

Sausages today are generally made with good-quality ingredients, so you don't need to prick them to drain away excess fat, as Grandma often did. They'll stay more moist and flavoursome if you keep the casing intact.

Prepare and relax **Thrifty**

Pork goulash with caraway dumplings

Goulash is hearty, warming and, with its paprika flavouring, a little exotic. This pork version is served with dumplings with the distinctive flavour of caraway. Or, instead of the dumplings, serve it with potato or buttered egg noodles.

1kg diced pork
2 tablespoons olive oil
1½ tablespoons butter
2 large onions, halved and
    thinly sliced
2 tablespoons sweet paprika
1 tablespoon plain flour
375ml chicken stock (see Basics),
    plus 125ml if needed
1 tablespoon soft brown sugar
400g can chopped tomatoes
2 large tomatoes, chopped
125ml sour cream

CARAWAY DUMPLINGS
3 tablespoons butter
300g self-raising flour
1 teaspoon caraway seeds
125ml sour cream

Serves 6
Preparation 15 minutes
Cooking 1 hour 30 minutes

1 Preheat the oven to 180°C/gas 4. Season the pork with salt and black pepper. Heat the olive oil in a large frying pan over a medium heat. Brown the pork in batches, removing each batch to a casserole dish with a tight-fitting lid.

2 Reduce the heat to low. Melt the butter in the frying pan, then add the onions and sauté for 2 minutes. Sprinkle with the paprika and flour and stir for 1 to 2 minutes so the flour coats the onion. Add the 375ml stock, sugar and tomatoes, scraping up the residue from the bottom of the pan. Cook, stirring constantly, until the mixture boils.

3 Take the frying pan off the heat. Remove a few spoonfuls of the hot liquid and mix with the sour cream until smooth. Pour the mixture back into the pan and stir to mix. Carefully pour it over the pork in the casserole dish.

4 Cover the casserole dish and transfer to the oven. Bake for 1 hour, or until the pork is just tender, stirring occasionally during cooking and adding a little water if needed to keep the pork covered.

5 Meanwhile, make the dumplings. Rub the butter into the flour, stir in the caraway seeds and make a well in the centre. Whisk the sour cream with 125ml water until smooth, then add to the flour, mix to a soft dough and season with salt and freshly ground black pepper. Set aside until needed.

6 When the pork is tender, carefully drop large round spoonfuls of the dough on top of the goulash. If necessary, add about 125ml more stock to the goulash to keep the meat just covered and to help to cook the dumplings. Cover and bake for a further 10 minutes, or until the dumplings are fluffy and cooked through. Serve hot.

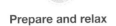
Toad-in-the-hole

Traditionally, this dish of sausages in batter was cooked in lard, but we've used olive oil as a healthier option. The onion gravy is a delicious extra.

150g plain flour
½ teaspoon salt
2 eggs
125ml milk
8 thin pork sausages,
    or 12 pork chipolatas
60ml olive oil
2 to 3 small sprigs
    fresh rosemary

QUICK ONION GRAVY
3 teaspoons olive oil or
    softened butter
1 large onion, halved, then sliced
1 tablespoon plain flour
250ml beef stock (see Basics)
60ml red wine (optional)

Serves 4
Preparation 15 minutes,
    plus 15 minutes resting
Cooking 40 minutes

1 Sift the flour and salt into a bowl. Crack the eggs into a bowl, add the milk and 185ml water and whisk until well combined. Pour into the flour mixture and whisk to a smooth batter. Set aside to rest for at least 15 minutes.

2 Meanwhile, preheat the oven to 200°C/gas 6. Pan-fry the sausages in a non-stick frying pan over a medium heat until lightly golden on all sides.

3 Place a 23cm deep-sided roasting tin on a baking tray. (Cooking the 'toad' in a metal cake tin on a metal baking tray is an excellent way to conduct heat; the hotter the oil is when the batter first hits it, the more it will puff up.) Pour the olive oil into the cake tin and brush some up the sides. Add the sausages, transfer to the oven and bake for 5 minutes.

4 Remove the baking tray from the oven. Whisk the batter well, then pour it over the sausages in the tin. Add the rosemary sprigs and bake for a further 20 to 30 minutes, or until the batter is puffed, brown and crisp. Serve immediately, with the onion gravy if desired.

5 If making the onion gravy, begin while the toad is baking. Heat the olive oil or butter in a small frying pan or saucepan over a medium heat. Add the onion and sauté for 3 minutes, or until soft. Add the flour and stir for 1 minute, then gradually stir in the stock and the wine, if using. Stir constantly until the mixture thickens, then reduce the heat and simmer for a minute. Transfer to a gravy boat and serve with the toad.

Variation
Cut a small peeled green apple into thin wedges and a small red onion into wedges, then quickly sauté until just soft. Spread into the roasting tin before adding the sausages.

Express

Thrifty

Pork sausages, tomato and beans

Super-speedy, this one-pot marvel is equally good as a simple weekday dinner or a hearty weekend breakfast. Serve with thick toasted slices of Italian-style bread.

1 tablespoon olive oil
1 large green pepper, chopped
8 thin herby or spicy
   pork sausages
2 cloves garlic, sliced
425g tomato passata
125ml beef stock (see Basics)
400g can cannellini beans,
   drained and rinsed
3 tablespoons shredded
   fresh basil

Serves 4
Preparation 5 minutes
Cooking 15 minutes

1 Heat the olive oil in large frying pan over a medium heat. Add the pepper and sauté for 1 to 2 minutes, then push the pepper to one side and add the sausages. Cook, turning, until golden brown and cooked through. Remove the sausages and set aside.

2 Add the garlic, passata and stock to the frying pan. Bring to the boil, then reduce the heat to low and simmer, stirring, until the mixture is slightly thickened.

3 Stir in the beans and basil and simmer for a minute to warm them. Return the sausages to the pan and stir gently until the sausages are heated through. Serve hot.

Variations
We've used thin sausages in this version as they pan-fry easily and absorb the lovely tomato and basil flavours, but beef sausages are good here too. For extra zing, add a little chopped fresh chilli.

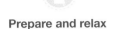
Baked sweet and sticky pork ribs

Serve these glazed ribs with mashed potato and green beans for a simple but really tasty family meal.

750g thick-cut pork ribs
3 cloves garlic, crushed
60g soft brown sugar
60ml barbecue sauce
185ml tomato sauce
1 tablespoon soy sauce

Serves 4
Preparation 5 minutes
Cooking 45 minutes

1 Preheat the oven to 190°C/gas 5. Place the ribs in a large saucepan and cover with cold water. Bring slowly to the boil, then reduce the heat to low and simmer for 5 minutes. Drain the ribs and rinse under cold-running water.

2 Place the ribs in a bowl, add the remaining ingredients and mix well to coat the ribs completely.

3 Line a baking dish with baking parchment or greaseproof paper (to make washing up easier). Spread the ribs in the dish and roast for 15 minutes. Pour 125ml water into the dish to ensure the ribs don't stick. Roast for a further 20 minutes, or until the meat is cooked. Carefully turn each rib to coat with the glaze, and serve.

Prepare and relax   Thrifty

Pork cassoulet

In rural France, where the dish originated, a cassoulet may involve a number of different cuts of meat and take several days to cook. Our version is much quicker and simpler to prepare, but still hearty and delicious.

800g diced pork
2 tablespoons olive oil
3 pork and garlic sausages
1 onion, chopped
3 cloves garlic, sliced
1 carrot, peeled and finely
**   chopped**
125ml white wine
400g can chopped tomatoes
2 tablespoons tomato purée
375ml chicken stock
**   (see Basics)**
3 to 4 sprigs fresh thyme
400g can butter beans or
**   cannellini beans, drained**
**   and rinsed**
160g fresh breadcrumbs
3 tablespoons butter, melted
1 tablespoon chopped
**   fresh parsley**
2 teaspoons fresh thyme

Serves 6
Preparation 20 minutes
Cooking 1 hour 30 minutes

1 Preheat the oven to 180°C/gas 4. Season the pork well with salt and freshly ground black pepper.

2 Heat the olive oil in a large frying pan over a medium heat. Brown the pork in batches, removing each batch to a casserole dish. In the same frying pan, brown the sausages all over (they don't need to be cooked through). Set the sausages aside.

3 Reduce the heat to low, then add the onion, garlic and carrot to the pan and sauté for 2 minutes. Stir in the wine and bring to the boil, then add the tomatoes, tomato purée, stock and thyme sprigs. Cook, stirring occasionally, until the mixture boils, then carefully pour it over the pork in the casserole dish. Slice the sausages thickly and arrange around the pork.

4 Cover the casserole dish tightly, transfer to the oven and cook for 1 hour, or until the pork is nearly tender, stirring occasionally and adding a little water if needed to keep the pork covered. Add the beans and gently stir to mix.

5 In a bowl, mix together the breadcrumbs, butter, parsley and thyme. Sprinkle over the casserole and bake, uncovered, for a further 15 minutes, or until the mixture is hot and the breadcrumbs are golden brown. Serve hot.

Kitchen wisdom

For extra flavour, add a bouquet garni to the dish. Tie together a bay leaf and a few sprigs of fresh thyme, parsley and sweet marjoram. Tuck them into the cavity of a 5cm length of celery, then tie some string around the bundle to secure.

Prepare and relax   **Extra thrifty**

Sausage rolls

Children and adults alike will love these sausage rolls. With onion and mixed herbs enriching the sausage meat, this version is particularly tasty.

3 slices white bread,
    crusts removed
125ml milk
500g pork mince, or a mixture of
    pork and veal mince
1 small onion, very finely chopped
1 to 2 tablespoons dried
    mixed herbs
2 teaspoons salt
½ teaspoon ground white pepper
    or freshly ground black pepper
4 sheets frozen ready-rolled puff
    pastry, thawed
1 egg, lightly beaten
tomato or barbecue sauce,
    to serve

Makes 48 (serves 10 as a nibble)
Preparation 20 minutes,
    plus 5 minutes soaking
    and 15 minutes chilling
Cooking 25 minutes

1 Place the bread in a large bowl, pour the milk over and soak for 5 minutes. Line two baking trays with baking parchment or greaseproof paper.

2 Using a fork, blend the bread and milk to a paste. Add the mince, onion, herbs, salt and pepper and mix, using your hands to bring the ingredients together.

3 Lay the pastry sheets on a large work surface, then cut each one in half lengthways. Spoon six even-sized mounds of the mince mixture down the centre of each pastry strip. Brush a little beaten egg along one edge of each strip, then roll the pastry over to enclose the filling. Cut each roll into six pieces, making 48 rolls in all.

4 Place the sausage rolls, seam side down, on the baking trays. Place the trays in the fridge for 15 minutes to firm the pastry. Meanwhile, preheat the oven to 200°C/gas 6.

5 Brush each sausage roll with a little more beaten egg. Bake for 10 minutes, then reduce the oven temperature to 180°C/gas 4 and bake for a further 10 to 15 minutes, or until the pastry is golden and puffed. Serve hot, with tomato or barbecue sauce.

Kitchen wisdom

The soaked bread absorbs any fat from the pork as the sausage rolls cook and stops the mince shrinking inside the pastry. You can prepare the rolls a day ahead, up to step 4; cover the trays with cling film before refrigerating. Brush the rolls with beaten egg just before baking.

Quick

Extra thrifty

Pork hash

In the 1960s, family cooks discovered the versatility of canned soups, and began using them in a range of quick, innovative dishes. Here's a speedy recipe in which a can of mushroom soup is put to excellent use.

2 teaspoons olive oil

400g pork mince

1 small onion, finely chopped

2 stalks celery, finely chopped

150ml chicken stock
   (see Basics)

295g can condensed cream of
   mushroom soup

210ml milk or single cream

80g frozen peas

3 leftover cooked potatoes, sliced

1½ tablespoons softened butter

75g dry breadcrumbs

60g grated Cheddar

1 teaspoon sweet paprika

Serves 4
Preparation 10 minutes
Cooking 35 minutes

1 Preheat the oven to 180°C/gas 4. Lightly grease a shallow baking dish.

2 Heat the olive oil in a large non-stick frying pan over a medium heat. Add the mince and cook for 5 minutes, breaking up any lumps with a wooden spoon.

3 Add the onion and celery and sauté for 2 minutes, or until the onion is soft. Add the stock, soup, milk and peas and bring to the boil, then reduce the heat and simmer, uncovered, for 5 minutes.

4 Spoon the mixture into the baking dish. Arrange the potato slices over the top and dot with the butter. Combine the breadcrumbs and cheese, then sprinkle over the potatoes. Sprinkle with the paprika.

5 Bake, uncovered, for 20 minutes, or until the mixture is thoroughly hot and the breadcrumbs are golden brown. Serve hot.

Variation

The peas can be replaced with your favourite varieties of frozen mixed vegetables.

Time saver

Using leftover cooked pork (such as our roast pork on page 146) makes this dish even quicker to prepare. Chop the pork and add it to the sautéed onion and celery in step 3.

poultry
and game

In Grandma's day, chicken was a special treat and not the everyday meal we take for granted all too often today – and being free-range, it always tasted sublime. These simple recipes will take you straight down memory lane.

Prepare and relax   **Thrifty**

Roast chicken and vegetables with pan gravy

Here's how Grandma would have roasted a chicken for a special meal. She would also have made the most of the hot oven by roasting plenty of vegetables to serve with it.

1.6kg whole chicken
a few sprigs fresh thyme
1 small onion, halved
olive oil, for rubbing and drizzling
2 tablespoons melted butter
125ml chicken stock (see Basics),
    plus 125ml extra, for basting
4 roasting potatoes, peeled and
    cut in half
300g pumpkin or butternut
    squash, cut into chunks
    (leave the skin on if you like)
2 carrots, topped and tailed,
    then cut in half horizontally

PAN GRAVY
2 tablespoons plain flour
250ml to 375ml chicken stock
    (see Basics)

Serves 4
Preparation 15 minutes
Cooking 1 hour 45 minutes,
    plus 15 minutes resting

1 Preheat the oven to 180°C/gas 4. Rinse the chicken inside and out and pat dry with kitchen paper. Put the thyme sprigs and onion inside the cavity, generously rub the chicken with olive oil and season well with salt and freshly ground black pepper. Secure the wings and legs with string.

2 Place the chicken in a roasting tin. Drizzle with the melted butter and pour the stock into the dish. Cover with foil and roast for 45 minutes.

3 Remove the chicken from the oven. Discard the foil and baste the chicken with some extra stock. Move the chicken around a bit so that it doesn't stick to the roasting tin. Place the vegetables in another large roasting tin, drizzle well with olive oil and season with salt and black pepper.

4 Roast the chicken and vegetables for 30 minutes, leaving the chicken uncovered and basting occasionally. Turn the vegetables and roast for another 15 minutes, or until the vegetables are golden and tender and the chicken is cooked (the juices will run clear when the thickest part of the thigh is pierced with a skewer).

5 Remove the chicken to a serving platter. Cover with foil and rest for 15 minutes while making the gravy.

6 Place the roasting tin on the cooker top over a medium heat. Stir in the flour with a wooden spoon, scraping up any residue from the base of the pan. Slowly stir in the stock and bring to the boil, then reduce the heat and simmer for a few minutes.

7 Carve the chicken and serve with the pan gravy and roasted vegetables.

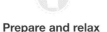

Prepare and relax   **Extra thrifty**

Chicken curry

When you crave a curry, don't call for a takeaway but try this richly aromatic version with its creamy coconut sauce boosted with plenty of classic oriental spices. If you like your curry fiery, add a little more chilli powder to the mix.

2 tablespoons vegetable oil

1 onion, chopped

2 cloves garlic, crushed

3cm piece of fresh ginger, peeled and grated

1 teaspoon ground turmeric

1 teaspoon chilli powder

3 teaspoons ground coriander

1 teaspoon ground cumin

½ teaspoon cinnamon

¼ teaspoon salt

400g can chopped tomatoes

250ml chicken stock (see Basics)

600g boneless, skinless chicken thighs, cut into 2cm cubes

60ml coconut cream (or single cream)

chopped fresh coriander leaves, to serve

steamed rice, to serve

poppadums, to serve

Serves 4

Preparation 10 minutes

Cooking 45 minutes

1 Heat the oil in a saucepan over a medium heat. Add the onion, garlic and ginger and sauté for 4 to 5 minutes, or until the onion is soft.

2 Add the spices and salt and cook, stirring, for 1 minute, or until fragrant and to your taste.

3 Add the tomatoes and stock and bring to the boil, then reduce the heat and simmer, covered, for 10 minutes. Add the chicken and simmer for a further 20 minutes, or until the chicken is cooked through. Stir in the coconut cream or single cream and simmer for a final 5 minutes.

4 Sprinkle with the coriander leaves and serve with poppadums and steamed rice.

Time saver

For a speedy curry that will beat any takeaway, replace the raw chicken with 400g cooked, diced chicken. Reduce the simmering time to 5 minutes just to heat the chicken through.

Prepare and relax   **Thrifty**

Chicken and mushroom sauté

This simple recipe, flavoured with tomatoes, white wine, butter, onion and herbs, produces wonderfully tender chicken and is so versatile – see our variations below, and enjoy experimenting with your own.

1½ tablespoons butter
1 tablespoon olive oil
1.6kg whole chicken, cut into
    pieces (see Basics)
1 onion, chopped
200g button mushrooms, sliced
125ml white wine
125ml chicken stock (see Basics)
2 sprigs fresh thyme,
    plus extra, to serve
2 tomatoes, peeled, seeded
    and chopped
2 tablespoons chopped
    fresh parsley

Serves 4
Preparation 10 minutes
Cooking 50 minutes

1 Heat a large heavy-based saucepan over a medium-high heat. Add the butter and olive oil. When the butter starts to foam, brown the chicken pieces for 3 to 4 minutes on all sides – you may need to do this in batches if your pan isn't big enough. Remove and set aside.

2 Add the onion to the pan and sauté for 5 minutes, or until lightly coloured. Add the mushrooms and sauté for a further 5 minutes, then pour in the wine and bring to the boil. Add the stock, thyme sprigs, tomatoes and chicken pieces. Bring to a gentle simmer, then cover and cook for 10 minutes.

3 Remove the lid and simmer for a further 15 minutes, or until the chicken is tender and the sauce has thickened and reduced. Season to taste with salt and freshly ground black pepper, sprinkle with the parsley and extra thyme sprigs and serve.

Variations
Add a tablespoon of sherry with the wine for enhanced flavour – or use red wine instead of white. To make a Basque-style chicken, use 100g mushrooms and add 100g diced ham, along with 1 red and 1 green pepper, cut into strips.

Chicken schnitzel

Austria is the home of schnitzel, traditionally made with veal or pork escalopes. It has evolved to incorporate a variety of meat cutlets, including chicken, that have been flattened, tenderised and then fried in a crumbed batter coating.

2 large boneless, skinless chicken breasts (about 650g in total)
75g plain flour
2 eggs
100g cornflake crumbs
2 tablespoons olive oil
1½ tablespoons butter
lemon wedges, to serve

Serves 4
Preparation 10 minutes,
    plus 30 minutes chilling
    (optional)
Cooking 10 minutes

1 Using a sharp knife, cut the chicken breasts in half, to make four thin fillets. Using a mallet, gently beat until the meat is around 5mm thick. Place the flour in a wide bowl. Beat the eggs in a separate bowl with some salt and freshly ground black pepper. Put the cornflake crumbs in a third bowl.

2 Working one at a time, dip each chicken piece in the flour, then the egg, letting the excess drain off. Dip them in the crumbs and place in a single layer on a tray. If you have time, refrigerate for 30 minutes to set the coating.

3 Heat the olive oil and butter in a large frying pan over a medium heat until the butter foams. Fry the schnitzels, in two batches, for 2 minutes on each side, or until golden. Serve hot with lemon wedges.

Variations

To vary the flavour, add 2 tablespoons grated Parmesan and 2 teaspoons chopped fresh parsley (or other herbs) to the crumbs, or add a splash of Tabasco to the eggs. Serve with pesto sauce or heat up a small jar of pasta sauce.

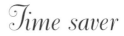 *Time saver*

Try leftover schnitzel in a sandwich with lettuce and mayonnaise.

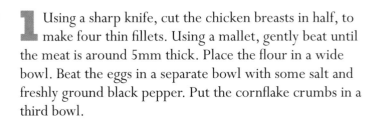

Super quick

Thrifty

Chicken with cashew nuts

Another dish with Chinese origins, tender chicken and creamy cashews are a winning combination, tossed with peppers and green beans in this speedy stir-fry for crispness and crunch.

4 boneless, skinless
    chicken thighs
1 egg white, lightly beaten
1 tablespoon cornflour
2 tablespoons sherry
60ml vegetable oil
1 red pepper, sliced
2 spring onions, sliced
125g green beans, cut into
    4cm lengths
1 tablespoon soy sauce
250ml chicken stock (see Basics)
80g roasted cashews
fresh coriander, to garnish
    (optional)

Serves 4
Preparation 15 minutes
Cooking 10 minutes

1 Cut the chicken into 1cm slices. Place in a bowl with the egg white, 2 teaspoons of the cornflour and half the sherry. Season with salt and freshly ground black pepper and mix well.

2 Heat the oil in a frying pan or wok over a medium-high heat. Add the chicken in two batches, and stir-fry each batch for 3 minutes, or until lightly browned. Remove and set aside.

3 Add the vegetables to the pan and stir-fry for 1 minute. Mix the remaining cornflour and sherry until smooth, then add to the pan with the soy sauce and stock. Stir for 1 to 2 minutes, or until the sauce has thickened.

4 Add the chicken and toss for 1 to 2 minutes, or until warmed through and coated with the sauce. Sprinkle with the cashews and coriander, if using. Serve with steamed rice or noodles.

Prepare and relax **Luxury on a budget**

Chicken provençale

Here's a much-loved dish from the sun-drenched countryside of southern France, which incorporates garlic, white wine and tomatoes along with a sprinkling of herbs. A handful of black olives can be added for extra flavour.

1.6kg whole chicken, cut into
   pieces (see Basics)
2 tablespoons butter
2 tablespoons olive oil
1 onion, finely chopped
150g button mushrooms, sliced
2 cloves garlic, crushed
250ml white wine
1 stalk fresh parsley
1 sprig fresh rosemary
1 bay leaf
400g can chopped tomatoes
125ml chicken stock (see Basics)
mashed potato (see Basics),
   to serve

Serves 4
Preparation 10 minutes
Cooking 1 hour 40 minutes

1 Preheat the oven to 180°C/gas 4. Dry off the chicken pieces with kitchen paper.

2 Heat the butter and oil in a large flameproof casserole dish over a medium heat. Fry the chicken pieces in batches for 5 to 7 minutes, or until golden on all sides. Remove from the dish and set aside.

3 Sauté the onion in the casserole dish for 5 minutes, or until softened. Add the mushrooms and garlic and sauté for a further 2 minutes, or until starting to colour. Pour in the wine and bring to the boil, stirring to scrape up the residue from the bottom of the dish. Add the chicken with all the remaining ingredients and bring back to the boil.

4 Cover, transfer to the oven and bake for 1¼ hours, or until the chicken is tender. If you need to thicken the sauce, remove the chicken pieces and place the casserole dish on the hob over a high heat and boil until the sauce thickens. Serve with mashed potato.

Variations
You can use thighs and drumsticks instead of a jointed chicken. For a healthier option, increase the quantity of olive oil in proportion to the butter.

Waste not, want not

Leftovers from this dish are particularly delicious for lunch the next day.

Prepare and relax   **Luxury on a budget**

Rabbit in red wine sauce

In bygone years it was a cheap meat popular with thrifty cooks; these days rabbit is less ubiquitous. This recipe, another French country classic, is something a little special to share with discerning friends.

1.5kg rabbit joints
35g plain flour
150g rindless bacon, cut
   into strips
olive oil, for pan-frying
1 onion, finely chopped
2 carrots, peeled and
   finely chopped
2 cloves garlic, crushed
1 tablespoon tomato purée
500ml red wine
1 bouquet garni
250ml to 500ml chicken stock
   (see Basics)

Serves 6
Preparation 10 minutes
Cooking 1 hour 50 minutes

1 Dust the rabbit joints with the flour and season generously with salt and freshly ground black pepper.

2 Heat a flameproof casserole dish or large heavy-based saucepan over a medium heat. Add the bacon strips and sauté for 3 to 4 minutes, or until most of the fat has been released. Remove from the pan and set aside.

3 Add the rabbit joints in batches and brown all over for 5 to 7 minutes, adding a little olive oil if necessary. Remove from the pan and set aside.

4 Add the onion, carrots and garlic to the pan and sauté for 5 minutes, or until browned. Stir in the tomato purée until combined, then add the wine, scraping up the residue from the bottom of the pan.

5 Return the bacon and rabbit to the pan with the bouquet garni and add enough stock to just cover the rabbit. Bring to a simmer, then cover and cook over a low heat for 1 hour, or until the rabbit is tender. Remove the lid and simmer for a further 30 minutes, or until the sauce has reduced. Serve with mashed potatoes and steamed vegetables.

Money saver

Rabbit can be found in a number of supermarkets, but if cost is an issue, or you're not a fan of rabbit, chicken is a delicious alternative in this dish. Use 1.5kg chicken pieces and reduce the cooking time by 30 minutes.

Prepare and relax   **Luxury on a budget**

Roast stuffed chicken with bacon

Draping bacon slices over the chicken infuses it with flavour and keeps it succulently moist as it roasts. Serve with pride and watch the sumptuous sage stuffing quickly disappear.

1.6kg whole chicken
2½ tablespoons butter, softened
8 slices bacon

STUFFING
1½ tablespoons butter, melted
1 small onion, finely chopped
1 clove garlic, crushed
125g fresh breadcrumbs
5 to 6 fresh sage leaves,
   finely chopped
1 egg
2 tablespoons milk

Serves 4
Preparation 15 minutes
Cooking 1 hour 30 minutes,
   plus 15 minutes resting

1 Preheat the oven to 190°C/gas 5. Rinse the chicken inside and out and pat dry with kitchen paper.

2 In a bowl, mix together all the stuffing ingredients and season well with salt and freshly ground black pepper.

3 Spoon the stuffing into the chicken cavity, then secure the opening with a skewer, or tie the legs together with kitchen string. Season the chicken with salt and black pepper and rub the softened butter over the skin. Lay the bacon slices over the chicken and place in a roasting tin.

4 Roast for 1¼ hours, basting three or four times with the pan juices. Remove the bacon and place in the roasting tin with the chicken, or set it aside if it has become crisp. Turn the oven up to 220°C/gas 7 and roast for a further 15 minutes, or until the chicken is golden and the juices run clear when the thickest part of the thigh is pierced with a skewer.

5 Remove the chicken from the oven, cover loosely with foil and allow to rest for 15 minutes before serving.

Waste not, want not

Leftovers are excellent in Chicken à la king (page 188) and Chicken noodle soup (page 50), and delicious in sandwiches or salads the next day.

Turkey curry

Although it makes a great centrepiece for a celebration meal, a large turkey can land you with the problem of an excess of leftovers. Here's a really quick and easy way to use up roast turkey.

2½ tablespoons butter
1 large onion, finely chopped
2 stalks celery, finely diced
1 small red pepper, finely diced
1 clove garlic, crushed
1 tablespoon curry powder
1 tablespoon plain flour
125ml chicken stock
250ml milk
500g cooked turkey, diced
2 tablespoons mango chutney
coriander sprigs, to garnish

Serves 4
Preparation 10 minutes
Cooking 15 minutes

1 Melt the butter in a saucepan over a medium heat until frothy. Add the onion, celery, pepper and garlic and sauté for 5 minutes, or until just starting to colour.

2 Add the curry powder and flour and cook, stirring, for 1 minute. Pour in the stock and milk, stirring constantly for 2 minutes, or until thickened.

3 Stir in the turkey and chutney and simmer for 5 minutes, or until heated through. Serve garnished with coriander.

Variations

Use your favourite curry paste instead of curry powder, replace the milk with coconut milk, add some diced pineapple or apple, and use whatever chutney you fancy. Serve with steamed rice, naan bread and extra chutney, and maybe banana pieces tossed in desiccated coconut. Use chicken instead of turkey if you have a roast to use up.

Coq au vin

French peasants devised this dish to deal with a tough old rooster who'd had his day. The bird would be slowly simmered with onions, herbs and good red wine to render its gamy meat flavoursome and tender. It works just as well with more tender meat.

2kg chicken pieces
60ml olive oil
150g rindless bacon, diced
12 baby onions, peeled
2 stalks celery, finely diced
2 cloves garlic, crushed
200g whole button mushrooms
2 tablespoons brandy
750ml red wine
2 bay leaves
½ teaspoon dried mixed herbs
knob of butter
2 tablespoons plain flour

Serves 6
Preparation 10 minutes
Cooking 1 hour 30 minutes

1 Season the chicken with salt and freshly ground black pepper. Heat the olive oil in a flameproof casserole dish over a medium-high heat. Brown the chicken in batches for 3 minutes on each side; remove from the dish and set aside.

2 Fry the bacon for 3 minutes, or until crisp; remove and set aside. Sauté the onions, celery and garlic for 3 minutes, then add the mushrooms and sauté for 2 minutes, or until softened. Pour in the brandy, then the wine, stirring to scrape up the residue from the bottom of the dish. Add the chicken, bacon, bay leaves and herbs, then cover and simmer for 1 hour.

3 Mix the butter and flour to a smooth paste, then stir into the sauce, a teaspoon at a time, to thicken it. Serve with mashed or boiled potatoes.

Variation

Fresh chopped parsley can be stirred into the sauce just before serving, and instead of dried mixed herbs you could use three fresh sprigs of thyme.

Chicken kiev

Bursting with rich garlicky flavour, chicken kiev may seem a little complex to prepare but the results are worth it. The dish traditionally uses chicken breasts with the wing bones attached – as these can be hard to get, we've used breast fillets instead.

100g butter, slightly softened

3 cloves garlic, crushed

4 boneless, skinless chicken breasts

150g plain flour

4 eggs, lightly beaten

320g fresh breadcrumbs (made from bread that's one or two days old)

vegetable oil, for deep-frying

Serves 4
Preparation 30 minutes,
   plus 1 to 2 hours chilling
Cooking 25 minutes

1 Mix the butter and garlic in a small bowl and season with salt and freshly ground black pepper. Form the butter into four logs about 5cm long. Wrap in cling film and place in the freezer while preparing the chicken.

2 Using a sharp knife, butterfly each chicken breast by cutting through the side, almost all the way through. Open out each chicken breast and place between two sheets of cling film. Carefully beat with a mallet or rolling pin until 5mm thick, or as thin as possible, taking care not to create holes in the flesh. You may need to trim the edges to neaten – the resulting chicken pieces should be roughly rectangular. Season well with salt and pepper.

3 Put the flour, eggs and breadcrumbs into separate wide, shallow bowls.

4 Place a log of butter on one side of each breast and roll the chicken up, folding the sides inward to create a larger log. Dust each chicken piece with the flour, then dip them in the egg, letting the excess drain off. Next, roll each piece in the breadcrumbs, dip into the egg again, letting the excess drain off, and then finally roll them in the breadcrumbs again. Place on a tray or plate and refrigerate for 1 to 2 hours to set the coating.

5 Heat the oil in a deep-fryer or saucepan to 160°C/ gas 3, or until a cube of bread dropped into the oil browns in 30 to 35 seconds – you need enough oil in the pan to cover the chicken completely. Deep-fry the chicken in two batches for 10 minutes each time, reducing the heat slightly if it's browning too quickly. Keep the first batch warm while frying the remaining chicken and serve at once.

Variation

Jazz up the butter by adding dried red chilli flakes or fresh herbs of your choice, such as chives or parsley.

Quick

Extra thrifty

Chicken and vegetable stew

This versatile hotpot lends itself to whatever vegetables are in season – good candidates include sweetcorn, turnips, sweet potato and green beans. But you can vary the ingredients depending on which vegetables are easily available.

2 tablespoons olive oil

700g boneless, skinless chicken thighs, cut into 2cm dice

1 large onion, finely chopped

2 cloves garlic, crushed

2 stalks celery, cut into 1cm dice

2 carrots, peeled and cut into 1cm dice

1 tablespoon tomato purée

2 potatoes, peeled and cut into 1cm dice

500ml chicken stock (see Basics)

½ teaspoon dried oregano or mixed herbs

1 tablespoon Worcestershire sauce

1 courgette, cut into 1cm dice

80g frozen peas

1 to 1½ tablespoons cornflour

2 to 3 tablespoons chopped fresh parsley

crusty bread or mashed potatoes (see Basics), to serve

Serves 6
Preparation 10 minutes
Cooking 35 minutes

1 Heat the olive oil in a large saucepan over a medium-high heat. Fry the chicken in two batches for 2 to 3 minutes each time, or until lightly browned. Remove and set aside.

2 Sauté the onion, garlic, celery and carrots in the pan for 5 minutes, or until softened. Stir the tomato purée through, then add the potatoes, stock, herbs, Worcestershire sauce and chicken. Bring to the boil, then reduce the heat, cover and simmer for 15 minutes.

3 Add the courgette and peas and cook for a further 10 minutes, or until all the vegetables are soft.

4 Mix the cornflour with 60ml water until smooth, then add to the saucepan and stir for 2 minutes, or until thickened. Season to taste with salt and freshly ground black pepper and stir in the parsley. Serve with crusty bread or mashed potatoes.

Variation

If you have herbs growing at home or a ready source of fresh herbs, use them instead of the dried herbs. Increase the quantity and stir them through at the end.

Waste not, want not

Leftovers from the stew can be frozen for another meal. You can also use leftover cooked chicken in this dish – just add it to the stew for the last 5 minutes to heat through thoroughly.

Quick

Thrifty

Chicken Maryland

There are probably as many recipes for this crumbed chicken dish as there are home cooks in Maryland, the US state from which it hails. Grandma would have served hers with grilled canned pineapple rings for sunshine on a plate.

150g plain flour
2 eggs, lightly beaten
100g dry breadcrumbs
4 small chicken legs
vegetable oil, for deep-frying
2 bananas, peeled and halved
mini corn on the cob, cooked,
   to serve
grilled tomatoes, to serve

Serves 4
Preparation 10 minutes
Cooking 15 minutes

Kitchen wisdom

If you can't find chicken legs, just use chicken pieces. For extra flavour, try adding a teaspoon or two of dried herbs to the flour.

1 Put the flour in a wide, shallow bowl and season with salt and freshly ground black pepper. Put the eggs and breadcrumbs in separate wide bowls.

2 Coat the chicken pieces with the flour, then dip into the eggs, allowing the excess to drain off. Coat each piece throughly with the breadcrumb mixture.

3 Heat the oil in a large deep frying pan, saucepan or deep-fryer to 160°C/gas 3, or until a cube of bread dropped into the oil browns in 30 to 35 seconds – the oil needs to be deep enough to cover the chicken. Add the chicken and turn the heat up slightly to maintain the temperature, then deep-fry the chicken for 10 to 12 minutes, turning it over halfway through, and reducing the heat slightly if it's browning too quickly. Pierce the chicken at its thickest point with a skewer – if the juices run clear, it's cooked. Drain well on kitchen paper.

4 Meanwhile, coat the bananas with the flour, then with the remaining egg and breadcrumbs. Deep-fry the banana pieces for 3 minutes, or until they appear golden. Drain well on a bed of kitchen paper.

5 Serve the chicken and banana pieces with mini corn on the cob and grilled tomatoes or pineapple rings.

Chicken à la king

Here's a lighter version of a super-rich, ultra-creamy dinner-party classic from the 1970s. It's a cinch to make, but the results are entirely delicious.

knob of butter
60ml olive oil
1 small green pepper, diced
125g button mushrooms, sliced
600g boneless, skinless chicken breasts, diced
375ml chicken stock (see Basics)
2 tablespoons plain flour
250ml soured cream
1 tablespoon sherry
fresh parsley, to garnish
steamed rice, to serve

Serves 4
Preparation 10 minutes
Cooking 15 minutes

1 Heat the butter and 1 tablespoon of the olive oil in a large frying pan over a medium heat. Add the pepper and mushrooms and sauté for a few minutes, or until they are starting to soften. Remove and set aside.

2 Reduce the heat and add the chicken to the pan. Sauté for 3 to 4 minutes, or until lightly browned and almost cooked, then add 125ml of the stock and cook until the liquid has evaporated. Remove the chicken and set aside.

3 Add the remaining olive oil to the pan, stir in the flour until smooth and cook for 1 minute. Remove from the heat and whisk in the remaining stock.

4 Return the saucepan to the heat and whisk the gravy for 2 minutes, or until it has thickened, then whisk in the soured cream.

5 Return the chicken and vegetables to the pan with the sherry and season to taste with salt and freshly ground black pepper. Bring to a simmer for 2 to 3 minutes to heat the chicken through. Garnish with parsley and serve with steamed rice.

Waste not, want not

Leftovers can be used as a filling for crêpes, or in mini pies. You could even mix them through leftover cooked pasta and gently reheat.

fish, seafood and shellfish

Nutritionists and doctors are always saying that we should eat more fish and seafood – it's good for our brains and our overall health. While fresh seafood isn't always cheap, a little good-quality fish goes a long way and canned varieties can be very economical. Here are some of Grandma's favourite recipes for the fruits of the sea.

Prepare and relax   Luxury on a budget

Fish pie

This fantastic fish pie is so versatile and simple to prepare. For a real treat, try replacing some of the fish with smoked fish – haddock, for example – or add some prawns or a mixture of seafood, such as crab or scallops.

1kg firm white fish fillets
750ml milk
1 onion, chopped
1 bay leaf
1 teaspoon white peppercorns
75g butter
75g plain flour
80g frozen peas
3 tablespoons chopped
    fresh parsley
1 x 375g sheet chilled, ready
    rolled puff pastry
1 egg, lightly beaten

Serves 6
Preparation 10 minutes,
    plus 5 to 10 minutes cooling
Cooking 45 minutes

1 Put the fish, milk, onion, bay leaf and peppercorns in a large frying pan over a medium heat. Bring to the boil, then reduce the heat and simmer for 10 minutes. Remove the fish and set aside to cool. Strain the milk mixture and set aside. When the fish has cooled, break it into chunks and discard any skin and bones.

2 Melt the butter in a saucepan and stir in the flour to make a smooth paste. Cook for 1 minute, then remove from the heat and whisk in the reserved milk. Return to the heat and whisk until thickened. Stir in the peas and parsley and season to taste with salt and plenty of freshly ground black pepper.

3 Place the fish in a small baking or casserole dish and pour the sauce over – the dish should be just large enough to accommodate the mixture. Stir gently to combine, then set aside to cool slightly. (Allowing the filling to cool a little will stop the pastry going soggy when it's placed on top.)

4 Preheat the oven to 200°C/gas 6. Top the fish mixture with the pastry sheet, trimming the edges to fit. Brush the top generously with the beaten egg and bake for 25 to 30 minutes, or until the pastry is golden.

Grandma's secret

Instead of topping the pie with pastry you can use mashed potato, or slices of leftover potatoes. You can also make this dish ahead, up to the end of step 3.

Super quick   **Luxury on a budget**

Steamed fish with soy and garlic

A whole steamed fish makes a spectacular feast — we've used red snapper in this version but all sorts of varieties could be used instead — go for what's fresh in that day. Drizzling hot oil over the fish before serving makes the skin delightfully crisp.

700g whole fish (ask your fishmonger which fish is best on the day), gutted and scaled (ask your fishmonger to do this)
4 spring onions, trimmed, plus extra spring onion slices, to serve
60ml chicken stock (see Basics)
2 tablespoons soy sauce
2cm piece of fresh ginger, peeled and cut into matchsticks
2 tablespoons peanut oil
1 tablespoon sesame oil
fresh coriander leaves, to serve
steamed rice, to serve

Serves 4
Preparation 5 minutes
Cooking 20 minutes

1 Pat the fish dry with kitchen paper and make three diagonal cuts on each side through the thickest part of the flesh. Place the spring onions on a heatproof plate large enough to hold the fish and fit in a steamer. Place the fish on top.

2 Mix together the stock and soy sauce and pour over the fish. Scatter with the ginger. Put the plate in the steamer and set the steamer over a pot or wok of boiling water. Cover and steam the fish for 15 minutes, or until just cooked (the flesh will be opaque and flake easily when tested with a fork). Remove the plate from the steamer and scatter the fish with extra spring onion slices.

3 Heat the oils in a small saucepan until just smoking, then pour over the cooked fish. Garnish with coriander leaves and serve with steamed rice.

Variations
Steaming is a superb way to cook fish as it preserves its sea-fresh sweetness and keeps it succulently moist. Be adventurous and experiment with Thai aromatics such as lime juice, lime leaves, lemongrass, galangal and chilli.

Kitchen wisdom

If the fish is too large for your steamer, or you don't have one, wrap the fish in a large sheet of foil – bring the two ends up and fold them over to form a tent, then roll the two short sides up to seal in all the liquid and flavours. Bake at 200°C/gas 6 for 15 to 20 minutes, or until cooked through.

Quick

Extra thrifty

Kedgeree

In the days of the Raj in India, kedgeree was a popular breakfast dish, but it tastes just as good when served for lunch or dinner. For a completely different but equally delicious flavour, try canned salmon instead of the smoked fish.

400g smoked cod (or any other
　　smoked fish such as haddock)
500ml milk, approximately
2 tablespoons butter
1 small onion, finely chopped
1 teaspoon curry powder
550g cold, cooked long-grain rice
2 tablespoons chopped fresh
　　parsley
4 hard-boiled eggs (see Basics),
　　shelled and quartered
lemon wedges, to serve

Serves 4
Preparation 10 minutes
Cooking 25 minutes

1 Place the fish in a saucepan just large enough to contain it, then pour in enough milk to just cover. Bring to a simmer over a medium heat, then reduce the heat to low. Cover and simmer gently for 15 minutes, or until the fish is just cooked (the flesh will be opaque and flake easily when tested with a fork). Drain, then break into large flakes.

2 Melt the butter in a large frying pan over a medium heat. Add the onion and curry powder and gently sauté for 3 to 4 minutes, or until the onion is softened.

3 Add the rice and stir to coat in the butter. Add the fish and stir gently for 2 to 3 minutes, or until it's heated through. Top with the parsley and hard-boiled eggs and serve with lemon wedges.

Waste not, want not

This is an ideal recipe for using up leftover rice and any leftover cooked fish.

Impossible salmon pie

An 'impossible' pie is one that miraculously makes its own crust. It sounds hard to believe, but follow our instructions and you'll find out for yourself.

4 eggs
125g butter, softened and
    roughly diced
75g self-raising flour
500ml milk
213g can salmon, drained,
    any bones removed and
    flesh flaked
1 small onion, chopped
60g grated Cheddar
2 tablespoons chopped
    fresh parsley

Serves 6
Preparation 10 minutes
Cooking 50 minutes

1 Preheat the oven to 180°C/gas 4. Thoroughly grease a 26cm diameter pie dish.

2 Put the eggs, butter and flour in a food processor and blend until smooth.

3 Combine the milk, salmon, onion, cheese and parsley into a bowl, then add the egg mixture. Stir to combine and season well with salt and freshly ground black pepper. Pour the mixture into the pie dish and bake for 50 minutes, or until firm and golden.

Variation

Instead of salmon, you can use canned tuna or leftover cooked fish here, and instead of parsley any herbs that happen to be in your garden or fridge. Top with pine nuts or a little extra cheese and serve with a green salad.

Waste not, want not

This pie can be eaten cold the next day and is also suitable for packed lunches.

Express

Luxury on a budget

Grilled fish with lemon butter sauce

Grilled fish is probably the easiest and quickest meal in the world to cook and is supremely nutritious as well as delicately flavoured. A simple lemon sauce is all it needs to dress it up.

4 x 175g fish fillets
1 tablespoon olive oil

LEMON BUTTER SAUCE
80g butter
60ml lemon juice
1 tablespoon chopped
    fresh parsley

Serves 4
Preparation 5 minutes
Cooking 10 minutes

1 Preheat the grill to high. Brush the fish with the olive oil and season with salt and freshly ground black pepper. Cook the fish under the grill until just cooked through (the flesh will be opaque and flake easily when tested with a fork). This will probably take 6 to 8 minutes, depending on the thickness of the fillets.

2 Meanwhile, melt the butter in a small saucepan over a medium heat, then add the lemon juice and parsley. Cook until foaming, then pour over the fish.

Variation
Try this dish with our pesto from page 41, or a horseradish sauce made by mixing 1 tablespoon horseradish cream with 125ml soured cream.

Pan-fried fish with braised lentils

Make an accompaniment of lentils that have been gently braised with onions, carrots, tomatoes and garlic to go beautifully with pan-fried fish, a perfect complement to its silky texture and subtle sweetness.

4 x 180g white fish fillets
2 tablespoons olive oil
2 tablespoons butter
grilled lemon halves,
    to serve

BRAISED LENTILS
1 tablespoon olive oil
1 onion, chopped
1 carrot, peeled and diced
1 stalk celery, thinly sliced
2 tablespoons tomato purée
250g Puy or small green lentils,
    rinsed
2 cloves garlic, crushed
450ml chicken stock
    (see Basics)
1 bouquet garni
3 tablespoons chopped
    fresh parsley

Serves 4
Preparation 5 minutes
Cooking 40 minutes

1 To braise the lentils, heat the olive oil in a saucepan over a medium heat and sauté the onion, carrot and celery for 5 minutes, or until softened and lightly coloured. Stir in the tomato purée, then add the lentils, garlic, stock, bouquet garni and enough water to just cover the lentils. Bring to the boil, reduce the heat and simmer for 30 minutes, or until the lentils are tender, stirring regularly and adding a little more water if required. (If there's too much liquid, increase the heat and gently boil to reduce the liquid.) Season well with salt and freshly ground black pepper and stir the parsley through.

2 When the lentils are nearly ready, season the fish fillets with salt and black pepper. Heat the olive oil and butter in a large non-stick frying pan over a medium heat until the butter has melted and the oil is just sizzling. Add the fish fillets and cook for 3 minutes on each side, or until just cooked and golden. Serve on a bed of lentils, with grilled lemon halves.

Kitchen wisdom

Puy lentils are small dark lentils grown in the volcanic soils of the Puy region of France. They are prized for their delicate flavour and texture and hold their shape well during cooking.

Quick

Extra thrifty

Tuna and lemon fishcakes

Grandma was a real whizz at making something good from practically nothing. These little breaded cakes are a perfect example, turning a little canned fish and leftover mashed potatoes into a scrumptiously thrifty meal.

425g canned tuna, drained
    and flaked
500g potatoes, peeled, cooked
    and mashed
2 spring onions, finely chopped
2 tablespoons chopped
    fresh parsley
grated zest and juice of 1 lemon
75g plain flour
1 egg
100g dry breadcrumbs
olive oil, for pan-frying
tartare sauce, to serve

Serves 4
Preparation 15 minutes,
    plus 30 minutes chilling
Cooking 10 minutes

1 In a large bowl, mix together the tuna, mashed potatoes, spring onions, parsley, lemon zest and lemon juice. Season well with salt and freshly ground black pepper. Roll the mixture into 12 balls and flatten them slightly.

2 Put the flour in a bowl. Crack the egg into another bowl and beat lightly. Put the breadcrumbs in a third bowl. Dip each fishcake into the flour, coating on all sides. Dip them into the egg, then the breadcrumbs. Place on a tray and refrigerate for at least 20 to 30 minutes to set the coating.

3 Heat enough olive oil in a large frying pan to generously cover the base. Fry the fishcakes over a medium heat for 4 to 5 minutes on each side, or until golden (you may need to do this in two batches). Serve warm.

Variation
The tuna can be replaced with canned salmon or any leftover fish that's available. For a stronger flavour, try adding a teaspoon of mustard to the fish mixture.

Grandma's secret

These fishcakes can be prepared ahead of time and cooked when required.

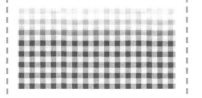

Quick

Luxury on a budget

Fish stew

Based on the famed French seafood stew bouillabaisse, this elegantly simple but fully flavoured version doesn't take hours to prepare. You can put it together with any combination of your favourite kinds of fish and shellfish.

2 tablespoons olive oil
1 onion, finely chopped
1 stalk celery, finely chopped
3 cloves garlic, crushed
¼ teaspoon saffron threads
    (optional)
125ml white wine
680ml to 700ml jar tomato
    passata
500ml fish or chicken stock
    (see Basics)
2 bay leaves
1.5kg prepared fish and seafood
    (such as fish fillets cut into
    chunks, shelled raw prawns,
    calamari, scallops, mussels)
2 tablespoons fresh parsley
lemon wedges, to serve

Serves 6
Preparation 15 minutes
Cooking 30 minutes

1 Heat the olive oil in a large saucepan over a medium heat. Add the onion, celery and garlic and sauté for 5 minutes, or until softened. Stir the saffron through, if using, then add the wine and bring to the boil.

2 Stir in the passata, stock and bay leaves, then reduce the heat and simmer for 10 minutes.

3 Add the prepared seafood and simmer until it's all cooked. Depending on their size, the fish pieces will take 8 to 10 minutes to cook through, and the prawns, calamari, scallops and mussels 4 to 5 minutes.

4 Season the finished stew with salt and freshly ground black pepper, sprinkle with parsley and serve with lemon wedges.

Variations

A finely shredded fennel bulb can be added with the onion; for some extra warmth, add a pinch of dried red chilli flakes or chilli powder with the saffron.

Curried prawns

Serve prawns in a creamy coconut sauce piled on a mound of steamed rice for the easiest seafood curry.

1½ tablespoons butter
1 onion, finely chopped
2 cloves garlic, crushed
1 to 2 tablespoons curry powder
    (or to taste, depending on the
    strength of the powder)
270ml coconut cream
700g raw prawns, peeled
    and the veins removed
1 tablespoon lemon juice
steamed rice, to serve

Serves 4
Preparation 15 minutes
Cooking 15 minutes

1 Melt the butter in a frying pan over a medium heat. Add the onion and garlic and sauté for 3 to 4 minutes, or until softened. Add the curry powder and stir for 1 minute, or until fragrant. Add the coconut cream and simmer for 5 minutes, or until the mixture starts to thicken.

2 Add the prawns, then cover and simmer for 5 minutes, or until the prawns are cooked through. Stir in the lemon juice and season with salt. Serve with steamed rice.

Variations
Fresh coriander or parsley can be stirred through the prawns just before serving. If you prefer a more fiery curry, add some chopped fresh chilli to your taste.

Time saver
You can use cooked prawns and just add them for the last 4 minutes of cooking.

Prawn cocktail

All the rage as a dinner party highlight in the 1970s, this simple summer starter requires no cooking, just a little assembly. Try this recipe and you'll remember why prawn cocktail was so popular.

1 iceberg lettuce, outer leaves discarded
60g mayonnaise
1 tablespoon tomato sauce
½ teaspoon Worcestershire sauce
1 teaspoon lemon juice
a pinch of ground white pepper
500g cooked prawns, peeled and the veins removed
lemon wedges, to serve

Serves 4
Preparation 15 minutes
Cooking nil

1 Shred the lettuce and divide among four serving dishes.

2 Combine the mayonnaise, sauces and lemon juice, whisking until smooth. Season well with salt and ground white pepper.

3 Divide the prawns among the serving dishes on top of the lettuce and drizzle with the mayonnaise dressing. Serve immediately, with lemon wedges.

Variations

You could also serve the prawns and dressing on top of avocado halves. For those who like it spicy, add a few drops of Tabasco sauce to the mayonnaise dressing, or for more mature tastes add a teaspoon of brandy.

Quick

Luxury on a budget

Baked fish with onion and tomatoes

A dish that showcases no-fuss cooking at its finest: all you have to do is put all the ingredients in a baking dish and into the oven and allow the heat to infuse the fish with wonderful flavours of lemon, garlic, wine and herbs.

1 onion, thinly sliced
1 garlic clove, crushed
2 sprigs fresh thyme
4 x 180g thick white fish fillets, skin and bones removed
1 lemon, thinly sliced
4 tomatoes, cut into wedges
2 bay leaves
1 tablespoon olive oil
60ml white wine
125ml chicken stock (see Basics)
1 tablespoon chopped fresh parsley (optional)

Serves 4
Preparation 15 minutes
Cooking 20 minutes

1 Preheat the oven to 200°C/gas 6.

2 Spread the onion, garlic and thyme sprigs in a baking dish that will be large enough to hold all the fish fillets, with a little space in between. Place the fish on top and season well with salt and freshly ground black pepper. Arrange the lemon slices over the fish and place the tomatoes and bay leaves around the fish.

3 Mix together the olive oil, wine and stock and pour over the fish. Bake for 20 minutes, or until the fish is just cooked through. Sprinkle with parsley, if desired, and serve.

Variation
This dish is also excellent – and very Mediterranean – with a handful of black olives added to the mix.

Kitchen wisdom

Many varieties of fish are suitable for baking, including cod, red snapper, John Dory, salmon and tuna. Choose the freshest fillets you can find.

Quick

Luxury on a budget

Battered fish and chips

Evoke happy memories of holidays by the sea without leaving home with our best-ever fish and chips, with the fish deep-fried in a beery batter. If you're not a beer fan, use milk or soda water in the batter instead.

**750g fish fillets, such as plaice,
    cod or haddock**
275g plain flour
½ teaspoon salt
375ml beer
**4 large all-purpose potatoes,
    cut into thin wedges**
vegetable oil, for deep-frying
lemon wedges, to serve

Serves 4
Preparation 10 minutes
Cooking 30 minutes

1 Carefully remove any bones from the fish. If the fillets are large, cut them into pieces – aim to get each one measuring about 5cm x 10cm.

2 Sift the flour and salt into a bowl, then gradually whisk in the beer until smooth – the mixture should have the consistency of thick cream. If it becomes too thick, stir in a little water.

3 Dry the potato wedges with kitchen paper. Half-fill a deep-fryer or large saucepan with oil and heat to 180°C/gas 4, or until a cube of bread dropped into the oil browns in 15 seconds. Cook the potatoes for 5 to 6 minutes, or until almost tender but not coloured. Remove and drain on kitchen paper.

4 Dip the fish pieces in the batter, coating well. Deep-fry the fish (you may need to do this in batches to maintain the oil temperature) for 8 to 10 minutes, or until golden and crisp. Drain well on kitchen paper.

5 Return the potato wedges to the hot oil and fry for a final 3 to 4 minutes, or until golden and crisp. Sprinkle with salt and serve with the battered fish and lemon wedges.

Smoked fish with creamy parsley sauce

An old Scottish favourite that's traditionally known as 'finnan haddie', this dish can be enjoyed for breakfast, brunch or supper.

700g smoked fish fillets,
**   such as cod or haddock**
375ml milk

CREAMY PARSLEY SAUCE
625ml milk
1 onion, roughly chopped
6 black peppercorns
1 bay leaf
3 tablespoons butter
35g plain flour
2 tablespoons chopped
**   fresh parsley**
1 teaspoon lemon juice

Serves 4
Preparation 10 minutes
Cooking 20 minutes

1 Place the fish and milk in a shallow saucepan just large enough to hold all the fish in a single layer. Add enough water to cover the fish. Bring to a simmer, then cover and cook for 15 minutes, or until the fish is just cooked (the flesh will be opaque and flake easily when tested with a fork). Remove the fish with a slotted spoon.

2 Meanwhile, make the creamy parsley sauce. Put the milk, onion, peppercorns and bay leaf in a saucepan. Bring to a simmer, then remove from the heat and allow to infuse for 5 minutes. Strain the milk into a bowl and reserve.

3 Melt the butter in a small saucepan over a medium heat. Stir in the flour to make a smooth paste and cook, stirring, for 1 minute. Add the reserved milk, whisking until smooth. Continue to stir until the mixture thickens and comes to the boil. Reduce the heat to low and cook, stirring, for 4 to 5 minutes.

4 Season the sauce with salt and freshly ground black pepper and stir in the parsley and lemon juice. Serve the sauce drizzled over the poached fish fillets.

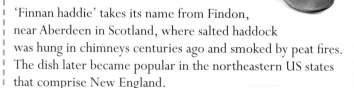

Kitchen wisdom

'Finnan haddie' takes its name from Findon, near Aberdeen in Scotland, where salted haddock was hung in chimneys centuries ago and smoked by peat fires. The dish later became popular in the northeastern US states that comprise New England.

Quick

Extra thrifty

Tuna and macaroni bake

Some dishes never fall out of favour. This ultra-easy bake is great for using up leftover cooked pasta and is just the ticket when the cupboard is running bare as it uses a range of the ultimate storecupboard staples.

250g macaroni
80g butter
1 small onion, finely diced
2 tablespoons plain flour
750ml milk
90g grated Cheddar
**425g canned tuna, drained and
    flaked**
**2 tablespoons chopped
    fresh parsley**
80g fresh breadcrumbs

Serves 4
Preparation 10 minutes
Cooking 35 minutes

1 Preheat the oven to 180°C/gas 4. Cook the macaroni according to the packet instructions. Drain well.

2 Meanwhile, melt 3 tablespoons of the butter in a saucepan over a medium heat. Add the onion and sauté for 2 to 3 minutes, or until starting to soften. Stir in the flour until smooth, then cook, stirring, for a minute. Gradually add the milk, whisking until smooth and thickened. Bring to the boil, then reduce the heat and simmer for a minute. Remove from the heat.

3 Add 60g of the cheese, then all the tuna, parsley and pasta. Transfer the mixture to a baking dish and sprinkle with the breadcrumbs and the remaining cheese and butter. Bake for 25 minutes, or until the topping is golden. Serve hot.

Variations

For extra flavour, add 1 teaspoon mustard to the white sauce. Instead of tuna you can also use canned salmon.

Super quick

Luxury on a budget

Moules marinière

It's always worth using a good-quality wine when preparing this dish to make a really superb broth. Serve the moules (mussels) with plenty of crusty bread so that you don't miss out on any of the buttery juices.

100g butter
2 onions, finely chopped
500ml white wine
2kg mussels, scrubbed, hairy beards removed and any opened or damaged shells discarded
3 tablespoons chopped fresh parsley
crusty bread, to serve

Serves 4
Preparation 20 minutes
Cooking 10 minutes

1 Melt the butter in a saucepan large enough to hold all the mussels. Add the onions and sauté over a medium heat for 4 to 5 minutes, or until softened. Pour in the wine and bring to the boil.

2 Add the mussels, then cover and cook for 4 to 5 minutes, or until the mussels open, shaking the pan from time to time.

3 You may need to stir gently once or twice to ensure that the mussels on top are cooked. Mix the parsley through and season to taste with salt and freshly ground black pepper. Discard any mussels that have not opened. Serve immediately, with crusty bread.

Variation
A little cream or soured cream can be stirred through the sauce to make it richer.

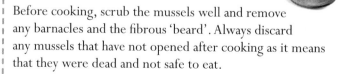

Kitchen wisdom

Before cooking, scrub the mussels well and remove any barnacles and the fibrous 'beard'. Always discard any mussels that have not opened after cooking as it means that they were dead and not safe to eat.

vegetables
and salads

A meal isn't complete without fresh vegetables on the table —
whether as part of the main dish or an accompaniment.
If you can't pick your own from the garden or allotment
like Grandma often did, follow her lead and eat
with the seasons, when produce is at its best.

Prepare and relax   **Extra thrifty**

Roast potatoes and root vegetables

There's nothing nicer with a juicy roast than crispy roast potatoes. You can use any combination of root vegetables to go with the potatoes: carrots, parsnips, swedes, turnip and beetroot are all terrific when roasted.

4 roasting potatoes
3 carrots
3 parsnips
3 small swedes or turnips
3 beetroots
olive oil, for drizzling

Serves 6
Preparation 10 minutes
Cooking 45 minutes

1 Preheat the oven to 210°C/gas 6.5. Wash and scrub all the vegetables, then pat dry with kitchen paper. Peel the potatoes and cut each in half.

2 Top and tail the carrots and parsnips, then peel them and cut them in half horizontally. Peel the swedes or turnips and cut into quarters. Leave the beetroot whole and the skin on.

3 Place all the vegetables in a large roasting tin, add a good splash of olive oil and season well with salt and freshly ground black pepper. Roast for 30 minutes, then turn the vegetables over and roast for a further 15 minutes, or until golden and tender. Serve hot.

Variation

In summer, try Provençal-style roast vegetables. Trim and cut in half some courgette, red and green peppers, yellow squash and red onions; toss with olive oil, salt and fresh thyme. Bake in a roasting tin in a moderately hot oven for 45 minutes.

Kitchen wisdom

Root vegetables such as parsnips, turnips, swedes and carrots are at their peak in late autumn and winter. Store them in the vegetable compartment in the fridge.

Quick   **Extra thrifty**

Mushrooms filled with bacon and buttery breadcrumbs

Stuff mushrooms with garlicky bacon and top with crisp breadcrumbs for a really tasty treat that's great as a starter, or serve alongside a good steak. To make this a real meal, try using big Portobello mushrooms.

8 mushrooms, or
    4 large mushrooms
knob of butter
1 tablespoon olive oil
2 slices bacon, rind removed,
    finely chopped
2 cloves garlic, crushed
80g fresh breadcrumbs
2 teaspoons finely chopped
    fresh thyme leaves

Serves 4
Preparation 15 minutes
Cooking 20 minutes

1 Preheat the oven to 180°C/gas 4. Line a baking tray with baking parchment or greaseproof paper.

2 Wipe the tops of the mushrooms with kitchen paper, then remove the stems and chop them finely.

3 Warm the butter and olive oil in a frying pan over a medium heat. Add the bacon and sauté for 4 to 5 minutes, or until brown and crisp. Add the chopped mushroom stems and cook for a further minute, or until soft. Add the garlic and cook for another 30 seconds.

4 Stir in the breadcrumbs and thyme and sauté the mixture for 3 to 4 minutes. Season with freshly ground black pepper.

5 Place the mushrooms on the baking tray, cup side up, and spoon the crumb mixture on top. Bake for 10 minutes, or until the mushrooms are tender and the topping is crisp.

Kitchen wisdom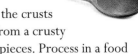

To make fresh breadcrumbs, cut the crusts from day-old bread (preferably from a crusty Italian-style loaf) and break into pieces. Process in a food processor until chunky crumbs form.

Cauliflower cheese

Cauliflower is always sublime with a cheesy sauce. To give the dish extra crunch, sprinkle with three tablespoons of fresh breadcrumbs and the same of finely grated Cheddar before grilling.

1 small cauliflower (about 800g),
   cut into florets
2 tablespoons butter
2 tablespoons plain flour
310ml milk
60g strongly flavoured
   grated Cheddar
ground white pepper, to taste

Serves 6
Preparation 15 minutes
Cooking 15 minutes

1 Steam the cauliflower over a saucepan of boiling water for 5 to 7 minutes, or until just tender. Drain and arrange in a single layer in a heatproof serving dish.

2 Meanwhile, melt the butter in a small saucepan over a medium heat until foaming. Add the flour and stir over a low heat for 1 minute. Add the milk, a little at a time, stirring after each addition until smooth.

3 Bring to the boil and simmer for 2 minutes, stirring occasionally. Remove from the heat and stir in the cheese. Season to taste with salt and ground white pepper.

4 Pour the cheese sauce over the cauliflower. Place under a hot grill (but at least 15cm from the heat) and cook for 5 minutes, or until the sauce is golden brown. Serve immediately.

Variations
You can serve the cauliflower simply drizzled with the sauce, without grilling it. To season the sauce, try a pinch of cayenne pepper or nutmeg instead of white pepper.

Prepare and relax   **Extra thrifty**

Potato gratin

Layer thickly sliced
baked potatoes in
a creamy cheese
sauce for a luxurious
accompaniment to a
range of meat and
fish recipes.

250ml milk
300ml single cream
2 cloves garlic, sliced
1.25kg baking potatoes
60g grated Cheddar

Serves 8
Preparation 20 minutes
Cooking 1 hour 30 minutes

1 Preheat the oven to 190°C/gas 5. Lightly grease a shallow 1.5 litre baking dish.

2 Warm the milk, cream and garlic in a saucepan over a medium-low heat until hot. Turn off the heat and leave to infuse while you prepare the potatoes.

3 Peel the potatoes and slice to 5mm thick. Arrange a layer of potatoes in the baking dish, overlapping slightly. Season with salt and freshly ground black pepper, then pour one-third of the milk mixture over the potatoes. Make another two layers using the remaining potatoes and milk. Cover with lightly oiled foil.

4 Bake for 30 minutes; remove the foil and cook for a further 30 minutes. Sprinkle with the cheese and bake for a final 10 minutes. Leave to stand for 5 minutes before serving.

Kitchen wisdom

To make it easier to slice the potatoes finely, cut a small slice from the bottom of each potato so that they sit securely and don't move during slicing.

Quick

Extra thrifty

Bubble and squeak

Perhaps the ultimate way to use leftover potatoes and other veggies, bubble and squeak is also a tasty way to get reluctant children to eat vegetables. Try it for a special weekend brunch with a fried egg or bacon.

2 large potatoes (about 500g)
2 tablespoons milk
knob of butter
1 carrot, peeled and chopped
75g chopped cabbage
80g frozen peas, thawed
olive oil, for pan-frying
1 onion, chopped

Serves 4 (makes 8)
Preparation 15 minutes
Cooking 30 minutes

1 Peel the potatoes and cut into large, even-sized pieces. Cook in a large saucepan of boiling water for 10 minutes, or until tender. Drain well, then roughly mash. Stir in the milk and butter.

2 Meanwhile, cook the carrot in a steaming basket over a saucepan of boiling water until tender, adding the cabbage and peas for the last 2 minutes of cooking. Drain, mash roughly, then add to the mashed potato.

3 Heat 2 teaspoons of olive oil in a large non-stick frying pan over a medium heat. Add the onion and sauté for 5 minutes, or until soft. Combine all the vegetables in a large bowl and season well with salt and freshly ground black pepper.

4 Heat some extra oil in the frying pan. Drop in about 80g of the mixture at a time and flatten out slightly to a patty shape – you should be able to fry four patties in the pan at a time. Cook for 3 to 4 minutes on each side, or until well browned – take care when turning as they will be soft. Remove and keep warm. Add a little more oil to the frying pan and cook the remaining patties. Serve hot.

Variations

Bubble and squeak is a brilliant way to use up any kind of leftover cooked vegetables – include some mashed potato, sweet potato or pumpkin to bind it. For enhanced flavour, fry some chopped bacon and/or garlic with the onion.

Quick

Extra thrifty

Red cabbage with apples

A real favourite of eastern European grandmas, this recipe also works with green cabbage, or a mix of red and green. For a different, slightly sharper flavour, add a teaspoon of caraway seeds along with the onion.

1 tablespoon olive oil
2 slices bacon, rind removed, chopped
1 small onion, finely chopped
300g red cabbage, any damaged outer leaves and thick ribs discarded, the remaining leaves shredded
2 dessert apples, peeled, cored and thinly sliced
1 tablespoon red wine vinegar
1 tablespoon soft brown sugar

Serves 6
Preparation 20 minutes
Cooking 25 minutes

1 Heat the olive oil in a large saucepan over a medium heat. Add the bacon and cook for 5 minutes, or until lightly browned. Add the onion and sauté for 5 minutes, or until the onion is soft.

2 Add the cabbage, apples and 60ml water to the pan. Cook, uncovered, for 15 minutes, or until the cabbage is soft, stirring occasionally.

3 Stir in the vinegar and sugar. Season to taste with salt and freshly ground black pepper and serve.

Variation

For an excellent accompaniment to roast pork, omit the bacon and add a cinnamon stick and/or a few whole cloves while the cabbage and apples are cooking.

Waste not, want not

Leftovers can be used in our Bubble and squeak, on page 227.

Super quick **Extra thrifty**

Minted peas

Minted peas have a particular affinity with lamb dishes, but they are also good with beef and sweet poultry such as duck. Just before serving, you can roughly crush the peas if you like or try puréeing them.

500g peas in the pod
2 sprigs fresh mint
knob of butter
pinch of caster sugar

Serves 4
Preparation 20 minutes
Cooking 10 minutes

1 Remove the peas from their pods. Pick the mint leaves from the sprigs. Finely shred the leaves and set aside (you will need about 1 tablespoon shredded mint). Trim the ends of the stalks.

2 Bring a saucepan of water to the boil over a medium heat. Add the mint stalks and peas and cook for 10 minutes, or until the peas are tender. Drain, discarding the mint stalks.

3 Return the peas to the pan with the butter and chopped mint. Season with salt and freshly ground black pepper and add the sugar. Toss over low heat until the butter has melted. Top with some extra mint and serve immediately.

Kitchen wisdom

Shelling 500g fresh pods will yield about 250g peas, but when they're not in season simply use 250g frozen peas.

Creamed spinach

Popeye the sailor man loved his spinach, and so will you when you try our creamed spinach recipe, which makes a fabulous side dish for all kinds of meat, fish and poultry. Don't overcook spinach or it will lose its vibrant colour and nutrients.

1kg spinach
knob of butter
2 cloves garlic, crushed
125ml single cream
pinch of ground nutmeg

Serves 4
Preparation 15 minutes
Cooking 5 minutes

Waste not, want not

Leftovers can be used in our Bubble and squeak, on page 227.

1 Pull the spinach leaves from their stems and immerse in a large bowl of cold water to loosen the dirt. Leave for 5 minutes, then lift out of the water (any dirt will have sunk to the bottom). Drain well, then dry in a salad spinner or a clean tea towel to remove as much water as possible. Finely shred the leaves.

2 Melt the butter in a large frying pan over a medium heat. Add the garlic and sauté for 1 minute, then pour in the cream. Bring to the boil, then add the spinach and cook until wilted and soft. Season with nutmeg, salt and freshly ground black pepper and serve.

Prepare and relax   **Extra thrifty**

Vegetable pie

Packed with a delicious array of vegetables and topped with puff pastry, this pie is a meal in itself – perfect for lunch or a light supper.

½ small butternut squash (about 800g), peeled, seeded and cut into 1.5cm cubes
2 carrots, peeled and chopped
1 small head broccoli, cut into small florets
3 tablespoons butter
1 onion, chopped
1 red pepper, chopped
3 tablespoons plain flour
500ml milk
60g grated Cheddar
55g frozen peas
1½ sheets frozen puff pastry, thawed
1 egg, lightly beaten

Serves 6
Preparation 20 minutes
Cooking 45 minutes

1 Preheat the oven to 200°C/gas 6. Steam the squash and carrots over a saucepan of boiling water for about 10 minutes, or until tender, adding the broccoli for the last 2 minutes of cooking. Drain and place in a large bowl.

2 Meanwhile, melt the butter in a large saucepan over a medium heat until bubbling. Add the onion and pepper and sauté for 5 minutes, or until soft. Sprinkle the flour over and cook, stirring, for 1 minute.

3 Add the milk, 60ml at a time, stirring between each addition. Bring to the boil, then reduce the heat to medium-low and simmer for 2 minutes, stirring occasionally. Stir in the cheese. Add the sauce to the bowl of vegetables, along with the peas. Season with salt and freshly ground black pepper and fold together until combined.

4 Transfer the vegetables to a 1.5 litre pie dish. Cut 2cm wide strips from the half-sheet of pastry and press them around the rim of the dish, overlapping the joins, and trimming to fit. Lay the other sheet of pastry over the dish. Using a small sharp knife, trim the excess pastry and use the trimmings to fill any gaps around the edge. Use a fork or your thumb to press the two layers of pastry together around the rim. Brush with beaten egg and cut small slits into the top of the pastry to allow steam to escape.

5 Bake for 35 minutes, or until the pastry is puffed and golden brown. Serve hot.

Variation
Sprinkle the pastry with sesame or poppy seeds after brushing with the beaten egg.

Quick **Extra thrifty**

Potato latkes

Another eastern European treat, latkes – simply made with grated potato, onion and eggs – are often served with a dollop of soured cream or with apple sauce, but you can serve them just sprinkled with salt, as part of a meal.

1kg potatoes, peeled
1 small onion, finely chopped
2 eggs, lightly beaten
50g plain flour
1 teaspoon baking powder
vegetable oil, for pan frying

Serves 6 (makes 12)
Preparation 20 minutes
Cooking 20 minutes

1 Grate the potatoes and combine with the onion. Take a handful of the mixture at a time and squeeze over a bowl to remove as much liquid as possible. Transfer the mixture into a clean bowl.

2 Add the eggs, then sift in the flour and baking powder. Mix together until combined.

3 Heat about 5ml of oil in a large frying pan over a medium heat. Drop 50g of the mixture into the pan at a time and flatten slightly to about 8cm – you should be able to cook about four at a time, but don't overcrowd the pan. Cook for 3 minutes on each side, or until golden brown and crisp. Drain on kitchen paper and keep warm while cooking the remaining latkes. Serve immediately.

Variation
You could make smaller latkes and top them with a little smoked salmon and a small spoonful of soured cream to serve as an appetiser.

Grandma's secret

Crisp on the outside but creamy in the middle, these grated potato pancakes are a traditional food of Hanukkah, an eight-day Jewish holiday. They are especially delicious for breakfast.

Kitchen wisdom

Starchy (floury) potatoes are good for mashing and roasting and give a lovely crisp result here. Starchy potatoes have a thin skin, which comes away a little like tissue paper as you rub it. Waxy (boiling) potatoes feel much denser and their skin is firmer, not flaky.

Glazed carrots

Shiny and bright, glazed carrots bring a splash of colour to any plate. You can serve them sprinkled with a little chopped fresh parsley or dill. For a taste of the Middle East, add a pinch of ground cumin to the glaze.

3 carrots
knob of butter
1 tablespoon honey

Serves 6
Preparation 10 minutes
Cooking 10 minutes

1 Peel the carrots and cut into 5mm slices on a slight diagonal. Cook in a saucepan of boiling water over a medium heat for 5 minutes, or until just tender. Drain.

2 Add the butter and honey to the pan. Cook over a low heat, stirring and tossing, for 2 minutes, or until well glazed. Season with a pinch of salt and serve.

Variation
For a really attractive accompaniment on a special occasion, use a bunch of whole baby carrots instead – trim the tops, leaving about 1.5cm of green stalk, then peel and cook as directed. You can also cook parsnips this way.

Oven-baked chips

Our chunky, golden, guilt-free chips are truly irresistible. Baking chips in the oven, rather than deep-frying them, saves a lot of oil and makes good use of a hot oven in which other items are baking.

3 large roasting potatoes (about 750g)
1 tablespoon olive oil

Serves 4
Preparation 10 minutes
Cooking 40 minutes

1 Preheat the oven to 200°C/gas 6. Lightly oil a baking tray.

2 Wash and peel the potatoes, then cut into chips about 1.5cm thick. Rub the chips dry in a clean tea towel.

3 Spread the chips on the baking tray, drizzle with the olive oil and toss to coat. Bake for 40 minutes, or until golden brown, turning occasionally. Season with salt and serve hot with ketchup, mayonnaise or barbecue sauce.

Variation

Desiree potatoes make great potato wedges. Don't bother peeling them, just cut them lengthwise into thick wedges and toss in olive oil. Bake for 40 minutes, or until golden brown.

Ratatouille

A delicious mélange of sautéed vegetables, this colourful dish works well hot or cold. In an old-style ratatouille, the vegetables are cooked separately and the dish is assembled at the end. This quick method is just as tasty.

2 tablespoons olive oil
1 onion, chopped
2 cloves garlic, crushed
1 red pepper, cut into 2cm pieces
2 courgettes, cut in half lengthways, then into 2cm slices
1 aubergine, cut into 2cm cubes
5 ripe tomatoes, cored and chopped
2 tablespoons shredded fresh basil, plus extra leaves, to garnish

Serves 6
Preparation 20 minutes
Cooking 35 minutes

1 Heat the olive oil in a large, heavy-based saucepan over a medium heat. Add the onion and sauté for 7 minutes, or until soft and golden. Add the garlic and cook for a further minute.

2 Add the pepper and cook for 2 minutes, stirring occasionally. Add the courgette and aubergine and stir until well combined.

3 Stir in the tomatoes and bring to the boil. Reduce the heat to low and partially cover with a lid. Simmer, stirring occasionally, for 20 minutes, or until the vegetables are tender. Stir in the basil and season with salt and freshly ground black pepper. The dish can be served hot, warm or cool, scattered with extra basil.

Variation

To make a delicious hearty meal, add a drained 400g can of chickpeas towards the end of cooking and heat through. Serve with crusty bread.

Kitchen wisdom

If your tomatoes aren't super-ripe, you can enrich the flavour of the dish by adding 1 tablespoon of tomato purée, or use 800g of canned chopped Italian tomatoes. When seasoning tomato-based dishes, a good pinch of sugar often enhances the flavour.

Prepare and relax   Extra thrifty

Stuffed jacket potatoes with leeks and cheese

Jacket potatoes are a perfect light lunch or supper – and provide a backdrop for a host of interesting fillings. As well as the variations below, you can top or fill them with – among other ideas – baked beans, bolognese sauce or a good con carne.

4 large potatoes (about 1kg)
1 large leek
1½ tablespoons butter
125g grated Cheddar

Serves 4
Preparation 15 minutes
Cooking 1 hour 45 minutes

1 Preheat the oven to 200°C/gas 6. Scrub the potatoes with a stiff-bristled brush and pat dry with paper towels. Prick them a few times with a fork. Place them in the oven, directly onto an oven rack. Bake for 1½ hours, or until the potatoes are soft when tested with a small sharp knife and the skin is crisp.

2 Meanwhile, trim the darker green section from the leek and discard. Cut the white stalk in half lengthways and rinse to remove any grit. Drain well and finely slice.

3 Melt the butter in a frying pan over a medium heat. Add the leek and sauté for 5 minutes, or until soft.

4 Using tongs, remove the potatoes from the oven. Allow to cool slightly, then cut a slice from the top of each potato. Scoop out the flesh using a spoon and place in a bowl. Add the sautéed leek and the cheese to the flesh, season with salt and freshly ground black pepper and mix to combine.

5 Spoon the mixture back into the potatoes and replace the tops. Place the potatoes on a baking tray and bake for a final 10 minutes. Serve hot.

Variations
Add ham or fried bacon to the filling, or sweetcorn and sautéed red pepper. Replace the Cheddar with cream cheese or blue cheese, or scoop out the potato and mash it with avocado and grated cheese. Alternatively instead of the leek, add canned salmon or tuna, chopped fresh chives and grated cheese.

Express   **Extra thrifty**

Pan-fried brussels sprouts with bacon

Not just for Christmas, goodness-packed brussels sprouts are too often underrated and overcooked, which can make them mushy and sulphurous. Here, roasted hazelnuts and bacon lend intriguing flavours to lightly cooked sprouts.

300g brussels sprouts
1 tablespoon olive oil
knob of butter
2 slices bacon, rind removed,
cut into short, thin strips
2 tablespoons roasted hazelnuts,
chopped (optional)

Serves 4
Preparation 10 minutes
Cooking 10 minutes

1 Pull off any loose or discoloured outer leaves from the brussels sprouts. Cut the sprouts in half lengthways. Cook in a steaming basket over a saucepan of boiling water for 5 minutes, or until just tender.

2 Meanwhile, heat the olive oil and butter in a large frying pan over a medium heat. Add the bacon and cook for 3 to 4 minutes, or until crisp.

3 Add the brussels sprouts to the pan and toss to coat in the butter mixture. Cook, tossing regularly, for 5 minutes, or until the sprouts are softened and well glazed. Toss through the hazelnuts, if using, and serve.

Waste not, want not

Leftovers can be used in our Bubble and squeak, on page 227.

Kitchen wisdom

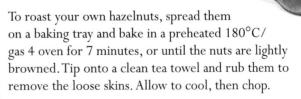

To roast your own hazelnuts, spread them on a baking tray and bake in a preheated 180°C/ gas 4 oven for 7 minutes, or until the nuts are lightly browned. Tip onto a clean tea towel and rub them to remove the loose skins. Allow to cool, then chop.

Pasta picnic salad

When you're cooking a batch of pasta for a hot dish, make double and you can use the rest as the backdrop for a versatile salad that's great for picnics, barbecues and packed lunches.

1 Cook the pasta in a large saucepan of boiling water according to the packet instructions. Drain and rinse under cold-running water, then drain well again.

2 Tip the pasta into a large bowl and add the mayonnaise and lemon juice. Gently toss to combine.

3 Add the remaining ingredients and toss again to thoroughly mix in the dressing. Serve at room temperature, or cover and refrigerate until required.

Variations

For a smart twist, use prosciutto or salami instead of ham. Replace the vegetables and parsley with olives, roasted red pepper, semi-dried tomatoes and fresh basil, and dress with olive oil and balsamic vinegar instead of the mayo dressing.

300g spiral pasta, or other short
    pasta, such as penne or farfalle
60g mayonnaise
3 teaspoons lemon juice
310g sweetcorn, drained
1 carrot, peeled and grated
100g cherry tomatoes, quartered
150g sliced ham, chopped
2 tablespoons chopped
    fresh parsley

Serves 4
Preparation 15 minutes
Cooking 10 to 12 minutes

Rice salad

On hot summer nights, a cool rice salad is the perfect partner for grilled or barbecued chicken or fish. In this version, soft fluffy rice is generously speckled with raw, diced vegetables for vibrant colour and a palate-pleasing crunch.

200g long-grain white rice
310g sweetcorn, drained
4 spring onions, sliced
1 small red pepper, diced
1 small cucumber, diced
2 stalks celery, sliced
60ml lemon juice
2 tablespoons olive oil

Serves 8
Preparation 20 minutes
Cooking 10 minutes

Kitchen wisdom

Rice left unrefrigerated can pose a food poisoning risk. If you're not using it immediately, keep the rice covered in the fridge. Take the rice out 20 minutes prior to serving to take off the chill.

1 Cook the rice in a large saucepan of boiling water for 10 minutes, or until just tender. Drain well. Leave to cool, turning the rice over occasionally with a large metal spoon to release the heat.

2 Once the rice has cooled to room temperature, fold all the vegetables through. Whisk together the lemon juice and olive oil, then pour over the rice and fold through. Serve immediately at room temperature, or cover and refrigerate until required.

Super quick

Thrifty

Caesar salad

A real meal in a bowl, this famously crunchy salad is a wonderful mix of flavours and textures. Modern versions often include cooked prawns or chicken to make them even more substantial.

1½ tablespoons extra virgin
    olive oil
1 clove garlic, crushed
3 thick slices crusty
    Italian-style bread
2 eggs
3 slices bacon, rind removed,
    cut into thin strips
2 small cos lettuces
125g piece of Parmesan
3 anchovy fillets, drained and
    finely sliced

DRESSING
½ small clove garlic, crushed
1 to 2 tablespoons single cream
    or good-quality mayonnaise
2 teaspoons lemon juice
1 teaspoon Worcestershire sauce
80ml olive oil

Serves 4
Preparation 15 minutes
Cooking 15 minutes

1 Preheat the oven to 180°C/gas 4. In a small bowl, combine the olive oil and garlic. Cut the bread into 1cm cubes and spread them on a baking tray. Drizzle the olive oil mixture over the bread cubes and gently toss to coat. Bake for 10 minutes, or until the croutons are crisp and golden.

2 Meanwhile, place the eggs in a small saucepan and cover with cold water. Bring to the boil and cook for 10 minutes, timing from when the water starts to boil. Cool under cold-running water, then peel and cut into quarters.

3 Cook the bacon in a small frying pan over a medium heat until crisp. Drain on kitchen paper and set aside.

4 Wash, dry and tear each lettuce into bite-sized pieces. Using a vegetable peeler, shave the Parmesan into fine slices.

5 To make the dressing, whisk together the garlic, cream, lemon juice and Worcestershire sauce. Slowly whisk in the olive oil in a thin, steady stream.

6 Place the lettuce in a serving bowl and scatter the croutons, bacon, Parmesan and anchovies over the top. Toss well, then arrange the egg quarters over the top. Drizzle with the dressing and serve immediately.

Express

Extra thrifty

Salad of green beans and bacon

A great light meal or accompaniment to cold meats; if you add a large can of drained, flaked tuna and some cherry tomatoes to this salad, it becomes a more substantial, protein-packed main course.

155g frozen broad beans
500g small green beans, topped and tailed
5 slices bacon, rind removed
60ml red wine vinegar
80ml extra virgin olive oil
1 teaspoon Dijon mustard
pinch of soft brown sugar
¼ teaspoon salt

Serves 6
Preparation 10 minutes
Cooking 10 minutes

1 Cook the broad beans in a saucepan of boiling salted water for 5 minutes, or until just tender. Drain and run under cold water until cool, then peel off the skins.

2 Meanwhile, cook the green beans in a saucepan of boiling salted water for 1 to 2 minutes, or until just tender. Drain and run under cold water until cool.

3 Cook the bacon in a small frying pan over a medium heat until crisp. Drain on kitchen paper.

4 Combine the vinegar, olive oil, mustard, sugar, salt and some freshly ground black pepper in a small screw-top jar. Seal tightly and shake well to combine.

5 Place the green beans and broad beans in a wide serving bowl and pour the dressing over. Chop the bacon, pile it over the salad and serve immediately.

Express **Extra thrifty**

Coleslaw

So popular that we take it for granted, coleslaw is a quite different proposition when homemade rather than bought from a supermarket. Try a large dollop with barbecued or roast meats as well as cold cuts.

¼ small white cabbage
1 large carrot, coarsely grated
1 small red onion, finely chopped
60g good-quality mayonnaise
2 tablespoons lemon juice

Serves 8
Preparation 15 minutes
Cooking nil

1 Discard any damaged outer leaves from the cabbage. Using a large sharp knife, shred the cabbage as finely as possible, discarding any thick ribs. Toss in a large bowl with the carrot and onion.

2 Combine the mayonnaise and lemon juice. Add to the vegetables and toss to combine. Serve immediately, or cover and refrigerate until required.

Variations

To add a new dimension, use red cabbage, or a combination of red and green, and use four finely sliced spring onions instead of the red onion. For extra kick, add 2 teaspoons of wholegrain or Dijon mustard to the dressing.

Kitchen wisdom

Replace the lemon juice with white wine vinegar if you don't have a lemon.

Express

Thrifty

Turkey salad

Here's a fresh way to dish up leftover roast turkey from the Christmas table. You can also use leftover roast chicken and just about any fresh salad vegetables at hand.

100g mixed salad leaves
250g cherry tomatoes, halved
1 cucumber, sliced
1 small red pepper, cut into thin strips
2 stalks celery, thinly sliced
1 small avocado, sliced
250g leftover roast turkey, shredded or thinly sliced
2 spring onions, finely sliced
60ml olive oil
2 tablespoons white wine vinegar
1 teaspoon wholegrain mustard

Serves 4
Preparation 20 minutes
Cooking nil

1 Place the salad leaves in a serving bowl. Top with the tomatoes, cucumber, pepper, celery, avocado and turkey, then sprinkle with the spring onions.

2 Combine the olive oil, vinegar and mustard in a screw-top jar. Seal tightly and shake well to combine. Drizzle over the salad and serve immediately.

Variations

For extra interest, toss some bean sprouts through the salad. For a Waldorf-inspired salad, omit the tomatoes and pepper, add two chopped red apples and sprinkle with chopped toasted walnuts or almonds.

Super quick   **Extra thrifty**

Creamy potato, egg and bacon salad

A substantial salad that's great with ham, pastrami and cold roast beef. You can peel the potatoes if you prefer, although the red skin gives an attractive colour to the dish and also helps to hold the potatoes together.

1kg red-skinned potatoes (such as Desiree)
2 eggs
2 teaspoons olive oil
3 slices bacon, rind removed, chopped
60g soured cream
60g good-quality mayonnaise
1 teaspoon Dijon mustard
1 tablespoon white wine vinegar
3 spring onions, sliced, plus extra, to garnish

Serves 8
Preparation 15 minutes
Cooking 15 minutes

1 Cut the potatoes into 3cm chunks and place in a large saucepan. Cover with cold water and bring to the boil. Cook for 10 minutes, or until tender. Drain well.

2 Meanwhile, place the eggs in a small saucepan and cover with cold water. Bring to the boil and cook for 10 minutes, timing from when the water starts to boil. Cool under cold-running water, then peel and cut into quarters.

3 Heat the olive oil in a non-stick frying pan over a medium heat. Cook the bacon for 5 minutes, or until crisp. Drain on kitchen paper and allow to cool.

4 Combine the soured cream, mayonnaise, mustard and vinegar and mix until smooth. Add to the potatoes, along with the spring onions, egg quarters and most of the bacon. Season to taste and turn gently to combine. Sprinkle with some extra spring onion and the remaining bacon. Serve at room temperature, or cover and refrigerate until required.

Super quick

Extra thrifty

European potato salad

A favourite of German and eastern European grandmas and flavoured with parsley, dill and the sharpness of pickled gherkins, this herbaceous version of potato salad is especially good with seafood dishes and chicken.

1kg small new potatoes
60ml olive oil
60ml white wine vinegar
2 tablespoons chopped fresh parsley
2 tablespoons chopped fresh dill
½ red onion, finely chopped
45g finely chopped gherkins or pickled cucumber

Serves 8
Preparation 15 minutes
Cooking 15 minutes

1 Place the whole potatoes in a large saucepan and cover with cold water. Bring to the boil and cook for 10 minutes, or until tender when pierced with a skewer. Drain and allow to cool slightly, then slice thickly.

2 Layer one-third of the potatoes in a serving dish. Mix together the olive oil and vinegar and drizzle one-third over the potatoes. Reserve a little of the herbs for the top, then sprinkle half the remaining herbs over the potatoes, then add half the onion and pickles. Season generously with salt and freshly ground black pepper.

3 Repeat the layers, finishing with the dressing, and season each layer well. Sprinkle with the reserved herbs and serve at room temperature.

Kitchen wisdom

You can use any boiling (or waxy) potatoes here, as distinct from roasting (or floury) potatoes, which are more starchy and suited to baking. Boiling (waxy) potatoes often have a deeper-coloured yellow flesh, and hold their shape well during cooking.

Bean salad

Bean salads are so nutritious and tasty. Use just one type of canned bean if you like instead of the mix suggested here — borlotti or cannellini work well. Adding 2 teaspoons of chopped fresh rosemary will enhance the flavour beautifully.

200g green beans, stalk ends
   trimmed (you can leave the
   'tails' on)
420g can mixed beans, drained
   and rinsed
½ small red onion, finely sliced
200g small cherry tomatoes,
   halved
3 tablespoons roughly chopped
   fresh parsley
2 tablespoons olive oil
1 tablespoon red wine vinegar
pinch of sugar

Serves 6
Preparation 15 minutes,
   plus 30 minutes standing
Cooking 5 minutes

1 Add the green beans to a saucepan of boiling water. Cover and bring back to the boil, then remove the lid and cook for 2 minutes. Drain the beans and plunge into a bowl of iced water to stop them cooking, then drain well. Cut into thirds and place in a bowl.

2 Add the canned beans, red onion, tomatoes and parsley. Then add the olive oil and vinegar, sugar, and salt and freshly ground black pepper to taste, and toss to combine.

3 Cover and stand at room temperature for 30 minutes to allow the flavours to develop. If you're preparing the salad ahead, cover and refrigerate until needed, then return to room temperature before serving.

Express

Extra thrifty

Mixed leaf salad

A truly versatile salad – you can use any mixture of salad leaves, add fresh herbs and try different kinds of oils and vinegars in the dressing. For a cool-weather salad, add curly radicchio, rocket or watercress.

150g mixed salad leaves
2 tablespoons extra virgin olive oil
3 teaspoons white wine vinegar
½ teaspoon Dijon mustard

Serves 6
Preparation 10 minutes
Cooking nil

Kitchen wisdom

A basic vinaigrette always includes oil, an acid such as vinegar or lemon juice, and mustard, which helps to emulsify the dressing. You can experiment with types of oil (fruity extra virgin olive oil, or walnut or sesame oil) and vinegar (red or white wine vinegars, sherry vinegar or luscious balsamic). For a mild garlic flavour, add half a garlic clove to the jar, infuse for 15 minutes, then discard before dressing the salad.

1 Place the salad leaves in a large bowl of cold water and stand for 5 minutes. Working in batches of a handful at a time, lift the leaves out and let the excess water drain away. Dry them in a salad spinner and place in a salad bowl; repeat with the remaining leaves. Cover tightly with plastic wrap and refrigerate if not using immediately.

2 Combine the olive oil, vinegar and mustard in a small screw-top jar. Seal tightly and shake well to combine.

3 Season to taste with salt and freshly ground black pepper. Just before serving, pour the dressing over the lettuce and toss to coat the leaves. Don't add the dressing too early or the lettuce will become soggy.

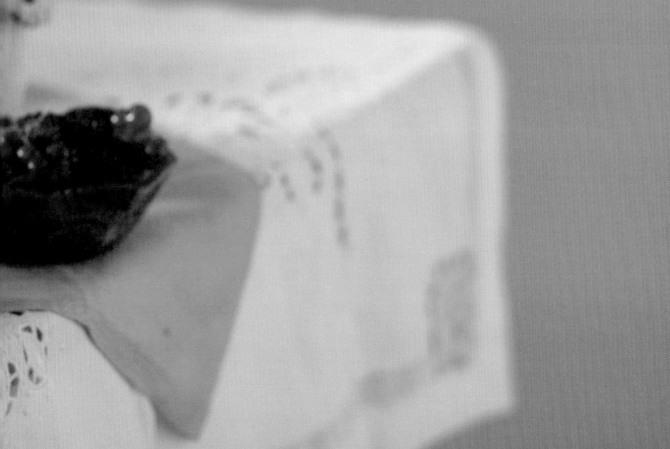

desserts

Lovingly prepared on the day, and making the most of simple ingredients, Grandma's desserts had a host of devoted admirers. Here's a great selection of delicious and nostalgic favourites.

Quick **Extra thrifty**

Chocolate puddings

These indulgent little puddings are deliciously rich, with a wonderful deep chocolate flavour. They are also surprisingly inexpensive to make. You can serve them in fanciful teacups as here or, more elegantly, in small glass dishes.

melted butter, for brushing, plus
   3 tablespoons extra
150g self-raising flour
2 tablespoons cocoa powder
115g caster sugar
1 egg
125ml milk
1 teaspoon vanilla extract
50g walnuts, roughly chopped
sifted icing sugar, for dusting
whipped cream, to serve

CHOCOLATE SAUCE
170g caster sugar
30g cocoa powder

Serves 6
Preparation 15 minutes
Cooking 25 minutes

1 Preheat the oven to 180°C/gas 4. Brush the base and side of six 330ml capacity ramekins or heatproof dishes with melted butter.

2 Sift the flour and cocoa powder into a bowl, then stir in the sugar. Whisk together the extra 3 tablespoons of melted butter, egg, milk and vanilla, then pour into the flour mixture and stir until smooth. Add the walnuts and mix lightly. Carefully spoon or pour the mixture into the ramekins.

3 To make the chocolate sauce, put the sugar and cocoa powder in a bowl, add 500ml boiling water and stir well to dissolve the sugar.

4 Slowly pour the chocolate sauce over each pudding, then bake for 25 minutes. Spoon into serving dishes if you wish and dust the puddings with icing sugar. Serve with a dollop of whipped cream.

Variation
You can also make one large pudding, using a 2 litre baking dish. Increase the cooking time to 40 minutes.

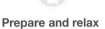

Prepare and relax   **Extra thrifty**

Pavlova

A real old-fashioned classic that's as impressive now as it was in Grandma's time. Fill a crisp meringue shell with whipped cream and pile it high with fresh seasonal fruit – from berries to slices of tropical fruit.

4 egg whites
230g caster sugar
2 teaspoons cornflour
1 teaspoon vanilla extract
1 teaspoon white vinegar
300ml double cream,
**   whipped**
fruit, to decorate, such as sliced
**   bananas (brushed with lemon**
**   juice to stop them browning),**
**   kiwi fruit and strawberries**
passionfruit pulp, for drizzling
**   (optional)**

Serves 8
Preparation 20 minutes
Cooking 1 hour 30 minutes

1 Preheat the oven to 120°C/½ gas. Using a 20cm cake tin or plate as a guide, draw a circle on a sheet of baking parchment or greaseproof paper with a pencil. Lightly grease a baking tray (so the paper doesn't slip), and place the paper on it pencil side down.

2 Using a very clean electric whisk, beat the egg whites in a large bowl with a pinch of salt until soft peaks form. Add the sugar gradually, about 1 tablespoon at a time at first, beating after each addition until dissolved.

3 Sift the cornflour over, then add the vanilla and vinegar. Beat just to combine. Spread the mixture out on the circle of baking parchment or greaseproof paper. Using a small non-serrated knife, make vertical ridges around the side of the meringue.

4 Bake for 1½ hours, then turn off the oven and open the oven door slightly (prop the door if necessary so it remains open). Leave the pavlova shell to cool completely.

5 Slide a knife under the cooled pavlova shell to loosen it from the baking paper. Carefully slide the pavlova shell onto a serving plate. Spread the whipped cream over, then top with the sliced fruit and drizzle with passionfruit pulp, if using. Serve within 30 minutes of topping.

Variations
In summer, top the pavlova with fresh mixed berries, dusted lightly with icing sugar, or tropical fruits such as mango and pineapple. For a gorgeous special-occasion dessert, top with sliced fresh figs and a sprinkling of chopped pistachios.

Prepare and relax   Extra thrifty

Bread and butter pudding

Still a great way of using up a loaf of bread that's a little past its best, this simplest of puddings is just like the one Grandma used to make, except that it uses honey instead of sugar, to enrich the flavour.

8 thick slices of bread
1½ tablespoons butter, plus some
**   melted butter, for brushing**
175g honey, plus extra,
**   for drizzling**
4 eggs
250ml single cream
500ml milk
¼ teaspoon ground cinnamon
ice cream, to serve

Serves 6
Preparation 10 minutes,
    plus 10 minutes standing
Cooking 45 minutes

1 Preheat the oven to 160°C/gas 3. Brush a shallow rectangular baking dish with a little melted butter.

2 Spread each slice of bread with the butter and honey. (To make the honey easy to spread, warm it for 30 seconds in the microwave.) Cut each slice into four triangles, then arrange them in the baking dish, overlapping the slices as needed.

3 In a bowl, lightly whisk together the eggs, cream, milk and cinnamon. Pour the egg mixture over the bread and place a saucer on top. (Weighing the bread down with a saucer allows the egg mixture to soak into the bread, giving a really rich, dense pudding.) Stand for 10 minutes, then remove the saucer.

4 Place the dish in a larger baking dish and transfer to the oven. Carefully pour enough hot water into the larger baking dish to come halfway up the side of the smaller dish.

5 Bake for 45 minutes, or until the pudding is just set and golden. Serve warm with ice cream and a drizzle of extra honey.

Variations

Instead of honey, use 55g caster sugar and whisk it with the eggs in step 3. Replace the plain bread with fruit bread, or sprinkle 100g mixed dried fruit or 60g sultanas over the bread before adding the eggs.

Waste not, want not

In this pudding you can use up any leftover dried fruit from our Roast shoulder of lamb with fruity stuffing (page 98) – and at the same time save electricity by baking the pudding while the oven is still hot from the roast.

Prepare and relax   **Thrifty**

Pear, brown sugar and oat crumble

Pears are always at their very best in early autumn. When cooking, select firmer examples rather than the ripest ones as they hold their shape better. If you really need to save time, you can use drained canned pears.

220g sugar

6 firm pears, such as Conference or Comice, peeled and thickly sliced

melted butter, for brushing, plus 60g cold butter, cubed

95g soft brown sugar

75g rolled oats

35g plain flour

¼ teaspoon baking powder

2 teaspoons ground cinnamon

double cream or custard (see Basics), to serve

Serves 4
Preparation 15 minutes
Cooking 40 minutes

1 Put the sugar in a saucepan with 500ml water. Stir over a low heat until the sugar has dissolved. Bring slowly to the boil and boil for 2 minutes, then reduce the heat to a simmer. Add the pears and cook for 15 to 20 minutes, or until the pears are just tender.

2 Meanwhile, preheat the oven to 180°C/gas 4. Brush a small round baking dish (about 23cm in diameter) with a little melted butter.

3 Place the brown sugar, oats, flour, baking powder and cinnamon in a bowl. Using your fingertips, rub in the cold, chopped butter.

4 Remove the pears from the syrup and arrange in the baking dish. Sprinkle the crumble mixture evenly over the top and bake for 20 minutes, or until the crumble is golden. Serve hot, with double cream or custard.

Waste not, want not

Don't discard the sugar syrup the pears are cooked in – drizzle it over fruit salad or use it to poach other fruits.

Kitchen wisdom

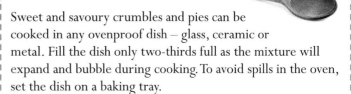

Sweet and savoury crumbles and pies can be cooked in any ovenproof dish – glass, ceramic or metal. Fill the dish only two-thirds full as the mixture will expand and bubble during cooking. To avoid spills in the oven, set the dish on a baking tray.

Quick

Extra thrifty

Jam roly poly

One of the most comforting of puddings and redolent of childhood winters, a jam roly poly is hearty and absolutely delicious. It flattens during cooking and the jam will ooze, but that's all part of the charm.

225g self-raising flour
100g frozen butter, grated
240g strawberry jam
custard (see Basics), to serve

Serves 6
Preparation 20 minutes
Cooking 30 minutes

Kitchen wisdom

Made with the humblest ingredients, this traditional dessert gave cheer to even the poorest households. It was also known as 'dead man's arm' or 'shirt-sleeve pudding' as it was often steamed in a sleeve cut from an old, worn-out shirt.

1 Preheat the oven to 200°C/gas 6. Sift the flour into a large bowl and stir the butter through. Make a well in the centre. Add 125ml water and mix with a non-serrated knife until the mixture starts to clump together.

2 Gather the dough (it will be slightly sticky) into a ball and turn out onto a sheet of lightly floured baking parchment. Roll out to a 26 x 20cm rectangle between two sheets of baking parchment or greaseproof paper.

3 Spread the jam over the dough, leaving a 2cm gap along the short sides. Roll up the dough, starting from a short side. Place the roll, still on the baking paper, onto a baking tray. Roll the baking paper up, twisting the ends to enclose.

4 Bake for 30 minutes, or until golden brown. Allow the roly poly to cool completely, then cut into slices. Serve with custard, within 1 hour of cooking.

Steamed fruit pudding

Something magical occurs when you turn this pudding out onto a plate and the citrus flavouring and fruits combine to create an enticing aroma. For extra spice, add 1 teaspoon ground mixed spice, ginger or cinnamon.

150g butter, at room temperature, chopped
170g caster sugar
2 teaspoons finely grated lemon or orange zest
2 eggs
300g self-raising flour, sifted
125ml milk
60g sultanas
75g currants
custard (see Basics), cream or vanilla ice cream, to serve

Serves 8
Preparation 20 minutes
Cooking 2 hours 15 minutes

Kitchen wisdom

If you have a metal or plastic pudding basin it will probably have a lid. In that case, just put a layer of pleated baking parchment (without the foil) over the basin, then secure the lid over the top.

1 Grease and flour a 1.5 litre pudding basin. Cut a sheet of foil and a sheet of baking parchment or greaseproof paper about 40cm long. Lay the paper onto the foil, then fold to create a 5cm pleat down the centre.

2 Using an electric mixer, beat the butter, sugar and citrus zest until light and creamy. Add the eggs, one at a time, beating well. Using a large metal spoon, fold in half the flour, all the milk and then the remaining flour. Fold in the fruit.

3 Spoon the mixture into the pudding basin. Place the paper and foil, paper side down, over the basin. Tie kitchen string securely around the side of the basin to seal the paper and foil (just under the lip if it has one). Place a trivet or upturned saucer in a large stockpot, sit the pudding basin on the trivet and pour enough boiling water into the pot to come two-thirds up the side of the basin. Cover with a lid and cook over a medium heat for 2¼ hours, topping up with boiling water as needed.

4 Carefully remove the pudding basin from the pot, then remove the foil and paper. Place a serving plate over the basin and invert to turn out the pudding. Serve with custard, cream or vanilla ice cream.

Variation

For a steamed jam pudding, grease (but don't flour) the basin. Omit the dried fruit and citrus zest; add 1 teaspoon vanilla extract to the butter and sugar. Spoon 210g jam into the pudding basin, spoon the batter over and cook as directed.

Quick

Extra thrifty

Lemon delicious

Treat yourself to this gorgeously light, spongy pudding with a soft centre. Lemon is the classic flavour, but the juice and zest of other kinds of citrus fruits, including limes or oranges, will also work beautifully here.

50g butter, at room temperature
170g caster sugar
1 tablespoon finely grated
** lemon zest**
3 eggs, separated
330ml milk
80ml lemon juice
35g self-raising flour
sifted icing sugar, for dusting
cream or ice cream, to serve

Serves 6
Preparation 15 minutes
Cooking 20 minutes

Grandma's secret

To evenly dust the top of the puddings, put a little icing sugar in a sieve and gently sift it over the top.

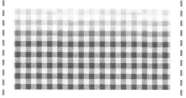

1 Preheat the oven to 180°C/gas 4. Lightly grease six 250ml ovenproof dishes.

2 Using an electric mixer, beat the butter, sugar, lemon zest and egg yolks for 3 to 4 minutes, or until the mixture is light and creamy.

3 Gradually add the milk, stirring with a wire whisk. Stir in the lemon juice. Sift the flour over and gently mix to combine.

4 Using a very clean whisk, beat the egg whites in a bowl until soft peaks form. Fold into the batter using a large metal spoon, taking care not to lose any volume.

5 Spoon the mixture into the prepared dishes and set them in a baking dish. Transfer to the oven and carefully pour enough boiling water into the baking dish to come halfway up the side of the dishes.

6 Bake for 20 minutes, or until the puddings spring back when gently touched (they will still be pale). Dust with icing sugar and serve immediately with cream or ice cream.

Variation
To make one large pudding, use a 1.5 litre baking dish and bake the pudding for 35 minutes, or until golden brown. Allow the pudding to stand for 5 minutes before serving.

Super quick **Extra thrifty**

Golden syrup dumplings

Economical and filling, these divinely sweet and hearty dumplings have sustained many generations of families through chilly winter nights.

150g self-raising flour
50g butter, chopped
125ml milk
350g golden syrup
cream or vanilla ice cream,
to serve

Serves 4
Preparation 15 minutes
Cooking 15 minutes

1 Sift the flour into a bowl. Using your fingertips, rub in 1 tablespoon of the butter until evenly combined. Make a well in the centre, add the milk and mix with a non-serrated knife until the mixture starts to clump together. Gather the dough into a ball. Pinch off level tablespoons and lightly roll into 12 small balls.

2 Put the remaining butter into a large, deep frying pan with the golden syrup and 250ml water. Stir over a medium heat until melted and combined. Bring to the boil. Carefully add the dumplings, then cover and cook for 5 minutes. Using a spoon, gently turn the dumplings over. Increase the heat to medium-high and cook, uncovered, for a further 5 minutes.

3 Drizzle the dumplings with the pan syrup and serve with cream or vanilla ice cream.

Grandma's secret

If you don't have a lid for your frying pan, cover it with a large baking tray.

Prepare and relax   **Extra thrifty**

Baked apples

When stuffing these golden baked apples you can use any combination of dried fruit (up to about 140g). If using large fruit, such as dried apricots or dates, chop them finely first.

6 dessert apples
50g butter, melted
60g brown sugar
30g sultanas
35g currants
40g chopped raisins
1 teaspoon mixed spice
custard (see Basics), cream or
**   vanilla ice cream, to serve**

Serves 6
Preparation 15 minutes
Cooking 45 minutes

1 Preheat the oven to 170°C/gas 3½. Remove the cores from the apples using an apple corer. Use a small sharp knife to score a line through the skin, around the middle of each apple.

2 Mix the remaining ingredients together in a large bowl. Press the mixture into the cavities in the apples, then place the apples in a large baking dish.

3 Bake for 45 minutes, or until the apples are tender. Drizzle the apples with the juices left in the baking dish and serve with custard, cream or vanilla ice cream.

Variations
Try substituting maple syrup for the brown sugar – and for a quick yet slightly more luxurious filling, use good-quality mincemeat, perhaps one with added brandy.

Prepare and relax   **Extra thrifty**

Classic chocolate mousse

Serve these dark, smooth, decadent ultra-rich delights with some extra whipped cream. Add fresh fruit, such as sliced strawberries, to cut the richness.

250g dark chocolate, plus extra shaved chocolate, to serve (optional)
3 eggs, at room temperature
300ml whipping cream, whipped, plus extra, to serve (optional)

Serves 6
Preparation 20 minutes,
    plus 3 hours chilling
Cooking 5 minutes

1 Roughly break up the chocolate and place in a heatproof bowl. Set the bowl over a saucepan of barely simmering water, making sure the bottom of the bowl doesn't touch the water. Stand for about 3 minutes, stirring occasionally, to soften. Remove from the heat and stir until smooth.

2 Separate the eggs. Add the egg yolks to the chocolate and stir until smooth. Fold a little cream through the chocolate mixture to loosen it, then fold in the remainder.

3 Using a very clean electric or hand whisk, beat the egg whites in a bowl until soft peaks form. Gently fold the egg whites through the chocolate mixture – use a large metal spoon or rubber spatula, folding until all the white streaks are gone, but taking care not to lose the volume.

4 Spoon the mixture into six 185ml glasses or small serving dishes. Cover with plastic wrap and refrigerate for 3 hours, or until the mousses have thickened slightly and are well chilled. Serve topped with whipped cream and shaved chocolate, if desired.

Variations
Add 2 tablespoons of your favourite liqueur, strong cold espresso or 1 teaspoon vanilla extract to the melted chocolate when adding the egg yolks.

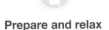
Pancakes

Rest the batter for a while before you cook it to make for lighter, airier pancakes. If time is short, combine the flour, egg and milk very gently and don't worry if there are a few small lumps in the pancake mix.

150g plain flour
1 egg
375ml milk
30g cold butter, in one piece
lemon juice, for drizzling
sugar, for sprinkling

Serves 4 (makes 8)
Preparation 5 minutes,
    plus 30 minutes resting
Cooking 20 minutes

1 Sift the flour into a bowl and make a well in the centre. Whisk the egg and milk together, then gradually add to the flour, whisking until smooth. Cover with plastic wrap and set aside to rest for 30 minutes.

2 Wrap the butter in a sheet of kitchen paper. Heat a 20cm non-stick frying pan over a medium-high heat and wipe around the inside with the butter-filled paper towel. Set the wrapped butter aside on a plate to use again.

3 Pour 60ml of the batter into the pan and quickly swirl to make a thin, even layer. Cook for 1½ minutes, or until lightly golden underneath, then turn and cook for a further minute. Transfer to a warm plate. Repeat with the remaining batter. (If you want to serve the pancakes all at the same time, keep them warm on a plate in a 120°C/ gas ½ oven, covered loosely with foil.)

4 To serve, fold the pancakes into quarters. Drizzle with lemon juice and sprinkle with sugar.

Variations

Fill with sliced poached pears and drizzle with melted dark chocolate, or top with sliced bananas and strawberries and drizzle with maple syrup. Or heat some blueberries or raspberries in a small saucepan until they are starting to soften, then sweeten with sugar and serve with the pancakes and ice cream.

Plum cobbler

In this old-fashioned pudding, plump, juicy plums gently stew beneath a light, scone-like topping. Use what's best in season — or a combination of your favourite plum varieties. Peaches, nectarines or apricots work equally well.

1kg plums, cleaned, halved and stoned
1 tablespoon caster sugar
225g self-raising flour
100g butter, chopped
60g soft brown sugar
80ml milk
1 egg
1 teaspoon vanilla extract
ice cream, cream or custard (see Basics), to serve
sifted icing sugar, for dusting (optional)

Serves 6
Preparation 20 minutes
Cooking 25 to 35 minutes

1 Preheat the oven to 180°C/gas 4. Arrange the plums in a 1.5 litre baking dish. Sprinkle the caster sugar over and toss to coat.

2 Sift the flour into a large bowl. Using your fingertips, rub in the butter until combined. Stir in the brown sugar and make a well in the centre.

3 Whisk together the milk, egg and vanilla extract, then add to the dry ingredients and fold together until just combined – don't overbeat.

4 Place large spoonfuls of the batter next to each other to cover the fruit (this gives the 'cobbled' effect). Bake for 25 to 35 minutes, or until the topping has risen and is golden brown. Serve hot, with ice cream, cream or custard, dusted with icing sugar if desired.

Variation

Try a quick crumble topping instead. Rub 100g chilled, chopped butter into 150g plain flour. Mix in 50g rolled oats, 95g soft brown sugar and perhaps ½ teaspoon ground cinnamon or mixed spice. Sprinkle over the fruit and bake for 30 minutes, or until golden brown.

Kitchen wisdom

If fresh plums aren't in season, use canned instead. You won't need to add sugar to canned fruit, but do drain well before using.

Chilled berry cheesecake

Biscuits, cream and the juiciest summer berries make for a truly luxurious cheesecake. If you like a little extra tang in the cheesecake mix, replace the vanilla with 1 teaspoon grated lemon zest and 2 teaspoons lemon juice.

**125g plain biscuits
   (such as digestives)**
3 tablespoons melted butter
2 teaspoons powdered gelatine
**250g cream cheese, at room
   temperature, chopped**
115g caster sugar
1 teaspoon vanilla extract
300ml double cream
**250g fresh blueberries or
   raspberries, or a combination**
**sifted icing sugar, for dusting
   (optional)**

Serves 8
Preparation 20 minutes,
   plus 4 hours chilling
Cooking nil

1 Lightly grease a 20cm spring-form cake tin and line the base with baking parchment or greaseproof paper.

2 Place the biscuits in a food processor and blend until finely chopped. Add the butter and process until combined. Transfer the biscuit mixture to the cake tin and use the back of a spoon to press it over the base of the tin. Refrigerate while making the filling.

3 Pour 2 tablespoons boiling water into a small bowl. Sprinkle the gelatine over. When it has softened, whisk with a fork until dissolved. Allow to cool.

4 Using an electric mixer, beat the cream cheese, sugar and vanilla in a bowl until smooth. Add the cream and the gelatine mixture and beat briefly to combine. Pour the mixture over the biscuit base and top with the berries. Refrigerate for 4 hours, or until firm. Serve sprinkled with icing sugar, if desired.

Variation

You can use frozen berries, but they don't hold their shape as well, so fold them through the cheesecake mixture rather than sprinkling them on top. It's best not to thaw them beforehand, so that the colour doesn't run.

Kitchen wisdom

If you don't have a food processor, put the biscuits in a plastic bag and gently crush them with a rolling pin. Transfer to a bowl and stir in the butter until evenly moistened.

Baked custard

If you want to make a really rich custard, replace 250ml of the milk with single cream. You can also infuse the heating milk with a wide strip of citrus rind.

625ml milk
4 eggs
115g caster sugar
1 teaspoon vanilla extract
a pinch of ground nutmeg

Serves 6
Preparation 5 minutes
Cooking 25 minutes

1 Preheat the oven to 180°C/gas 4. Lightly grease six 185ml ovenproof dishes. (If you'd prefer to make one large custard, use a 1.25 litre baking dish and extend the cooking time to 30 minutes.)

2 Heat the milk in a small saucepan over a medium heat until it nearly comes to the boil.

3 Meanwhile, whisk the eggs, sugar and vanilla in a large jug until the sugar has dissolved. Whisking constantly, gradually add the hot milk – but don't whisk too vigorously or you'll get too much froth on top of the custard. Pour the custard into the oiled dishes and sprinkle lightly with nutmeg.

4 Fold a clean tea towel and place it on the bottom of a large baking dish. Stand the dishes on the tea towel and then pour in enough boiling water so that it comes halfway up the sides of the dishes.

5 Bake for 20 minutes, or until the custards are just set but still wobbly (the tip of a small sharp knife should come out clean). Carefully lift the dishes out of the baking dish. Serve warm, at room temperature or chilled.

Variation

For a custard tart, make only half the custard. Set a pre-cooked 20cm tart shell on a baking tray, place it in the oven, then carefully pour in the custard. Sprinkle with nutmeg and bake for 30 minutes, or until set (as above). Cool, then cut into wedges.

Prepare and relax   **Extra thrifty**

Grandma's terrific trifle

Custard, jelly, cake, fruit, cream and a little bit of booze (sherry is the classic tipple) – trifle is for many the ultimate in indulgent desserts. Assemble it in a glass serving dish for maximum visual appeal.

135g packet jelly
   (any flavour you like)
250g madeira cake or trifle
   sponge cakes
1½ to 2 tablespoons
   strawberry jam
2 tablespoons sweet sherry
2 x 400g to 420g cans peach
   slices, drained
500ml cold ready-made custard
   (see Basics, or use the Banana
   custard recipe on page 289)
25g flaked almonds
125ml whipping cream, whipped

Serves 8
Preparation 20 minutes,
   plus 2 hours jelly setting
   plus 4 hours chilling
Cooking 5 minutes

1 Prepare the jelly according to the packet instructions. Pour the mixture into a 12cm x 16cm container and refrigerate for 2 hours, or until set.

2 Cut the cake into 1cm slices and spread half with the jam. Sandwich the other cake slices on top, then cut into 2cm cubes. Arrange half the cake cubes in a 1.75 litre glass serving dish – don't worry if they fall apart. Sprinkle with half the sherry.

3 Roughly cut the jelly into 3cm cubes. Arrange half the jelly cubes over the cake, then top with half the peaches. Spoon half the custard over them, spreading it out to cover the top.

4 Repeat the layers with the remaining ingredients. Cover with plastic wrap and refrigerate for 4 hours.

5 Preheat the oven to 180°C/gas 4. Spread the almonds on a baking tray and toast for 5 minutes, or until lightly golden – watch carefully as they can burn quickly. Allow to cool.

6 Just before serving, spoon the whipped cream over the trifle and sprinkle with the toasted almonds.

Variations
Use fresh soft fruit in season, such as berries, peaches, nectarines, cherries or plums. Instead of the madeira cake, you can use a jam-filled Swiss roll or day-old sponge cake.

Creamed rice

It's hard to believe that rice can taste so nice — so creamy, rich and tender. Serve by itself or with a range of fruity and spicy flavourings.

1 litre milk
115g caster sugar
2cm strip of lemon rind,
  white pith removed
110g medium-grain white rice
2 teaspoons cornflour
3 egg yolks
ground cinnamon, for sprinkling

Serves 6
Preparation 10 minutes
Cooking 1 hour 10 minutes

1 Put the milk and sugar in a large saucepan over a medium heat and stir to dissolve the sugar. Add the lemon rind and rice and bring to the boil, then reduce the heat to very low. Cover and cook for 1 hour, stirring occasionally, until the milk is absorbed and the rice is creamy and tender. Discard the lemon rind.

2 Whisk the cornflour and egg yolks in a small bowl. Stir a spoonful of the cooked rice into the egg yolk mixture until combined, then add to the rice. Stir over a low heat for 2 minutes, or until the rice is thick and creamy.

3 Spoon the rice into serving dishes and sprinkle with cinnamon. The dish is just as delicious served warm, at room temperature or chilled.

Variations

For a more pronounced cinnamon flavour, add a cinnamon stick when cooking the rice. You can top the finished rice with chopped toasted walnuts if you wish. This recipe also works well with low-fat milk.

Express

Extra thrifty

Banana custard

The basic recipe for this custard is suitable to use any time you need a classic custard. Keep the heat low so the egg mixture doesn't curdle or you'll find you've made scrambled eggs.

500ml milk
4 egg yolks
80g caster sugar
1 tablespoon cornflour
1 teaspoon vanilla extract
6 bananas, peeled and sliced
lightly toasted desiccated
   coconut, for sprinkling
   (optional)

Serves 6
Preparation 10 minutes
Cooking 10 minutes

1 Heat the milk in a saucepan over a medium heat until just at boiling point. Meanwhile, put the egg yolks, sugar and cornflour in a large heatproof bowl and beat with a whisk until creamy.

2 Pour the hot milk over the egg mixture, stirring constantly. Pour the mixture into a clean saucepan. Stir over a low heat for 5 minutes, or until the custard has thickened enough to coat the back of the spoon. Stir in the vanilla.

3 Spoon the bananas into serving dishes and pour the custard over. Serve immediately, sprinkled with coconut if desired.

Variation
Instead of vanilla extract, split a vanilla bean in half lengthways, scrape out the tiny seeds and add them to the milk with the pod when bringing it to the boil. Remove the pod before continuing with the custard.

Super quick   **Extra thrifty**

Stewed apples

As well as apples, a wide range of fruits can be stewed: berries, rhubarb, soft fruits, including apricots, plums and peaches, and dried fruit. Adjust the cooking time depending on variety so that the fruit is soft and plump but not mushy.

1kg dessert apples
2 tablespoons caster sugar
1 cinnamon stick
1 tablespoon finely grated
   lemon zest
cream, ice cream or custard
   (see Basics), to serve

Serves 6
Preparation 10 minutes
Cooking 20 minutes

1 Peel, quarter and core the apples. Cut each quarter into three wedges. Place in a wide saucepan and sprinkle with the sugar, stirring to combine. Add the cinnamon stick, lemon zest and 2 tablespoons water. Bring to the boil over a medium heat, then reduce the heat to medium-low.

2 Cover and simmer for about 15 minutes, or until the apples are tender, gently turning them occasionally so they cook evenly. Don't stir too much or the fruit will quickly become mushy.

3 Serve warm with cream, ice cream or custard, or allow to cool and use in another recipe (see below).

Variations

Drain the stewed apples, cool completely and use as a pie filling (see the pastry recipe on page 292). To use them in a crumble, uncover the pan when the apples are tender and cook for 5 minutes to evaporate the excess liquid; top with the crumble topping suggested in the 'Variation' on page 280.

Rhubarb and apple pie

Sprinkled with sugar and bursting with the tang of rhubarb and apples, this is a superb pie. If time is tight, you can use ready-made shortcrust pastry.

1kg dessert apples
80g caster sugar, plus extra,
    for sprinkling
½ teaspoon ground cinnamon
500g rhubarb, trimmed and cut
    into 2cm chunks
300g plain flour
3 tablespoons icing sugar
150g cold butter, chopped
3 to 4 tablespoons iced water
1 egg white, beaten
ice cream, to serve

Serves 8
Preparation 30 minutes,
    plus 15 minutes chilling
Cooking 1 hour 15 minutes

1 Peel, quarter and core the apples. Cut each quarter into thick wedges and place in a large saucepan with the sugar and cinnamon. Add 2 tablespoons water, cover and bring to the boil. Reduce the heat to low and cook for 10 minutes, or until tender, stirring occasionally.

2 Add the rhubarb and cook for 3 minutes. Remove the lid and cook for a further 7 minutes, stirring often, until the liquid has evaporated and the mixture is thick. Transfer to a large bowl and leave to cool, stirring occasionally to release the heat.

3 Meanwhile, sift the flour and icing sugar into a large bowl. Using your fingertips, rub in the butter until the mixture resembles fine breadcrumbs. Add 3 tablespoons of the chilled water and mix with a knife until the mixture starts to clump together, adding a little more water if it's still too dry – but not too much or it will become sticky.

4 Gather the dough into a ball, then divide in half. Roll out one piece on a sheet of baking parchment and use it to line a 3cm deep pie dish measuring 20cm across the base and 24cm across the top. Roll the other piece of dough out on the baking parchment, large enough to cover the pie dish, with some overhang. Place on a board and chill, along with the pastry-lined pie dish, in the fridge for 15 minutes.

5 Meanwhile, preheat the oven to 190°C/gas 5.

6 Spoon the rhubarb filling into the pastry shell. Let the top pastry soften slightly, then lay it over the pie dish. Crimp the edges to seal, then trim away any excess. Brush the top with egg white and sprinkle with extra sugar. Prick the centre of the pastry a few times with a fork. Bake for 50 minutes, until golden brown. Serve warm, with ice cream.

Prepare and relax   **Extra thrifty**

Apple strudel

A middle European classic in which layer upon layer of the lightest filo pastry encloses a soft fruit filling. For a special variation, replace some of the apple with stoned fresh cherries.

1kg dessert apples
40g raisins
2 tablespoons soft brown sugar
½ teaspoon ground cinnamon
6 sheets filo pastry
2 tablespoons melted butter
2 tablespoons ground almonds
sifted icing sugar, for dusting

Serves 6
Preparation 20 minutes
Cooking 40 minutes

1 Preheat the oven to 200°C/gas 6. Line a large baking tray with baking parchment or greaseproof paper.

2 Peel, quarter and core the apples. Cut each quarter into three wedges and place in a large frying pan with the raisins, sugar, cinnamon and 2 tablespoons water. Cover and cook over a medium heat for 5 minutes, stirring occasionally. Remove the lid and cook, turning gently, for a further 5 minutes, or until the liquid evaporates. Transfer to a large bowl and set aside to cool completely, turning occasionally to release the heat.

3 Lay the filo pastry sheets out on a clean work surface. Cover them with a clean, dry tea towel, then place a damp tea towel on top. Leaving the other pastry sheets covered, take one sheet of filo pastry, lightly brush with melted butter and sprinkle lightly with ground almonds. Repeat the layers, working with one filo sheet at a time, and finishing with a final sheet of pastry.

4 Spoon the cooled apple mixture along one long side of the pastry, about 7cm in from the edge and 9cm in from both ends. Fold the side and ends over, then roll up to enclose. Carefully place on the lined baking tray, seam side down. Brush with the remaining butter.

5 Bake for 30 minutes, or until the pastry is golden brown. Dust with icing sugar and cut into slices to serve.

Variations

For a lower-fat version, use olive oil spray on the filo pastry instead of brushing it with butter. You can use dry breadcrumbs instead of the ground almonds, which will also make the dish even thriftier.

Prepare and relax   Extra thrifty

Treacle tart

In Grandma's day, this frugal dessert was a way of using up stale breadcrumbs, but the end result belies its humble origins and it remains a deliciously sticky ending to a meal.

PASTRY
225g plain flour
100g butter, chopped and chilled
3½ tablespoons iced water

FILLING
350g golden syrup
25g butter
1 teaspoon finely grated
    lemon zest
2 tablespoons lemon juice
½ teaspoon ground ginger
160g fresh white breadcrumbs,
    made from day-old bread
1 egg, lightly beaten
ice cream, to serve

Serves 8
Preparation 20 minutes
Cooking 40 minutes

1 Preheat the oven to 180°C/gas 4.

2 To make the pastry, sift the flour into a large bowl. Using your fingertips, rub in the butter until the mixture resembles fine breadcrumbs. Add the iced water and mix with a flat-bladed knife until the mixture starts to clump together.

3 Turn the dough out onto a sheet of baking parchment and gather into a ball. Set aside one-third of the dough. Roll out the remaining dough on a sheet of baking parchment and use it to line a 20cm pie dish. Roll the other piece of dough to a 12cm x 25cm rectangle, then cut into long strips 1cm wide.

4 To make the filling, put the golden syrup, butter, lemon zest, lemon juice and ginger in a small saucepan over a medium heat. Stir until melted and combined. Place the breadcrumbs in a large bowl and pour the syrup mixture over. Stir well, then spoon into the pastry shell, spreading it to cover the pastry.

5 'Weave' the pastry strips over the pie. To do this, lay the first six strips over the pie, then fold every second one back. Lay one strip at right angles across the top, then fold the strips back. Fold the alternating strips back, and lay another strip across. Continue until all the strips are used. Trim any overhanging pastry, then press around the edges with a fork. Brush the pastry with beaten egg.

6 Bake for 40 minutes, or until the pastry is golden brown and the filling has browned. Cut into wedges and serve warm or at room temperature, with ice cream.

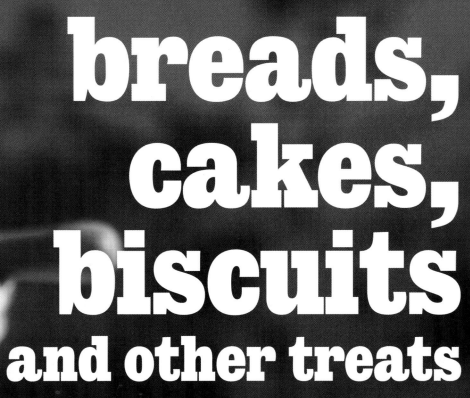

breads, cakes, biscuits
and other treats

Grandma always seemed to have something
lovely baking in the oven – a crusty loaf
of bread, a gorgeous cake perhaps, or sweet
treats for afternoon tea. We've collected a
selection of her favourites for you to enjoy.

Prepare and relax   **Extra thrifty**

Perfect white bread

When baking bread, it's worth making two loaves and freezing one. Wrap it in cling film and freeze in a ziplock bag and it will keep well for up to three months.

7g sachet (3 teaspoons) dried yeast
1 teaspoon caster sugar
melted butter, for brushing
450g plain flour
1 teaspoon salt
1 egg, beaten

Makes 1 loaf (about 12 slices)
Preparation 20 minutes,
   plus about 1 hour rising
Cooking 30 minutes

1 Combine the yeast, sugar and 330ml warm water in a jug. Stand in a warm place for 5 to 10 minutes, or until frothy.

2 Lightly brush a large bowl with melted butter. Sift the flour into another large bowl. Stir in the salt and make a well in the centre. Add the yeast mixture and mix until the dough comes together. Turn out onto a floured surface and knead for 5 to 8 minutes, or until smooth and elastic. (To test if you've kneaded the dough enough, push your thumb into the top, forming a dent – the dough should rise to the top of the dent.) Place in the buttered bowl, cover with cling film and rest for 45 minutes, or until doubled in size.

3 Brush an 8cm x 19cm (1lb) loaf tin with melted butter. Punch down the dough with your fist, then turn out onto a lightly floured surface and knead for 3 minutes, or until the dough has returned to its original size. Form into a loaf shape and place in the loaf tin. Rest for 20 minutes, or until the dough has risen just above the tin.

4 Meanwhile, preheat the oven to 200°C/gas 6. Brush the top of the loaf with more melted butter and the beaten egg. Bake for 30 minutes, or until the bread is golden and sounds hollow when tapped. Turn out onto a wire rack to cool. This loaf is best eaten on the day it's made, but will be perfect to toast for two to three days. Breadcrumbs can be made with any leftover bread.

Variations

For a fruit bread, add 2 tablespoons soft brown sugar and 125g sultanas to the flour. For a herb bread, add 45g chopped mixed fresh herbs such as parsley, chives or dill.

Irish soda bread

This crusty loaf gets its marvellous and unique taste from buttermilk, which reacts with the bicarbonate of soda to leaven the bread. The bread is best eaten on the day it's made — superb as an accompaniment to a big bowl of soup.

melted butter, for brushing
300g plain flour
150g self-raising flour
1 teaspoon salt
1 teaspoon bicarbonate of soda
80g butter, chopped
2 tablespoons caster sugar
375ml buttermilk
1 egg

Serves 4 to 6
Preparation 15 minutes
Cooking 25 to 35 minutes

1 Preheat the oven to 200°C/gas 6. Brush a baking tray with melted butter.

2 Sift the flours, salt and bicarbonate of soda into a large bowl. Using your fingertips, rub the butter into the flour. Stir in the sugar, then make a well in the centre.

3 Whisk the buttermilk and egg in a jug. Reserving 2 tablespoons for glazing, add the buttermilk mixture to the dry ingredients and stir with a flat-bladed knife until the dough comes together.

4 Turn the dough out onto a lightly floured surface and gently knead until smooth. Form into a 20cm round and place on the baking tray.

5 Cut a deep cross into the top of the bread. Brush with the reserved buttermilk mixture. Bake for 25 to 35 minutes or until the loaf is golden and sounds hollow when tapped.

Grandma's secret

Buttermilk is simply soured milk. You can make your own by adding a tablespoon of lemon juice or vinegar to ordinary milk.

Super quick **Extra thrifty**

Scones

Perhaps the ultimate traditional teatime treat, especially when served with a dollop of the thickest clotted cream and homemade strawberry jam. There's a bit of an argument as to whether the cream or jam goes first – we think it's up to you!

450g self-raising flour
80g butter, cut into cubes
310ml milk, plus extra,
 for brushing
jam, to serve
whipped cream, to serve

Makes 12
Preparation 10 minutes
Cooking 20 minutes

1 Preheat the oven to 200°C/gas 6. Grease and lightly flour a baking tray.

2 Sift the flour into a large bowl. Using your fingertips, rub in the butter until the mixture resembles fine breadcrumbs. Make a well in the centre. Stir in 250ml of the milk using a flat-bladed knife until it forms into a dough, adding more milk as needed.

3 Turn the dough out onto a lightly floured surface and lightly knead – don't overmix or the scones will be tough. Gently press the dough out into a round about 2cm thick. Using a 5cm round cutter, cut out 12 scones. Place on the baking tray, 1cm apart. Brush with a little milk and bake for 20 minutes, or until lightly golden and well risen. Transfer to a wire rack to cool slightly. Serve warm, with jam and cream.

Variations

To make cheese scones, add 90g grated Cheddar and a little cayenne pepper to the scone mixture. For fruit scones, add 125g sultanas or other mixed dried fruits.

Kitchen wisdom

To keep your scones soft, line a colander or basket with a tea towel, then wrap the scones in the towel.

Super quick

Extra thrifty

Pikelets

Feather-light golden pikelets never fail to delight. The trick to perfect pikelets is in getting the frying pan temperature just right so that they colour evenly.

150g self-raising flour
¼ teaspoon bicarbonate of soda
2 tablespoons caster sugar
250ml milk
1 egg
jam, to serve
whipped cream, to serve

Makes 30
Preparation 10 minutes
Cooking 20 minutes

1 Sift the flour and bicarbonate of soda into a bowl. Stir in the sugar and make a well in the centre.

2 Whisk the milk and egg together in a jug, then add to the flour mixture and whisk until a smooth batter forms.

3 Heat a non-stick frying pan over a medium heat. When hot, reduce the heat to medium-low. Drop dessertspoons of the batter into the pan, cooking two or three pikelets at a time and allowing room for spreading.

4 Cook for 2 minutes, or until bubbles form on the surface. Turn and cook for a further 1 to 2 minutes, or until golden on both sides and cooked through. Transfer to a large plate and repeat with the remaining batter. Serve warm or cold with jam and whipped cream.

Variation

You can also use our pikelet recipe to make crêpes – just add more milk until the mixture reaches a pourable consistency.

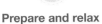

Prepare and relax   **Extra thrifty**

Big fruity tea bun

Shop-bought buns never taste or smell as good as Grandma's – this is a big, fat loaf bun with plenty of yummy sticky icing. Bake on the day and eat fresh and warm.

7g sachet (3 teaspoons)
   dried yeast
1 teaspoon caster sugar, plus
   2 tablespoons extra
300g plain flour
2 tablespoons cold butter,
   chopped, plus extra melted
   butter, for brushing
1 egg, lightly beaten
125g sultanas

GLAZE
1 tablespoon caster sugar
1 teaspoon powdered gelatine

ICING
60g icing sugar
1 tablespoon milk
2 teaspoons butter
a few drops of pink food colouring
1 tablespoon desiccated coconut

Makes a 20cm bun
   (about 12 slices)
Preparation 20 minutes,
   plus 40 minutes rising
Cooking 25 minutes

1 Combine the yeast, sugar and 185ml warm water in a jug. Stand in a warm place for 5 to 10 minutes, or until frothy.

2 Sift the flour into a large bowl. Rub in the butter using your fingertips, then stir in the extra caster sugar. Mix the yeast mixture, egg and sultanas into the flour mixture until the dough comes together. Cover with cling film and rest in a warm place for 25 to 30 minutes, or until the dough has doubled in size.

3 Meanwhile, preheat the oven to 200°C/gas 6. Brush a baking tray with melted butter.

4 Turn the dough out onto a lightly floured surface and knead for 5 to 8 minutes, or until smooth. Knead into a 20cm round shape, place on the baking tray and leave to rest for 10 minutes, or until well risen.

5 Bake for 20 to 25 minutes, or until the bun is golden and sounds hollow when tapped. Transfer to a wire rack. While still hot, brush with the glaze: combine the caster sugar, gelatine and 1 tablespoon hot water in a microwave-safe jug and microwave on high for 30 seconds, or until the gelatine is dissolved. Brush the glaze over the bun and allow to cool.

6 Meanwhile, make the icing. Sift the icing sugar into a bowl. In a small microwave-safe jug, microwave the milk and butter on high for 20 seconds, or until the butter has melted. Add to the icing sugar and stir until smooth, then add the food colouring, one drop at a time, until the desired colour is reached.

7 Spread the icing over the cooled bun and sprinkle with the coconut.

Super quick   **Extra thrifty**

Blueberry muffins

Muffins are so simple to bake, and homemade ones are far more delicious than the ones you can buy. We've added blueberries to this great basic mix, but try out the variations below, and have fun with your own ideas.

260g self-raising flour
115g caster sugar
125g butter, melted and cooled
2 eggs
185ml buttermilk
1 teaspoon vanilla extract
150g chopped fresh or
    frozen blueberries

Makes 12
Preparation 10 minutes
Cooking 20 minutes

1 Preheat the oven to 180°C/gas 4. Line a 12-hole muffin tin (one with 80ml holes) with large paper cases.

2 Sift the flour into a bowl. Stir in the sugar until well combined. In a large jug, whisk together the butter, eggs, buttermilk and vanilla. Add to the flour mixture with the berries (or any extra flavourings below) and stir until just combined – don't overbeat or the muffins will be tough.

3 Spoon the mixture into the paper cases. Bake for 15 to 20 minutes, or until a cake skewer inserted into the centre of a muffin comes out clean. Transfer to a wire rack to cool.

Variations

For chocolate-chip muffins, omit the berries, replace 35g of the flour with 30g cocoa powder and add 130g chocolate chips. For fruit and spice muffins, add 1 teaspoon mixed spice to the flour, and 185g mixed dried fruit with the buttermilk mixture.

Prepare and relax   **Extra thrifty**

Basic butter cake

A very easy, but light and fluffy cake that's really versatile. Try it with a delicately flavoured orange frosting – or use lemon if you prefer.

200g butter, softened
170g caster sugar
2 teaspoons vanilla extract
3 eggs, lightly beaten
185g self-raising flour
110g plain flour
125ml milk

ICING
155g icing sugar
finely grated zest of 1 orange
1½ tablespoons butter, softened
1 tablespoon orange juice or milk,
    as needed

Serves 8
Preparation 15 minutes
Cooking 45 minutes

1 Preheat the oven to 180°C/gas 4. Grease a deep 20cm round cake tin and line the base and sides with baking parchment or greaseproof paper.

2 Using an electric mixer, beat the butter, sugar and vanilla in a bowl until light and creamy. Add the beaten eggs gradually, beating well after each addition. Sift the flours together. Fold the flour and the milk alternately into the butter mixture.

3 Spoon the cake mixture into the cake tin and smooth the surface. Bake for 45 minutes. Remove the cake from the oven and leave in the tin for 10 minutes, before turning out onto a wire rack to cool completely.

4 To make the icing, sift the icing sugar into a bowl. Add the orange zest and butter and mix gently. Gradually add enough orange juice or milk so that the mixture becomes a thick but spreadable consistency. When the cake has cooled, spread the icing over the top.

Variation

For a chocolate version of this moist cake, add 4 tablespoons sifted cocoa powder to the flour and increase the milk by a tablespoon or so to ensure that it stays moist.

Waste not, want not

Any leftovers are delicious in our Grandma's terrific trifle recipe (see page 287).

Grandma's secret

A pinch of bicarbonate of soda keeps cake icing moist and stops it cracking. For easy spreading, have a tall glass of very hot water to hand. Dip a long, flat-bladed knife in the water, then quickly dry the blade on a clean tea towel. The hot knife helps the icing to glide over the cake for a smooth finish.

Express

Extra thrifty

Chocolate coconut squares

These little treats are a speciality of Australian grandmas, who know them as Lamingtons, after a former Governor of Queensland, 2nd Baron Lamington, who had a hand in their creation. Use shop-bought sponge cakes or make your own.

250g icing sugar
40g cocoa powder
60ml milk
180g desiccated coconut
2 x 20cm square sponge cakes
100g raspberry jam

Makes 16
Preparation 20 minutes
Cooking nil

1 To make the icing, sift the icing sugar and cocoa powder into a bowl. Add the milk and 60ml boiling water and stir until smooth.

2 Spread the coconut on a plate. Place one of the sponge cakes on a flat surface. Spread with the jam, top with the other sponge cake, then cut into 16 small squares.

3 Using two forks, roll a square of cake in the chocolate icing until well coated, allowing any excess to drip off. Drop the cake into the coconut and roll with your fingers to coat well. Transfer to a wire rack to set. Coat the remaining cake squares in the same way. The Lamingtons will keep in an airtight container for 3 to 4 days.

Variation

Try Grandma's quick '2-4-6-8' cake, so named for the ratio of imperial measurements it uses as a base. Lightly beat 2 eggs in a bowl, add 125g (4oz) softened butter, 175g (6oz) sugar and 225g (8oz) sifted self-raising flour and mix with a wooden spoon. Pour into a cake tin and bake at 200°C/gas 6 for 30 minutes. Cool, cut into squares and coat with jam, chocolate icing and coconut as above.

Kitchen wisdom

If using Grandma's never-fail sponge from page 323 in this recipe, bake the cakes in two shallow 20cm square cake tins. Once cooked, leave in the tins for 5 minutes, then turn out onto a wire rack to cool. Cut into squares and coat as directed.

Just-right rock cakes

Rock cakes are so simple that they are a perfect way to get even small children baking. Studded with currants and brightened with mixed peel, these small heaped cakes are always surprisingly delicious and moreish.

300g self-raising flour
½ teaspoon baking powder
½ teaspoon ground cinnamon
80g butter, chopped
80g caster sugar, plus extra,
    for sprinkling
150g currants
2 tablespoons mixed peel
125ml milk
1 egg

Makes 20
Preparation 10 minutes
Cooking 20 minutes

1 Preheat the oven to 200°C/gas 6. Line two baking trays with baking parchment or greaseproof paper.

2 Sift the flour, baking powder and cinnamon into a large bowl. Using your fingertips, rub in the butter. Stir the sugar, currants and mixed peel through.

3 Whisk the milk and egg together in a jug, then add to the flour mixture and stir through – the mixture should be quite stiff. Spoon heaped tablespoons of the mixture onto the baking trays, about 5cm apart, allowing room for spreading. Sprinkle with a little extra sugar and bake for 15 to 20 minutes, or until golden and cooked through. Remove from the oven and leave to cool on the baking trays.

Variations

The currants can be replaced with 240g chopped glacé cherries. If you don't like mixed peel, just leave it out.

Prepare and relax   Extra thrifty

Date and walnut loaf

Dark and caramel-rich with brown sugar, dates and walnuts, this rich loaf is wonderful served straight from the oven or spread with a little butter.

160g chopped dates
185g soft brown sugar
3 tablespoons butter
½ teaspoon bicarbonate of soda
1 egg, beaten
60g chopped walnuts
300g self-raising flour

Serves 6 to 8
Preparation 20 minutes
Cooking 45 minutes

1 Preheat the oven to 180°C/gas 4. Choose a 2lb loaf tin, or a 23cm x 8cm tin for a longer loaf. Grease and flour the tin, or grease and line it with greaseproof paper.

2 Combine the dates, sugar, butter and 250ml water in a saucepan over a medium-low heat and stir until the sugar has dissolved. Bring to the boil, remove from the heat and cool to lukewarm.

3 Add the bicarbonate of soda, egg and walnuts and mix well. Sift the flour over the mixture and stir until well combined. Spoon the mixture into the loaf tin.

4 Place the tin on a baking tray and bake for 45 to 50 minutes, or until a fine skewer inserted into the loaf comes out clean. Remove from the oven and leave on a wire rack to cool.

Prepare and relax   **Extra thrifty**

Devil's food cake

A cake that should probably carry a health warning, this sumptuous creation is wickedly indulgent. To make it slightly less sinful, you can replace the creamy chocolate ganache with a simple chocolate icing.

350g self-raising flour
90g cocoa powder
1 teaspoon bicarbonate of soda
345g caster sugar
160g butter
2 teaspoons vanilla extract
3 eggs, beaten

CHOCOLATE GANACHE ICING
185ml double cream
200g dark chocolate,
    roughly chopped

Serves 12
Preparation 20 minutes
Cooking 1 hour

1 Preheat the oven to 180°C/gas 4. Grease and line a 22cm round cake tin with baking parchment or greaseproof paper.

2 Sift the flour, cocoa powder and bicarbonate of soda into a large bowl. Stir in the sugar until well combined.

3 Combine the butter, vanilla and 250ml water in a saucepan over a medium heat. Stir until the butter has melted, then add to the flour mixture and whisk until well combined. Add the eggs and whisk until blended.

4 Spoon the mixture into the cake tin and smooth the top. Bake for 45 to 60 minutes, or until a cake skewer inserted into the centre of the cake comes out clean. Remove the cake from the oven and leave in the tin for 5 minutes, then turn out onto a wire rack to cool completely.

5 To make the icing, heat the cream in a small saucepan over a medium-low heat. When bubbles begin to form around the edge of the saucepan, remove the pan from the heat and stir in the chocolate until melted and smooth. Transfer to a bowl and stand at room temperature, stirring occasionally, until the icing is of a spreadable consistency.

6 When the cake is cold, spread the icing over the top.

Boiled fruit cake

Perfect for celebratory gatherings as well as simple afternoon tea or dessert, this rich, moist cake will keep for several months if you can hide it away from raiding fingers. It's also excellent as a base for a marzipanned and iced cake.

900g mixed dried fruit
320g chopped dates
100g chopped glacé cherries
125g butter
185g soft brown sugar
2 teaspoons mixed spice
185ml sherry, plus an extra
    60ml for drizzling
2 eggs
80g apricot jam
150g self-raising flour
150g plain flour
50g blanched almonds

Serves 12
Preparation 20 minutes,
    plus cooling time
Cooking 2 hours 10 minutes

1 Put the mixed fruit, dates, cherries, butter, sugar, mixed spice and the 185ml sherry in a large saucepan over a medium-low heat. Stir until the butter has melted and the mixture comes to the boil. Allow to boil for 3 minutes, then remove from the heat and leave to cool.

2 Meanwhile, preheat the oven to 160°C/gas 3. Grease and line a 20cm round cake tin or baking tin with a double layer of baking parchment or greaseproof paper. (Lining the tin with a double layer of paper ensures that the cake won't get too hot or cook too fast.)

3 When the fruit mixture is cold, stir in the eggs and jam, mixing well. Sift the flours over the top, then stir in using a large metal spoon until well combined. Spoon the mixture into the cake tin and smooth the top with the back of a wet spoon. Decorate with the almonds.

4 Bake for 2 hours, or until a cake skewer inserted into the centre of the cake has no raw mixture on it (the skewer will not be entirely clean). Pour the extra sherry onto the hot cake as soon as you remove it from oven, so it seeps into the cake.

5 Wrap the cake in a thick towel and leave to cool. When the cake is cold, remove the towel, wrap the cake in greaseproof paper or foil and store in an airtight container.

Kitchen wisdom

To save time and fuel, you can bake a slow-cooking cake such as this one while a casserole is cooking in the oven. As the casserole dish is covered, the savoury aromas will not affect the cake. Bake the cake on the top shelf of the oven.

Prepare and relax　　**Extra thrifty**

Honey cake

Soured cream and honey give a wonderful moistness to this buttery cake. A scattering of toasted flaked almonds adds a nutty richness and cuts the sweetness a little.

250g butter, softened
195g soft brown sugar
1 teaspoon vanilla extract
175g honey
3 eggs
225g self-raising flour
75g plain flour
1 teaspoon ground cinnamon
250ml soured cream

TOPPING
20g butter
260g honey
90g flaked almonds, toasted

Serves 10
Preparation 20 minutes
Cooking 1 hour 5 minutes

1 Preheat the oven to 160°C/gas 3. Grease and line a 22cm spring-form cake tin with baking parchment or greaseproof paper.

2 Using an electric mixer, beat the butter, sugar and vanilla in a bowl until light and creamy. Add the honey and beat until combined. Add the eggs, one at a time, beating well after each addition.

3 Transfer the mixture to a large bowl and sift the flours and cinnamon over the top. Gently stir in the soured cream using a large metal spoon until well combined. Spoon the mixture into the cake tin, smooth the surface and bake for 1 hour, or until a cake skewer inserted into the centre of the cake comes out clean.

4 Remove the cake from the oven and leave in the tin for 10 minutes, then turn out onto a wire rack to cool.

5 To make the topping, combine the butter and honey in a small saucepan over a medium heat. Stir until the mixture comes to the boil, reduce the heat and simmer for 2 minutes. Remove from the heat and stir in the almonds.

6 When the cake has cooled, spread the topping over the top and sides of the cake.

Grandma's secret

To cream butter and sugar quickly, first rinse the bowl with boiling water, then wipe it thoroughly dry. The heat of the bowl will soften the butter while you're beating, without melting it.

Quick

Extra thrifty

Grandma's never-fail sponge

Filled with jam and cream, Grandma's airy sponge is still as heavenly as ever. We've used raspberry jam, but apricot, blueberry or lemon curd are great, too. For a chocolate version, add 2 tablespoons of cocoa powder to the flour.

melted butter, for brushing
110g self-raising flour
50g cornflour
4 eggs, at room temperature
170g caster sugar
1 teaspoon vanilla extract
raspberry jam, to serve
whipped cream, to serve
sifted icing sugar, for dusting

Serves 8
Preparation 20 minutes
Cooking 20 minutes

1 Preheat the oven to 180°C/gas 4. Brush two shallow 20cm round cake tins with melted butter and line the bases with baking parchment or greaseproof paper.

2 Sift the flour and cornflour three times. Using an electric mixer, beat the eggs, sugar and vanilla in a bowl for 8 to 10 minutes, or until thick and pale.

3 Transfer the mixture to a large bowl. Using a large metal spoon, gently fold in the flour mixture.

4 Pour the mixture into the cake tins and bake for 20 minutes, or until the cakes are golden and beginning to shrink away from the side of the tins. Remove from the oven and leave in the tins for 5 minutes, then turn out onto a wire rack to cool.

5 When the cakes are cold, place one sponge on a serving plate. Spread generously with the jam and cream. Place the remaining sponge cake on top and dust with icing sugar.

Waste not, want not

Use any leftover sponge cake in our Grandma's terrific trifle recipe (see page 287).

Grandma's secret

For a wonderfully light, airy sponge, use room-temperature eggs, as these will beat to the highest volume. To make your cake look extra special, lay a paper doily on top and dust it with icing sugar. Then carefully remove the doily to reveal the icing sugar pattern.

Quick   **Extra thrifty**

Cinnamon teacake

A sprinkling of sugar and cinnamon is all it takes to turn this simple teacake into something special and wonderfully fragrant. If you really love cinnamon, you can add a pinch to the cake batter before you bake it.

80g butter, at room temperature
145g caster sugar
1 teaspoon vanilla extract
1 egg
200g self-raising flour, sifted
200ml milk

TOPPING
1 tablespoon melted butter
1 tablespoon caster sugar,
  mixed with ½ teaspoon
  ground cinnamon

Serves 8
Preparation 10 minutes
Cooking 35 minutes

1 Preheat the oven to 180°C/gas 4. Grease and line a 20cm round cake tin with baking parchment or greaseproof paper.

2 Using an electric mixer, beat the butter, sugar and vanilla in a bowl until the mixture is almost white. Add the egg and beat until well combined. Using a large metal spoon, gently fold the flour and milk into the batter until combined. Spoon the mixture into the cake tin and smooth the surface.

3 Bake for 30 to 35 minutes, or until a cake skewer inserted into the centre comes out clean. Remove from the oven and leave in the tin for 10 minutes, then turn out onto a wire rack.

4 While the cake is still warm, brush the top with the melted butter and sprinkle with the sugar mixture. Serve warm or cold.

Prepare and relax   **Extra thrifty**

Treacle gingerbread loaf

Thick, dark treacle, rich brown sugar and a generous measure of mixed spice and golden ground ginger — there's a lot to enjoy about this spicy loaf which will stay moist for days if properly wrapped and stored.

185g plain flour
110g self-raising flour
1 teaspoon bicarbonate of soda
1 tablespoon ground ginger
3 teaspoons mixed spice
140g soft brown sugar
260g black treacle
185ml milk
80ml olive oil
2 eggs

Serves 10
Preparation 20 minutes
Cooking 45 minutes

1 Preheat the oven to 180°C/gas 4. Grease a 10cm x 20cm x 7cm (1lb) loaf tin and line with baking parchment or greaseproof paper, ensuring that the paper extends 3cm above the tin.

2 Sift the flours, bicarbonate of soda, ginger and mixed spice into a large bowl. Stir in the sugar until well combined. Whisk the treacle, milk, olive oil and eggs in a jug. Add to the flour mixture and stir until just combined.

3 Pour the mixture into the loaf tin and bake for 40 to 45 minutes, or until a cake skewer inserted into the centre comes out clean. Remove from the oven and leave in the tin for 5 minutes, then turn out onto a wire rack and allow it to cool completely.

Variation
If you like, you can use golden syrup instead of black treacle.

Cinnamon star biscuits

Made with beaten egg whites, ground almonds and a little lemon and cinnamon, these macaroon-like biscuits are star performers at afternoon tea. Unusually, the topping is made from the same mixture as the biscuits.

2 egg whites
125g icing sugar, sifted
1 teaspoon ground cinnamon
grated zest of 1 lemon
175g ground almonds
55g caster sugar

Makes 16
Preparation 10 minutes,
    plus 1 hour resting
Cooking 20 minutes

1 Whisk the egg whites and a pinch of salt in a heatproof bowl until frothy. Add the icing sugar, cinnamon and lemon zest. Place the bowl over a saucepan of simmering water. Using an electric mixer, beat until the mixture is thick and holds its shape well. Remove the bowl from the saucepan.

2 Set aside about 80ml of the egg white mixture for decorating the biscuits. Using a large metal spoon, fold the ground almonds through the remaining mixture to form a dough. Fold more ground almonds into the mixture is too sticky. Then leave to stand for 1 hour.

3 Preheat the oven to 180°C/gas 4. Line two baking trays with baking parchment or greaseproof paper.

4 Sprinkle half the caster sugar on a sheet of greaseproof paper. Place the biscuit dough on top. Sprinkle with the remaining caster sugar and place another sheet of greaseproof paper on top. Using a rolling pin, gently roll out the biscuit dough until it's about 5mm thick, then remove the top sheet of greaseproof paper. Using star-shaped pastry cutters, cut out shapes from the dough and transfer to the baking trays.

5 Using a palette knife, spread the reserved egg white mixture over the biscuits. Bake for 15 to 20 minutes, or until just firm. Transfer to a wire rack to cool, then store in an airtight container.

Grandma's secret

To keep biscuits crisp, place half a teaspoon of sugar in the biscuit tin or jar when you put the biscuits in. Make sure that the tin is airtight.

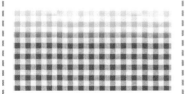

Prepare and relax   Extra thrifty

Shortbread

Buttery, crumbly shortbreads are a treat at any time of the year. At Christmas, cut them into star shapes and pack into decorative tins for a special homemade gift. You could also ice them for an additional festive touch.

250g butter, at room temperature
90g icing sugar
1 teaspoon vanilla extract
300g plain flour
60g cornflour or rice flour

Makes 24 to 28
Preparation 20 minutes,
    plus 15 minutes resting
Cooking 20 minutes

1 Using an electric mixer, beat the butter, icing sugar and vanilla in a bowl until light and creamy. Mix in the flour and cornflour using a wooden spoon.

2 Turn the dough out onto a lightly floured surface and gently knead until smooth. Divide the dough in half, then roll out each portion to form a disc about 2cm thick. Wrap the discs in greaseproof paper and refrigerate for 15 minutes.

3 Meanwhile, preheat the oven to 160°C/gas 3. Line two baking trays with baking parchment or greaseproof paper.

4 Roll the dough out between two sheets of baking parchment or greaseproof paper until about 5mm thick. Using a round, fluted 7cm pastry cutter, cut 12 to 14 rounds from each piece of dough.

5 Place the biscuits on the baking trays and bake for 15 to 20 minutes, or until firm to the touch. Remove from the oven and leave to cool on the trays for 10 minutes, then transfer to a wire rack to cool. Store in airtight containers for up to two weeks.

Variations
Try sandwiching the biscuits together with a citrus or passionfruit icing. To make a chocolate shortbread, add 2 to 3 tablespoons sifted cocoa powder to the flour mixture.

Super quick   **Extra thrifty**

Jam drop biscuits

Jam turns nicely chewy when baked. We've used raspberry jam for these lovely biscuits, but other flavours, including strawberry, apricot and peach jam or lime or lemon curd, will taste just as good.

125g butter, at room temperature
80g caster sugar
1 egg
150g self-raising flour
75g plain flour
30g cornflour
2 tablespoons raspberry jam,
** as needed**

Makes 28
Preparation 15 minutes
Cooking 15 minutes

1 Preheat the oven to 180°C/gas 4. Line two baking trays with baking parchment or greaseproof paper.

2 Using an electric mixer, beat the butter and sugar in a bowl until light and creamy. Add the egg and beat until well combined. Sift the three flours over the mixture, then stir in using a large metal spoon until well combined.

3 Roll teaspoons of the mixture into balls and place on the baking trays. Using your thumb, make small indentations in the centre of each biscuit, then spoon about ¼ teaspoon of jam into each dent.

4 Bake for 12 to 15 minutes, or until light golden brown. Transfer to a wire rack to cool, then store in airtight containers interleaved with layers of greaseproof paper.

Variations

Instead of topping the biscuits with jam, you can use sweets such as Smarties – or brush them with egg white before baking and sprinkle with hundreds and thousands.

Grandma's secret

If your biscuits become soft, heat them in a moderately low oven for a few minutes and they'll be as good as new.

Oat biscuits

Wholesome oats add loads of goodness to these chewy cookies. They will keep in an airtight container for up to seven days, or can be frozen for up to three months.

150g butter, chopped
115g caster sugar
2 tablespoons golden syrup
   or black treacle
150g rolled oats
150g plain flour
45g desiccated coconut
1 teaspoon bicarbonate of soda

Makes 25
Preparation 10 minutes
Cooking 15 minutes

1 Preheat the oven to 160°C/gas 3. Line two baking trays with baking parchment or greaseproof paper.

2 Combine the butter, sugar and golden syrup in a small saucepan over a medium heat. Stir until melted, then remove from the heat. Mix the oats, flour and coconut in a bowl.

3 Combine the bicarbonate of soda with 1 tablespoon boiling water. Add to the butter mixture, then stir through the dry ingredients until well combined.

4 Spoon tablespoons of the mixture onto the baking trays. Flatten them slightly with the back of a spoon, allowing room for spreading. Bake for 10 to 15 minutes, or until golden. Remove from the oven and leave to cool on the baking trays.

Variation
To reduce the saturated fat content of biscuits, you can replace the butter a low-fat spread.

Express   **Extra thrifty**

Gingersnap biscuits

Gratifyingly light, crisp and sweet, these decoratively dimpled biscuits are especially good with a steaming hot mug of coffee on a chilly day.

45g soft brown sugar
2 tablespoons butter
2 tablespoons golden syrup
   or black treacle
35g plain flour
1 teaspoon ground ginger

Makes 20
Preparation 10 minutes
Cooking 6 minutes

Grandma's secret

For extra ginger intensity, sprinkle some finely chopped glacé ginger over each biscuit before baking.

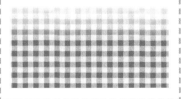

1 Preheat the oven to 180°C/gas 4. Line two baking trays with baking parchment or greaseproof paper.

2 Combine the sugar, butter and golden syrup in a small saucepan over a medium-low heat. Stir until the butter has melted and remove from the heat. Sift the flour and ginger over the mixture and stir until combined.

3 Place teaspoons of the mixture on the baking trays, allowing room for spreading. Bake for 5 to 6 minutes, or until lightly golden. Remove from the oven and leave on the trays for 1 to 2 minutes, or until the biscuits harden. Transfer to a wire rack to cool, then store in an airtight container for up to three days.

Melting moments

Sandwiched together with a gorgeous citrus icing, these golden melt-in-the-mouth biscuits are heaven on a plate. They make a special teatime treat or a delightful gift, presented in a decorative box or tin.

125g butter, at room temperature
30g icing sugar, plus extra, for dusting
110g plain flour
30g cornflour

CITRUS ICING
3 tablespoons butter, at room temperature
85g icing sugar
2 teaspoons finely grated lemon or orange zest
1 tablespoon lemon or orange juice

Makes 12 sandwiched biscuits
Preparation 20 minutes
Cooking 15 minutes

1 Preheat the oven to 160°C/gas 3. Line two baking trays with baking parchment or greaseproof paper.

2 Using an electric mixer, beat the butter and icing sugar in a bowl until pale and creamy. Sift the flour and cornflour over the mixture and stir until well combined.

3 With lightly floured hands, roll teaspoons of the dough into small balls. Place on the baking trays and lightly press with a fork dipped in icing sugar. Bake for 15 minutes, or until the biscuits are just cooked through. Remove from the oven, transfer to a wire rack and leave to cool.

4 To make the icing, beat the butter, icing sugar and citrus zest until smooth. Beat in the citrus juice.

5 When the biscuits are cold, spread the icing over half the biscuits, then top with another biscuit. Store in an airtight container.

Grandma's secret

When you only need a splash of lemon juice, pierce a lemon in a few spots with a knitting needle or skewer. You can squeeze out a little juice without wasting the rest of the lemon.

Prepare and relax   Extra thrifty

Cut-and-come-again cookies

The beauty of these biscuits, besides their taste, is that you can freeze or refrigerate the wrapped logs of dough, then simply slice off and bake up a batch whenever the need — or desire — arises.

250g butter, at room temperature
125g icing sugar, sifted
375g plain flour
90g dried apricots, finely chopped
70g roasted hazelnuts,
    finely chopped

Makes 50
Preparation 20 minutes,
    plus 1 hour resting
Cooking 10 minutes

1 Using an electric mixer, beat the butter and icing sugar in a bowl until light and creamy. Transfer to a large bowl.

2 Sift the flour over the butter mixture and stir in using a large metal spoon until well combined. Gently mix the apricots and hazelnuts through.

3 Turn the dough onto a lightly floured surface and knead until smooth. Divide the dough in half, then roll each piece into a 25cm log. Wrap each log in greaseproof paper or cling film and refrigerate for 1 hour, or until firm. (The refrigerated biscuit dough will keep in the fridge for seven to ten days, or can be frozen for up to three months.)

4 Preheat the oven to 180°C/gas 4. Line two baking trays with baking parchment or greaseproof paper.

5 Cut each log into slices 1cm thick and place on the baking trays about 3cm apart. Bake for 10 minutes, or until firm and cooked through. Remove from the oven and leave to cool on the trays. Store in airtight containers.

Variations
The apricots and hazelnuts can be replaced with other fruit and nuts — try raisins and pistachio nuts. For children, add a handful of small sweets to the plain dough mixture.

Quick   **Extra thrifty**

Gingerbread men

Always a winner — especially at Christmas — and so easy to make. Decorating the little men is almost as much fun as eating them. If you have a range of cutters, you can make a whole family of gingerbread people — and animals.

125g butter, at room temperature
115g caster sugar
1 egg
1 tablespoon milk
375g plain flour
1 teaspoon bicarbonate of soda
3 teaspoons ground ginger
2 tablespoons golden syrup
  or black treacle
icing and coloured sweets,
  to decorate

Makes about 20
Preparation 15 minutes,
  plus decorating time
Cooking 15 minutes

1 Preheat the oven to 180°C/gas 4. Line two baking trays with baking parchment or greaseproof paper.

2 Using an electric mixer, beat the butter and sugar in a bowl until light and creamy. Add the egg and milk and beat until well combined.

3 Sift the flour, bicarbonate of soda and ginger over the butter mixture. Put the golden syrup in a microwave-safe jug and microwave on high for 10 to 20 seconds, or until warm. Add to the butter mixture and stir until well combined.

4 Turn the dough out onto a lightly floured surface and gently knead. Roll the dough between two sheets of baking parchment or greaseproof paper until 3mm thick. Using gingerbread-men cutters, cut out shapes from the dough and place on the baking trays.

5 Bake for 15 minutes, or until golden and firm to the touch. Remove from the oven and leave to cool on the trays. Decorate as desired, using icing and sweets. Store in airtight containers.

Kitchen wisdom

You'll find decorating sweets and easy-to-use tubes of coloured icing in supermarkets. Or you can just use small, colourful sweets, such as Smarties or Dolly Mixtures, to decorate your gingerbread men.

Coconut macaroons

These light, meringue-like morsels with their vanilla and coconut flavouring are perfect for teatime or wrapped up as a special present.

2 egg whites
145g caster sugar
½ teaspoon cream of tartar
1 teaspoon vanilla extract
180g desiccated coconut

Makes 24
Preparation 15 minutes
Cooking 40 minutes

1 Preheat the oven to 150°C/gas 2. Line two baking trays with baking parchment or greaseproof paper.

2 Using an electric mixer, beat the egg whites in a bowl until soft peaks form. Add the sugar, 1 tablespoon at a time, beating after each addition until well combined and dissolved. Fold in the cream of tartar, vanilla and coconut.

3 Spoon or pipe the mixture onto the baking trays. Bake for 35 to 40 minutes, or until the macaroons are dry to the touch. Allow to cool in the oven with the door ajar. Store in airtight containers.

Variations

For a special occasion, add 1 teaspoon rosewater extract and some pink food colouring to the macaroons, or top each one with a halved glacé cherry or a blanched almond. You could also dip or drizzle them with melted chocolate.

Super quick **Extra thrifty**

Choc-chip biscuits

The rich choc-chip must be one of the most universally popular biscuits of all time. Once they are out of the oven, watch them disappear in double-quick time.

125g butter
80g caster sugar
1 teaspoon vanilla extract
2 tablespoons condensed milk
150g self-raising flour
125g dark cooking chocolate, chopped
sifted icing sugar, for dusting

Makes 30
Preparation 15 minutes
Cooking 15 minutes

Kitchen wisdom

To keep the biscuits fresh longer – assuming you can keep them out of reach of pilfering fingers – store them in an airtight biscuit tin lined with kitchen paper.

1 Preheat the oven to 160°C/gas 3. Grease or line two baking trays with baking parchment or greaseproof paper.

2 Using an electric mixer, beat the butter, sugar and vanilla in a bowl until light and creamy. Add the condensed milk and mix well. Fold the flour and chocolate into the butter mixture.

3 Drop half-tablespoons of the mixture onto the baking trays, allowing room for spreading. Bake for 15 minutes. Remove from the oven and leave to cool on the trays for 3 minutes, then carefully transfer to a wire rack and allow to cool completely.

4 Lightly dust with icing sugar and store in airtight containers for up to four days.

Quick

Extra thrifty

Jam and coconut slice

Raspberry jam and golden coconut make these soft slices so enticing. Served cool, they are a great teatime treat or cake stall favourite, or you could try serving them as a dessert, warmed and drizzled with cream.

3 tablespoons butter
170g caster sugar
225g self-raising flour
2 eggs
315g raspberry jam

TOPPING
2 eggs
115g caster sugar
135g desiccated coconut

Makes 24 slices
Preparation 15 minutes
Cooking 30 minutes

1 Preheat the oven to 180°C/gas 4. Line a shallow 20cm x 30cm baking tin with baking parchment or greaseproof paper.

2 Combine the butter, sugar and flour in a food processor and pulse until the mixture resembles fine breadcrumbs. Add the eggs and pulse until a dough forms. If necessary, add a little water to bring the mixture together.

3 Press the mixture into the baking tin and spread the jam evenly over the top.

4 To make the topping, beat the eggs and sugar in a large bowl until thick and pale, using an electric mixer. Add the coconut and stir through. Pour the topping over the jam, spreading to cover evenly.

5 Bake for 30 minutes, or until golden and firm. Remove from the oven and leave to cool in the tin. Cut into slices and store in airtight containers for up to four days.

Variations
Instead of raspberry jam, experiment with other jam flavours such as strawberry, apricot, rhubarb and ginger, or even your favourite marmalade.

Chocolate peppermint slice

Rich, sophisticated flavours and colours make this a perfect after-dinner treat — or treat at any time. Try going for the best grade of chocolate you can find — you'll really appreciate the difference in taste.

250g plain chocolate-flavoured biscuits
150g butter, melted
250g icing sugar, sifted
1 teaspoon peppermint extract
50ml milk, as needed
200g dark chocolate, roughly chopped
1 tablespoon vegetable oil

Makes 24 slices
Preparation 20 minutes, plus 10 minutes setting
Cooking 5 minutes

1 Line a shallow 20cm x 30cm slice tin with baking parchment or greaseproof paper.

2 Put the biscuits in a food processor and blend until finely chopped. Combine the biscuit crumbs and melted butter and press evenly into the slice tin. Place the tin in the freezer while preparing the topping – this will make the biscuit base harden, so that it will be easier to spread the topping over it.

3 In a bowl, mix together the icing sugar, peppermint extract and milk – the mixture should be of a spreading consistency, so add a little more milk if necessary. Spread the icing over the hardened biscuit base and return to the freezer.

4 Place the chocolate in a heatproof bowl over a saucepan of simmering water, ensuring the base of the bowl doesn't touch the water. Stir until melted, then stir in the vegetable oil.

5 Spread the chocolate mixture over the slice and set aside for about 10 minutes to harden. To serve, cut into 5cm squares using a hot knife. Store in airtight containers in the fridge for up to three days.

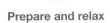

Prepare and relax **Extra thrifty**

Chocolate cherry slice

Another tempting slice with a really rich and chewy filling of coconut and cherries. And it's so easy to make – you don't even need to bake it. Seek out the best dark chocolate to create the perfect topping.

250g plain digestive biscuits
150g butter, melted

FILLING
397g can sweetened
condensed milk
250g desiccated coconut
400g finely chopped glacé
cherries
100g white vegetable shortening
such as Cookeen, melted

TOPPING
200g dark chocolate,
roughly chopped
1 tablespoon white vegetable
shortening

Makes 24 slices
Preparation 20 minutes,
plus up to 1 hour setting
Cooking 5 minutes

1 Line a shallow 20cm x 30cm slice tin with baking parchment or greaseproof paper.

2 Put the biscuits in a food processor and blend until finely chopped. Combine the biscuit crumbs and melted butter and press evenly into the slice tin. Place the tin in the freezer while preparing the topping – this will make the biscuit base harden, so it will be easier to spread the topping over it.

3 Combine all the filling ingredients in a large bowl and mix well. Press the filling evenly over the biscuit base, using wet hands to smooth the surface.

4 To make the topping, melt the chocolate and shortening in a heatproof bowl over a saucepan of simmering water, ensuring the base of the bowl doesn't touch the water. Stir until melted, then pour the mixture over the slice and spread evenly.

5 Set aside for up to 1 hour to harden. Cut into 5cm squares using a hot knife. Store in airtight containers for up to three days.

Prepare and relax   **Extra thrifty**

Lemon slice

Topped with a sweetly tangy custard, lemon slice is so delicious and moreish that you'll be hard pushed to limit yourself to just one square. For a tropical version, try the passionfruit variation below.

200g unsalted butter, chopped
60g icing sugar
225g plain flour

TOPPING
6 eggs
345g caster sugar
finely grated zest of 1 lemon
125ml lemon juice
75g plain flour
sifted icing sugar, for dusting

Makes 24 slices
Preparation 15 minutes
Cooking 40 minutes

Kitchen wisdom

To get more juice from citrus fruits, submerge them in hot water for 15 minutes before you juice them.

1 Preheat the oven to 180°C/gas 4. Line a 20cm x 30cm slice tin with baking parchment or greaseproof paper.

2 Combine the butter, icing sugar and flour in a food processor and process until the mixture comes together in a ball – it may be necessary to add a teaspoon of cold water to bring the mixture together.

3 Press the dough evenly into the slice tin and prick several times with a fork. Bake for 25 minutes, or until lightly golden.

4 Meanwhile, make the topping. Place the eggs in a bowl and whisk. Mix in the sugar, lemon zest and lemon juice. Sift the flour over the mixture and whisk to combine.

5 Pour the mixture over the biscuit base and bake for 15 minutes, or until the topping has just set. Remove from the oven and leave to cool in the tin. Cut into 5cm squares and dust with icing sugar. Store in airtight containers for up to two days.

Variation

For a passionfruit slice, omit the lemon zest from the topping and reduce the lemon juice to 2 tablespoons. Add 4 tablespoons strained passionfruit pulp to the topping, along with 1 tablespoon of the passionfruit seeds left after straining.

Brownies

Almost no one can resist these dark, moist, fudgy, chocolatey treats. Pull a batch out of the oven and watch them quickly vanish. Or if you can bear to, wait a day or two and enjoy them in chewy perfection.

250g unsalted butter, chopped

200g dark chocolate, roughly chopped, plus 100g dark chocolate chunks or dark chocolate chips

325g soft brown sugar

4 eggs, lightly beaten

1 teaspoon vanilla extract

185g plain flour, sifted

sifted icing sugar, for dusting (optional)

Makes 12 slices
Preparation 20 minutes
Cooking 40 minutes

1 Preheat the oven to 170°C/gas 3½. Line a 28cm x 18cm baking tin with baking parchment or greaseproof paper.

2 Melt the butter and the 200g chopped chocolate in a saucepan over a low heat. Whisk in the sugar until combined, then set aside for 5 minutes to cool.

3 Whisk in the eggs and vanilla, then stir the flour through. Add the chocolate chunks or chips and stir to combine.

4 Pour the mixture into the baking tin. Bake for 35 minutes, or until the top is firm and the cake is coming away from the sides of the tin – it should still be very moist inside.

5 Remove from the oven and allow to cool completely in the tin. Cut into 12 pieces and store in airtight containers for up to four days. Serve dusted with icing sugar if desired.

Variations

For triple-choc brownies, replace the dark chocolate chunks or chips with 50g white chocolate chips and 50g milk chocolate chips. For walnut or macadamia brownies, add 150g chopped walnuts or macadamias with the chocolate chips.

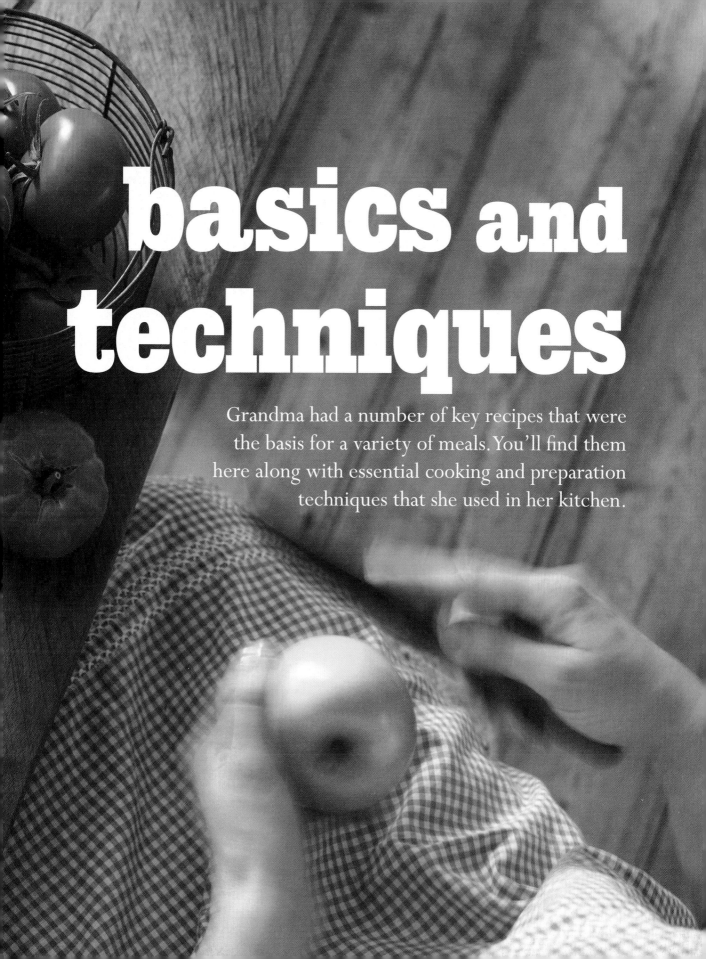

basics and techniques

Grandma had a number of key recipes that were the basis for a variety of meals. You'll find them here along with essential cooking and preparation techniques that she used in her kitchen.

Sauces

White sauce

2½ tablespoons butter
50g plain flour
600ml milk

Makes 600ml Prep 5 mins Cook 20 mins

1 Melt the butter in a small saucepan and stir in the flour. Cook, stirring continuously, for 1 minute, until the mixture forms a smooth paste (or 'roux').

2 Remove the pan from the heat and gradually pour in the milk, stirring or whisking constantly.

3 Return the pan to the heat and bring to the boil, still stirring or whisking. Reduce the heat and simmer the sauce gently for 2 minutes, stirring occasionally, until smooth and thick. Season to taste with salt and freshly ground black pepper and use as required.

Note This sauce doesn't keep well, so prepare it just before you need to use it. To vary the flavour of the sauce, add a sprinkling of cayenne pepper or ground nutmeg, or 1 teaspoon mustard.

Variations

Cheese sauce Stir 40g grated Cheddar into the sauce just before serving.

Mushroom sauce Gently cook 90g thinly sliced mushrooms in the butter before adding the flour.

Parsley sauce Stir 2 tablespoons chopped fresh parsley into the finished sauce.

Onion sauce Gently cook 1 small finely chopped onion in the butter for 5 minutes, or until softened, before adding the flour.

Vinaigrette dressing

125ml olive oil
1½ tablespoons red or white wine vinegar
  or lemon juice
a pinch of caster sugar
1 teaspoon mustard (optional)

Makes 150ml Prep 5 mins Cook nil

1 Put the olive oil, vinegar and sugar in a screw-top jar. Add the mustard, if using, and some salt and freshly ground black pepper to taste. Screw the lid on and shake well to combine. Alternatively, whisk all the ingredients together in a small bowl.

Traditional mayonnaise

1 large egg yolk
½ teaspoon mustard powder
a pinch of caster sugar
150ml olive oil
1 tablespoon white wine vinegar

Makes 185ml Prep 20 mins Cook nil

1 Whisk the egg yolk in a bowl until thick. Whisk in the mustard, sugar and some salt and freshly ground black pepper.

2 Add the olive oil, a drop at a time, whisking well after each addition; as the mayonnaise thickens and becomes shiny, add the oil in a thin stream. Blend in the vinegar. Cover and refrigerate for up to one month.

Variations

Herb mayonnaise Flavour the mayonnaise with 1 tablespoon chopped fresh herbs, such as chives or tarragon.

Garlic mayonnaise Stir 1 to 2 crushed garlic cloves into the mayonnaise.

Tartare sauce Stir in 3 small finely chopped gherkins, 2 tablespoons capers and 1 teaspoon snipped chives.

Fruit coulis

300g soft fresh or frozen summer fruits (such as strawberries, raspberries, blackberries, stoned cherries or peeled mangoes)
1 tablespoon lemon juice
icing sugar, to taste
1 to 2 tablespoons fruit liqueur (optional)

Serves 6 Prep 10 mins Cook nil

1 Place all the fruit in a food processor or blender and process to a smooth paste. For a smooth coulis, press the purée through a sieve to remove the seeds.

2 Stir in the lemon juice and sweeten to taste with icing sugar. Add a little fruit liqueur if you like, or if the coulis is too thick, stir in a little water to thin it to the desired consistency.

Custard

4 egg yolks
1 tablespoon cornflour
55g caster sugar
600ml milk
a few drops of natural vanilla extract (optional)

Makes 600ml Prep 5 mins Cook 10 mins

1 Put the egg yolks, cornflour and sugar in a heatproof bowl and beat until smooth.

2 Pour the milk into a saucepan and bring to the boil. Remove the milk from the heat and slowly pour it into the egg yolk mixture, stirring all the time.

3 Return the mixture to the pan and cook over a low heat, stirring constantly until thickened to a custard consistency. Stir in the vanilla extract, if using.

4 Remove from the heat and strain into a jug. Serve the custard warm or cold.

Variations

Instead of vanilla, add a little grated orange zest, or 2 tablespoons brandy, rum or liqueur.

Chocolate sauce

100g chopped dark chocolate
3 teaspoons unsalted butter
2 tablespoons golden syrup or honey

Serves 6 Prep 5 mins Cook 5 mins

1 Put the chocolate in a small saucepan with the butter, golden syrup and 1½ tablespoons water. Warm gently over a low heat until the chocolate has melted.

2 Remove from the heat and serve warm.

Butterscotch sauce

2½ tablespoons unsalted butter
140g light brown sugar
170g can evaporated milk

Serves 6 Prep 5 mins Cook 10 mins

1 Gently heat the butter in a small saucepan until melted. Add the sugar and stir until dissolved, then cook gently for 3 minutes.

2 Remove the pan from the heat and stir in the evaporated milk. Return to the heat and bring back to the boil. Serve warm, or cool, chill and reheat gently when required.

 # Stocks

Beef, veal or ham stock

750g to 1kg beef bones, veal bones or ham
bones (either fresh, or from a roast)
1 onion, roughly chopped
1 carrot, roughly chopped
1 celery stalk, chopped
1 bouquet garni (bay leaf, parsley and thyme)
6 black peppercorns
½ teaspoon salt

Makes 1 litre Prep 15 mins Cook 2 hours

1 Put the bones in a pot with 2.5 litres cold water. Bring to the boil, skimming off any froth, then add the remaining ingredients. Partially cover, reduce the heat and simmer for 2 hours.

2 Strain, discarding the solids. Leave to cool, then skim off the fat. Refrigerate for up to four days, or freeze for up to six months.

Note For a richer flavoured stock, roast the vegetables in a little oil in a very hot oven for 40 minutes first.

Vegetable stock

750g to 1kg mixed vegetables (beans, broccoli,
cauliflower, celery, fennel, leek, onion, root
vegetables), trimmed, peeled and chopped
1 bunch mixed fresh herbs
1 large strip of lemon zest
6 black peppercorns
1 teaspoon salt

Makes 1 litre Prep 15 mins Cook 1 hour

1 Put all the ingredients in a pot with 1.5 litres cold water. Bring to the boil. Partially cover, reduce the heat and simmer for 1 hour.

2 Strain, discarding the solids. Leave to cool, then refrigerate for up to four days, or freeze for up to six months.

Note For a darker stock, include aubergines, mushroom stalks and clean onion skins.

Chicken stock

1 chicken carcass (raw or from a roasted chicken)
chicken giblets, but not the liver (optional)
1 onion, roughly chopped
1 carrot, roughly chopped
1 celery stalk, roughly chopped
1 leek, trimmed and sliced (optional)
5 mushrooms, chopped (optional)
1 bouquet garni (bay leaf, parsley and thyme)
6 black peppercorns
½ teaspoon salt

Makes 1 litre Prep 15 mins Cook 2 hours

1 Break the carcass into several pieces and place in a pot with 2 litres cold water. Bring to the boil, skimming off any froth. Add the remaining ingredients, partially cover, reduce the heat and simmer for 2 hours.

2 Strain, discarding the solids. Leave to cool, then skim off the fat. Refrigerate for up to four days, or freeze for up to six months.

Fish stock

900g trimmings from white fish, including skin,
bones and heads (but without gills), or
400g white fish fillets (such as hake)
1 onion, sliced
125ml dry white wine
1 bouquet garni (bay leaf, parsley and thyme)
1 tablespoon lemon juice
4 black peppercorns

Makes 1 litre Prep 10 mins Cook 30 mins

1 Put the fish trimmings in a pot, add the onion and cook gently over a low heat for 5 minutes. Add the wine and 1.25 litres cold water. Bring to the boil, skimming off any froth, then add the remaining ingredients. Partially cover, then simmer for 30 minutes.

2 Strain, discarding the solids. Leave to cool, then skim off the fat. Refrigerate for up to four days, or freeze for up to three months.

Eggs and batter

Perfect poached eggs

Per person:

½ **teaspoon salt**

6 drops vinegar

1 egg

Prep nil Cook 3 to 5 mins

1 Bring about 2.5cm water to the boil in a frying pan or saucepan that's large enough to hold the required number of eggs. Reduce the temperature to a bare simmer – the water should just be shimmering, not moving – and add the salt and vinegar.

2 Break the egg into a saucer, then carefully slide it into the water. Poach for 3 to 5 minutes, according to how well cooked you like your eggs; the white should be set.

3 Gently spoon a little water over the yolk to help it set on top. Lift the egg out with a spatula or slotted spoon. Drain all the water off the egg and serve immediately.

Perfect boiled eggs

1 Bring the eggs to room temperature.

2 Half-fill a saucepan with water and bring to a gentle simmer. Lower the eggs carefully into the water using a spoon.

3 Simmer for 3 to 5 minutes for soft-boiled eggs (depending on how runny you like your egg), and 10 minutes for hard-boiled.

Prep nil Cook 3 to 10 mins

Note Simmering the eggs, rather than boiling them, will help to prevent them from cracking while they cook. If hard-boiling eggs, drain them once cooked, then immerse in cold water. As soon as they are cool enough to handle, gently tap the eggs all over on a hard surface to make a network of fine cracks all over them. This will make them easier to peel. Return to the cold water, allow to cool, then peel off the shells.

Classic thick batter

150g plain flour

a pinch of salt

1 tablespoon caster sugar (if the batter is to be used for sweet fritters)

1 egg

150ml water, milk or beer (see Note)

Makes about 450ml Prep 5 mins Cook nil

1 Sift the flour, salt and sugar, if using, into a bowl, then make a well in the centre. Break in the egg and beat with a balloon whisk, wooden spoon or an electric hand mixer.

2 Beat in the liquid, little by little, mixing in the flour gradually, just until the batter is smooth. Do not overbeat or the batter may be tough when cooked.

3 The batter may be used straight away, but it is much better if it's left to sit for 30 minutes or so, allowing the starch grains to soften.

Note This is a thick batter used for coating meat or fish for deep-frying, or for making fruit fritters. The type of liquid used in the batter (milk, a mixture of milk and water, or beer) will influence the result. Water makes a light batter; milk helps to make it smoother and causes it to brown more quickly; beer adds lightness and flavour to a savoury batter.

Perfect rice and mash

Grandma's perfect rice

250g white long-grain rice

Serves 4 Prep 2 mins Cook 15 mins,
    plus 10 mins standing

1 Put the rice in a heavy-based saucepan with
a tight-fitting lid. (If the lid of the saucepan
doesn't fit tightly, put a double layer of foil
under it.) Add 500ml cold water and a pinch
of salt.

2 Leaving the pan uncovered, bring to the
boil. Stir the rice once, return it to a gentle
simmer, then cover and continue to simmer
over a very low heat for 10 minutes.

3 Remove the pan from the heat, but don't
remove the lid. Leave the rice undisturbed
for 10 minutes, then remove the lid.

4 Run a fork through the rice and serve
immediately.

Grandma's perfect mash

400g floury potatoes

1 teaspoon salt

200ml milk

40g butter

freshly ground nutmeg (optional)

Serves 4 Prep 5 mins Cook 30 mins

1 Peel the potatoes and remove any eyes. Rinse
well, then cut into even-sized pieces. Place in a
saucepan, add enough cold water to just cover
them and sprinkle with the salt.

2 Cover the pan and bring to the boil, then
reduce the heat to low and simmer for 15 to
30 minutes, or until the potatoes are tender
when pierced with a skewer or sharp knife.

3 While the potatoes are cooking, heat the
milk and butter in a small saucepan over a
low heat until the butter has melted.

4 Drain the potatoes, return them to the
saucepan and let them steam briefly on
the switched-off hotplate, shaking the pot
repeatedly to help to dry them out a little.

5 Mash the hot potatoes well using a potato
masher. (Don't use a food processor or they
will become gluey.)

6 Add the warm milk mixture and beat with
a wire whisk until the mash is nice and fluffy.
Add a little more hot milk if you prefer a softer
texture. Season to taste with salt and mix in
some nutmeg, if using. Serve immediately.

Variations

For extra flavour and interest, add some
snipped fresh chives to the finished mash.
You could also try some lightly sautéed finely
chopped leeks, shredded cabbage, spring onion
or tiny pieces of well-done bacon.

 # Pastry

Shortcrust pastry

150g plain flour
150g self-raising flour
100g chilled butter, diced
1 teaspoon lemon juice
3 tablespoons iced water
Makes sufficient pastry to line a 20cm to 23cm
    pie dish or flan tin Prep 10 mins, plus 20 mins
    resting and 1 hour chilling Cook nil

1 Sift the two kinds of flour and a pinch of salt into a large bowl. Add the butter and rub into the flour between your thumbs and fingertips until the mixture resembles coarse breadcrumbs.
2 Combine the lemon juice and water, pour over the flour mixture and stir in quickly with a round-bladed knife. When the dough starts to cling together, use your fingers to press the mixture gently together into a ball.
3 Knead the dough lightly by pressing and turning it in the bowl until fairly smooth, then place it on a sheet of cling film, press it into a disc and wrap tightly to exclude the air. Rest the dough for 20 minutes in the refrigerator before rolling out.
4 After rolling out and lining the pie dish or flan tin, place in the refrigerator to chill for 1 hour before baking.
Note The resting and chilling steps are very important for pastry, as this allows the dough to 'relax' so that it will not shrink when it's baked. Always handle pastry as little as possible to ensure a light result. For sufficient dough to line a 25cm pie dish or tin, or for a two-crust 20cm to 23cm pie, use 185g each plain and self-raising flour, 130g butter and 80ml iced water (the quantities of salt and lemon juice remain the same).

Choux pastry

150g plain flour
250ml milk, water or white wine
65g butter, or 80ml olive or sunflower oil
4 to 5 eggs
Prep 10 mins Cook 25 to 40 mins

1 Preheat the oven to 220°C/gas 7. Line a baking tray with baking parchment or greaseproof paper. Sift the flour into a bowl.
2 Pour the milk into a saucepan and add the butter and a large pinch of salt. Cover and bring to the boil. As soon as the liquid begins to boil, turn off the heat.
3 Tip in the flour all at once and stir vigorously while heating again, until a thick mixture, and then a lump, are formed. After about 2 minutes, as soon as a white film has formed on the pan base, remove from the heat. Transfer the mixture to a bowl and cool to lukewarm.
4 Using a wooden spoon, or the dough hooks of a hand mixer, beat in 1 egg. One at a time, beat 3 more eggs into the mixture. As soon as the pastry is shiny and falls off the spoon or dough hooks in fairly solid peaks, it's ready; the fifth egg won't be needed, but beat the last egg in if the pastry doesn't reach this stage.
5 Using two spoons, place small ovals of pastry on the baking tray, about 3cm apart. (Use teaspoons for small puffs and tablespoons for large ones.) Or pipe the dough into finger shapes for éclairs.
6 Bake on the middle shelf of the oven for 8 to 10 minutes for small puffs, or 20 minutes for large. (Don't open the oven door during this time or the puffs will collapse.) Turn the oven down to 180°C/gas 4 and bake for 2 to 5 minutes for small puffs, or 5 to 10 minutes for large. Transfer to a wire rack and cool.
Serving suggestion Using kitchen scissors, cut the puffs or éclairs in two horizontally; fill with cream.

Preserves

Preparing jars

Any clean glass jars can be used for storing homemade jams and preserves, provided they are free from cracks, chips or other flaws. Wash jars in very hot water and drain well.

Place on a baking tray, right side up, and dry in a preheated 140°C/gas 1 oven for 15 minutes. Turn the oven off and leave the jars in the oven until you're ready to pot the jam. It's important to warm the jars in this way before filling them, as the boiling hot jam will otherwise cause them to crack. For the same reason, never stand the hot jars on a cold surface. This method also sterilises the jars.

Wash the lids in the same way, but don't put them in the oven as any rubber seals will melt. Instead, dry them thoroughly with a clean dry tea towel. They must be absolutely dry; even a tiny droplet of water can cause the preserves to spoil.

Testing for setting point

When you begin making jam, place a saucer in the freezer to chill. Boil the jam for the minimum time given in the recipe, then test for set as follows.

Carefully remove the pan from the heat, then drop about 2 teaspoons of the jam onto the cold saucer. Allow it to cool, then push your fingertip across the centre of the jam. If the surface wrinkles and the two halves remain separate, the jam is at setting point.

If it forms only a thin skin or remains runny, return the pan to the heat and bring the jam back to a full rolling boil. Boil for another 5 minutes, then test again.

To prevent the jam overcooking, turn the heat off or remove the pan from the heat each time you test for a set.

Tomato sauce

1 tablespoon olive oil
1 onion, chopped
1 large clove garlic, crushed
750g ripe tomatoes, peeled and chopped
2 teaspoons chopped fresh basil or oregano,
  or 1 teaspoon dried oregano
1 teaspoon sugar
Makes 500ml Prep 10 mins Cook 50 mins

1 Heat the olive oil in a large saucepan, add the onion and fry gently for 5 minutes, or until softened. Add the garlic and cook, stirring, for a further minute.

2 Add the tomatoes with their seeds and juice, then stir in the herbs and sugar and season with salt and freshly ground black pepper. Bring to the boil, then reduce the heat, cover and simmer gently for 30 to 45 minutes, stirring occasionally, until the sauce is thick and pulpy.

3 Remove from the heat, then transfer to a blender or food processor and purée the sauce until smooth. Check the seasoning and adjust as required.

4 Toss the sauce through hot cooked pasta, or use in lasagne, soups and casseroles – or for longer storage, pour the hot sauce into sterilised jars.

Note If you have a glut of fresh tomatoes, you can double or triple this recipe.

Tomato and apple chutney

1kg ripe tomatoes, peeled and roughly chopped

1kg apples, peeled, cored and roughly chopped

450g onions, roughly chopped

4 cloves garlic, crushed

400ml malt or cider vinegar

310g demerara or light brown sugar

215g sultanas

2 teaspoons salt

15g whole pickling spices (such as peppercorns, allspice berries, ginger, dried chillies and celery seeds), in a muslin bag (optional)

Makes 1.8kg Prep 25 mins Cook 2½ hours

1 Put the tomatoes, apples, onions, garlic and vinegar in a preserving pan or large, heavy-based stainless steel saucepan. Slowly bring to the boil, then reduce the heat and simmer for 30 minutes, or until tender, stirring the mixture occasionally.

2 Add all the remaining ingredients, including the pickling spices, if using. Heat gently, stirring frequently until the sugar has dissolved. Bring back to the boil, then reduce the heat and simmer for 2 hours, stirring often towards the end of the cooking time to prevent sticking. By this time the chutney should be well-reduced and very thick; if necessary, cook for a little while longer.

3 Spoon into warm, sterilised jars. Cover the chutney with discs of baking parchment to cover the surface completely. Cover the jars with cellophane or plastic screw-topped lids (not metal lids, as they will corrode).

4 When the chutney is completely cold, tighten the lids. Label and date the jars and leave to mature in a cool dark place for at least one month before eating. Use within one year of making. Once opened, store in the fridge and use within one month.

Variation

Use pears or plums instead of some of the apples. This makes a sweeter chutney, but don't reduce the sugar or it won't keep well.

Piccalilli

40g salt

500g button onions, peeled

675g cauliflower, cut into small florets

500g mini cucumbers, or regular cucumbers quartered lengthways and cut into 1cm to 2cm pieces

500g fine green beans, trimmed and halved

3 small red chillies, cut into thin strips

220g sugar

110g plain flour

2 teaspoons ground allspice

2 tablespoons ground ginger

2 tablespoons mild curry powder

2 tablespoons mustard powder

2 teaspoons ground turmeric

½ teaspoon cayenne pepper

1.25 litres white or cider vinegar

2 teaspoons black peppercorns

Makes 4 cups Prep 30 mins, plus 24 hours standing Cook 20 mins

1 Pour 1.25 litres water into a large stainless steel or enamel saucepan, add the salt and bring to the boil. Add the vegetables and chillies and cook over a low heat for 5 minutes. Pour into a colander in the sink, rinse well under cold water, then drain well on kitchen paper or a clean tea towel.

2 Put the sugar, flour and ground spices in a bowl. Add 3 to 4 tablespoons of the vinegar and mix to form a thick paste, then place in a stainless steel or enamel saucepan. Stir in the remaining vinegar, add the peppercorns and bring to the boil, stirring continuously. Reduce to a simmer and cook, stirring, for 3 to 5 minutes, or until the sauce thickens. Remove from the heat and leave to cool, stirring occasionally to prevent a skin forming.

3 Put the drained vegetables in a large bowl, add the sauce and mix together. Cover and leave to stand for 24 hours.

4 The next day, stir the piccalilli to coat the vegetables evenly, then spoon into clean, dry jars and cover with vinegar-proof lids. Label and date the jars and leave to mature in a cool dark place for two to three months.

Strawberry jam

3.2kg strawberries, small and firm if possible
juice of 2 lemons
2.7kg sugar

Makes about 4.5kg Prep 20 mins Cook 30 mins

1 Wash the strawberries to remove any dirt, then cut away the green hulls. Place the strawberries in a preserving pan or large, heavy-based stainless steel saucepan and add the lemon juice.

2 Heat gently until the juices start to run, then use a potato masher to mash the strawberries to the required texture, keeping some of the strawberries whole if you like. Continue cooking until the mixture is reduced to a thick slush, stirring often.

3 Add the sugar and stir continuously over a low heat until it has completely dissolved. Bring the mixture to the boil and boil steadily for 8 to 10 minutes, stirring frequently, until setting point is reached (105°C on a sugar thermometer).

4 Ladle the jam into warm, sterilised jars, then cover and seal. Allow the jars to cool, then label and date. Store in a cool dark place and use within one year of making. Once opened, store in the fridge and use within one month.

Note Some people like to warm the sugar before adding it to the fruit, to prevent a sudden drop in temperature of the cooking fruit. Put the sugar in a heatproof bowl in a low oven for 10 minutes, or in a microwave oven on high for 1 to 2 minutes.

Variation

Raspberry jam Use 2.7kg fresh or frozen raspberries and 2.7kg sugar. Omit the lemon juice. Prepare as directed, but start testing for the setting point after 5 minutes.

Marmalade

900g oranges, or a mixture of oranges
and grapefruit
2 lemons
1.75kg sugar

Makes about 2.5kg Prep 30 mins Cook 2¼ hours

1 Wash the fruit, then cut in half. Squeeze the juice into a preserving pan or large, heavy-based stainless steel saucepan. Remove the seeds and membranes from the citrus, wrap them in a muslin bag, tie up into a parcel and add to the pan.

2 Cut the citrus peel into thin shreds (or coarse ones, if preferred), then add to the pan with 2.25 litres water.

3 Bring the mixture to the boil, then reduce the heat and simmer gently for 2 hours, or until the mixture is reduced by about half and the peel is very tender.

4 Remove the muslin bag, leave to cool, then squeeze any liquid from the bag back into the pan. Add the sugar to the pan and stir over a very low heat until completely dissolved. Bring to the boil and boil rapidly for 15 minutes, or until setting point is reached (105°C on a sugar thermometer).

5 Remove from the heat and skim off any froth from the surface with a draining spoon. Leave to cool for 5 minutes, or until a thin skin starts to form on top of the marmalade. Stir gently to distribute the peel evenly.

6 Ladle into warm, sterilised jars, then cover and seal. Allow the jars to cool, then label and date. Store in a cool dark place and use within one year of making. Once opened, store in the fridge and use within one month.

Lemon syrup cordial

440g sugar
500ml lemon juice
3 teaspoons citric acid
Makes 875ml Prep 15 mins Cook 25 mins

1 Place the sugar and lemon juice in a saucepan with 375ml water. Cook, stirring occasionally, over a high heat until the sugar dissolves and the syrup comes to the boil.

2 Reduce the heat to medium-low and simmer for 20 minutes, or until the syrup has thickened slightly.

3 Stir in the citric acid, then strain the cordial into a sterilised bottle. Refrigerated, the cordial will keep for up to one month.

Serving suggestion Pour some of the lemon syrup into glasses, top up with iced water or soda water, stir well and serve immediately. If serving the cordial to adults, you could add a measure of gin or vodka.

Variation

Lemon and passionfruit cordial Make in the same way as the lemon cordial, but pour the hot syrup over the pulp of 12 passionfruits and allow to stand for 30 minutes to cool. Strain the cordial into a sterilised bottle.

Lemon butter

finely grated zest of 2 large lemons
strained juice of 2 large lemons
90g unsalted butter, chopped into small pieces
285g caster sugar
3 eggs, beaten
Makes about 310g Prep 5 mins Cook 25 mins

1 Put the lemon zest and lemon juice in a double boiler or a heatproof bowl set over a saucepan of gently simmering water. Take care not to let the bottom of the bowl touch the water.

2 Add the butter and sugar and strain in the beaten eggs through a nylon sieve to remove any white threads. Stirring the mixture continuously, cook over a medium heat for 20 minutes, or until thick enough to coat the back of a spoon. Don't let the mixture boil or it will curdle.

3 Remove from the heat and immediately pour the fruit butter through a fine nylon sieve into a clean, dry and warm jar. Cover immediately with a disc of baking parchment and leave until completely cold.

4 Seal the jar, then label and date. Store in the fridge for up to six weeks.

Note Citrus fruits are often waxed for sale, so always wash the fruit under warm-running water before grating the zest.

Serving suggestion Fruit butters are delicious on toast or warm scones, or spooned into little tartlet cases.

Variations

Lime butter Use the finely grated zest and strained juice of 4 large limes, 90g unsalted butter, 170g caster sugar and 3 eggs.

Orange butter Use the finely grated zest and strained juice of 2 large oranges, 90g unsalted butter, 80g caster sugar and 3 eggs.

Chicken

Jointing a chicken

Cutting a whole chicken into joints is cheaper than buying legs, wings and breasts separately. Freeze any portions you don't need.

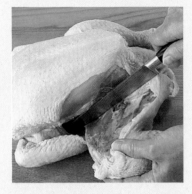

1 Gently pull one leg out from the body, then cut through the skin between the body and leg. Bend the leg until it pops out of the socket. Cut through the flesh under the joint. Repeat with the other leg.

2 To separate the drumstick and thigh, stand one leg on the board in a natural V-shape. Firmly hold the end of the drumstick in one hand and cut through the joint where the two bones meet.

3 To separate the wings from the body, make a deep cut in the breast, near the inside of each wing, angling the knife diagonally. Cut down into the meat, far enough to expose the bones.

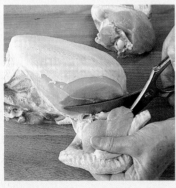

4 To free the wings from the carcass, cut between the ball and socket joints with poultry shears or strong kitchen scissors, through the remaining flesh and bone. Check there are no bone splinters left.

5 To remove the breast meat, lay the carcass on its side, then use shears or scissors to cut through the thin rib cage on either side of the backbone.

6 Divide the breast into two, carefully cutting crossways or lengthways through the flesh using a knife, and then through the bones and cartilage with shears or scissors.

Skinning chicken joints

Slip your fingers under the skin and ease the skin free of the flesh. Pull the skin off, using a small pointed knife, as needed, to cut through the underlying membrane. To pull skin off the legs, you may need to cut the skin around the bird's 'ankle' first.

Trussing a chicken

Shape the bird neatly with your hands, tucking the neck flap under the folded wings at the back. Place a piece of kitchen string across the bird, with the centre of the string just below the breastbone. Bring the string down over the wings to cross underneath, then bring the ends up to tie the legs and tail together. Remove the string before carving the cooked bird.

Roasting times for chicken

Chicken should be roasted at 200°C/gas 6 for 30 to 40 minutes per 1kg, plus an extra 15 to 20 minutes. To ensure that any harmful pathogens are killed, poultry should always be cooked thoroughly (see 'Testing for doneness', below).

Testing for doneness

To test whether a chicken is cooked, use one of these methods.

● Pierce the thickest part of the meat with a skewer or the point of a sharp knife. If the juices that run out are clear, the bird is cooked. If they are pink, roast the bird for a little longer.

● Lift the bird up with a carving fork and tip it up; check the colour of the juices that run out of the cavity.

● For more precise results, insert an instant-read thermometer into the thickest part of the meat. The dark thigh meat should reach at least 75°C, and the white breast meat 71°C.

Stuffing a chicken

● Always remove any giblets from the body cavity of the chicken before stuffing or roasting it.

● Although it's traditional to stuff the body cavity of the bird before roasting, this can stop heat penetrating to the centre of the bird. Also, the stuffing itself can harbour bacteria, which won't be destroyed unless the stuffing reaches a safe temperature inside the bird.

● If you do want to stuff the cavity, make sure you stuff it only two-thirds full, then weigh the bird and calculate the cooking time accordingly.

● After cooking, test the stuffing temperature with an instant-read thermometer: it should have reached at least 75°C.

● Alternatively, stuff the neck end only, or cook the stuffing in a separate pan.

● Don't stuff a bird more than 3 hours before cooking it as the raw meat may contaminate the stuffing.

● If using a warm stuffing, roast the bird straight away.

Tips for chicken

Stocking up When cutting up a chicken, keep the back, neck and gizzards. Freeze them, along with roast chicken carcasses. When you have enough, use them to make a delicious stock for a range of soups and sauces (see page 356).

Pounding alternatives You don't need a specialist meat mallet in order to flatten chicken breasts for recipes such as schnitzel. Place them between two sheets of plastic wrap, then pound them using the underside of a small heavy frying pan or saucepan.

Meat

For tender results

Lean meat is not self-basting because it doesn't have fat distributed through the flesh, so you need to take care that it doesn't dry out and become tough during cooking. Two ways to do this are to tenderise meat by pounding it with a meat mallet to break down some of the muscle fibres, or to marinate it.

Roasting times and temperatures

The cooking time for roasting meat is based on the weight of the joint, so weigh the meat – after stuffing it, if you're using stuffing – and then calculate the cooking time according to the chart on page 26. The times given are suitable for meat on or off the bone. If you're using one of the special 'mini roasts', follow the cooking instructions on the packaging. The ideal temperature for roasting is generally 180°C/gas 4, although lamb is sometimes slow-roasted at 160°C/gas 3.

Testing for doneness

Once the roasting time is reached, it can be difficult to tell if the meat is actually cooked – even if the outside is nicely browned, the inside might still be a little undercooked. The most accurate way to test for doneness is to use an instant-read thermometer to check the internal temperature. Always make sure the point of the thermometer goes into a thick part of the meat, not into fat or next to bone. The meat is cooked when it registers the thermometer temperatures given below.

BEEF AND LAMB	
Rare	60°C
Medium	70°C
Well-done	80°C

VEAL	
Well-done	80°C

PORK	
Medium	80°C
Well-done	85°C

Magic touch

With practice, you can tell how cooked a piece of meat is by gently pressing it with tongs. Medium-rare meat feels springy and soft; medium is slightly firm and springy. Any firmer and it's well-done.

Removing fat and tissue

Here's the correct way to trim meat for cooking or marinating so that you remove fat and tissue – not meat.

1 When you're preparing meat for a casserole or a stir-fry, you may need to trim it even further. Using a very sharp knife, first cut and pull away the surrounding fat from the meat.

2 Cut out the connective tissue, membrane and any gristle from each of the smaller pieces of meat. Boneless lamb is shown here.

Cutting meat for stir-frying

1 A stir-fry requires meat that's cut into uniform pieces. After the meat has been trimmed (boneless lamb is shown here), cut across the grain at right angles.

2 Then cut each piece crossways into strips about 5mm thick. It will be easier to slice the meat very finely if you partially freeze it first.

Deglazing a baking dish and making pan gravy

Grandma always saved the wonderful juices that dripped from meat during roasting in order to turn them into the most delicious gravy. Here's how she did it.

1 After roasting meat or poultry, add liquid (such as stock or wine) to the roasting pan and scrape up all the brown, caramelised bits from the bottom. Keep stirring until they have dissolved.

2 Pour the juices into a gravy separator, if you have one. Otherwise, pour the juices into a deep, narrow bowl and place it in the freezer for about 15 minutes, then spoon off the congealed fat.

3 Pour the de-fatted pan juices into a saucepan. Blend some flour or cornflour with a little water to a smooth paste and add to the pan juices. Cook, stirring, over a medium heat, until the gravy has thickened.

Seafood

Filleting a fish

1 Before you start to fillet a round fish (such as bream or snapper) first trim off the pectoral fins. Then cut deeply across one side of the fish, just below the head.

2 Gently slide the knife along the spine, towards the tail. Turn the fish over and repeat on the other side. Then pick out any remaining loose bones with tweezers.

Peeling and deveining prawns

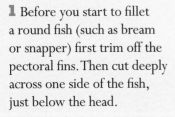

1 Hold the prawn with one hand and twist the head off with the other. Peel away the body shell and the legs; the tail shell can either be left on or gently pulled off, depending on what the recipe specifies.

2 If you can't get a good grip on the end of the back vein (the intestinal tract) with your fingers, use a small paring knife to cut down just next to the side of the vein to help you to remove it.

Extracting the meat from a crab

● If the crab is alive, place it in the freezer for 1 to 2 hours to make it comatose.

● Bring a large pot of salted water to the boil. Add a bouquet garni and simmer for 5 minutes. Drop in the crab, bring back to the boil and cook for 10 to 12 minutes, or until the shell turns red.

● Remove the crab from the water, cool under cold-running water and chill until serving time.

● To extract the meat, twist off the claws and legs and set aside. Pull off and discard the pointed tail flap. Hold the crab upright with the top shell facing you and the tail end uppermost. Holding the shell with both hands, use your thumbs to push the body free from the shell, then carefully pull the two sections apart.

● Remove the greyish-white bulbous gills and the attached feathery wisps. Spoon out the brown meat and set aside.

● With a fine skewer, prise out the white flesh from the leg and claw sockets, cutting the body in half to get all the meat out. With a kitchen weight or hammer, gently crack all the joints in the claws and legs; prise out the meat in the joints with a skewer.

Boning fish fillets

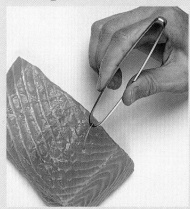

Fish fillets (salmon is shown here) sometimes contain pinbones. Feel for them with your fingers, then pull them out with large tweezers or needle-nose pliers.

Opening oysters

Hold each oyster firmly, flat side up, in a thick cloth to protect your hand and to stop the oyster slipping. Insert an oyster knife into the join between the halves of the shell, in about the middle of the straight edge. Slide the knife from end to end along the inside of the top shell to sever the muscle, then twist the knife to separate the shells. Run the knife gently under the oyster to loosen it from the bottom shell, keeping the shell horizontal to retain the juice. Pick out visible shards of shell but don't rinse.

Cooking prawns

To cook raw prawns, drop them into a large pot of boiling water with 2 teaspoons salt for every 1kg prawns. Boil until the prawns rise to the surface, then immediately plunge them into fresh cold water. If you aren't eating the prawns straight away, drain them again, mix with crushed ice and refrigerate.

Preparing lobster

Place the lobster in the freezer for 1 to 2 hours until it's comatose. Bring a large pan of salted water to the boil and drop in the lobster. Simmer for 10 minutes for the first 500g, and an extra 7 minutes for every extra 500g. Chill until serving time.

To serve, twist off the claws and set aside. Lay on a board, belly down. Using a large sharp knife, split the tail in half, starting where it meets the head, cutting down along the back. You may need to hit the back of the knife with a heavy weight to help it to penetrate the shell. Split the head down the centre, then separate the halves. Discard the transparent stomach sac and gills (in the head, near the tip). With the tip of a knife, remove the grey intestinal vein running down the tail. Remove the flesh from the claws as instructed for crabs (see opposite). Slice the claw and leg meat and arrange it over the lobster shells.

Cleaning mussels

Fill the sink or a large bowl with cold water. Add the mussels and sort through them, discarding any with damaged shells, and those that are open and don't close when their shells are tapped gently.

Using a small knife, scrape off any barnacles from the shells, then pull away the hairlike 'beards'. Scrub the shells under cold running water until clean.

Fruit and vegetables

Fruit and vegetable preparation

All vegetables should be washed before use. If you're peeling them, rinse them again afterwards. Most recipes assume that you will peel any vegetables that would normally be peeled, such as onions and potatoes. Here are useful preparation tips for some common produce.

Asparagus Bend each stalk gently not far from the bottom. The tough bit will snap off – then discard it. For white asparagus, which has thicker stems, peel the stalks with a vegetable peeler.

Berries These are delicate, so handle them carefully. Wash briefly if desired. Strawberries should always be washed, as they can be sandy; you should also remove the green leaf cap using the point of a small sharp knife.

Brussels sprouts Wash and cut off most of the stalk, but leave a bit attached or the sprouts will fall apart during cooking.

Cabbages Halve the cabbage lengthways; cut each half in half again lengthways. Core each quarter by cutting a wedge-shaped section from its base. Cut each quarter into strips or shreds.

Chillies Always wear gloves when handling chillies and never touch your eyes. Halve lengthways; remove the seeds if desired (these are the hottest part), then slice or chop.

Garlic To remove the skin, place a clove under the flat side of a knife blade; smack the blade with the heel of your hand. Discard the skin, then slice or chop the garlic as required.

Leeks Cut off the root end and leafy green end. Make a long cut in the top and fan back the leaves under cold-running water to wash away grit. Or slice the leek into rings, and flush under cold-running water in a colander. Save the leafy green end for stock.

Mushrooms Rather than rinsing, which makes the caps soggy, simply wipe the caps with damp kitchen paper. Cut off and discard the stems.

Stone fruits These should be washed. To stone them, cut along the natural line of the fruit right through to the stone, then twist and remove the stone. To stone cherries, use a cherry stoner or small sharp knife. To peel whole stone fruit, cover with boiling water for 30 seconds, then remove with a slotted spoon. When cooled, peel away the skins.

Sweetcorn Pull off the green husks, then pull away the silks. Boil the cobs whole, or cut down each side to remove the kernels.

Peeling tomatoes

Many recipes call for peeled tomatoes. Here's what to do.

1 Using a sharp knife, cut a shallow cross into the base of each tomato. (This will make it much easier to peel the skin off the tomatoes when they are cooked.) Gently lower the tomatoes into a saucepan of boiling water. Blanch them for about 1 minute, or until the skins shrivel. Remove from the pot and place in cold water until completely cooled.

2 Peel away the skin from each tomato with a paring knife, or simply by using your fingers. Use the tomatoes as instructed by the recipe.

Cutting onions

There's a simple but highly effective art to cutting onions, which holds the pieces together and also helps to contain the juice so that it doesn't sting your eyes.

1 Using a sharp cook's knife, cut the onion in half lengthways. Lay the cut sides on the chopping board and make several horizontal cuts, stopping about 1cm from the root end to keep it intact.

2 Next, make vertical cuts through the onion from top to bottom, slicing all the way through, but still keeping the root end intact.

3 Holding the onion by the root end, turn the onion around 90 degrees and make another series of vertical cuts through the onion, allowing it to fall apart into a series of small even pieces.

Grilling peppers

Grilling peppers intensifies their sweetness and gives a lovely, silky texture. Grilled peppers are especially popular in Mediterranean dishes.

1 Place the peppers on a grill tray or barbecue grill plate lined with foil. Grill at a high heat for 10 to 15 minutes, or until the skin is blackened and blistered.

2 Place the grilled peppers in a paper bag, or place in a bowl and cover with cling film. Allow them to sweat for 5 to 10 minutes, or until they are cool enough to handle.

3 Using your fingers or a small paring knife, peel away the charred skin. Cut into smaller pieces, then discard the inner seeds and membranes.

Baking

Before you bake

Read the recipe to check that you understand all the steps and to ensure you have all the necessary ingredients and equipment. Gather together everything you'll need, and measure out all the ingredients. Unless the recipe specifies that the ingredients should be chilled, remove cold ingredients from the refrigerator 1 hour before starting so that they will be at room temperature. Preheat the oven and prepare the baking tins or trays as specified in the recipe. Then just follow your recipe, step by step.

Baking terms and techniques

Adding eggs When adding eggs to a creamed mixture, do so gradually. If the mixture begins to separate and look curdled, the eggs have been added too quickly; to remedy this, stir a little flour into the mixture and then add the rest of the eggs gradually.

Beating eggwhites Have the eggwhites at room temperature. Use a clean, dry bowl and mixer. Starting at a medium-low speed, beat until frothy. Increase the mixer speed to medium and continue beating until the whites have become foamy and have increased in volume. Continue beating, occasionally tilting the bowl and moving the mixer around to take in as much air as possible. Beat until the eggwhites are stiff but still moist and glossy.

Creaming butter and sugar Many cake recipes will tell you to 'cream' butter and sugar. This refers to beating them together until they are pale, fluffy and increased in volume, using a hand whisk or electric mixer.

Folding in dry ingredients When a recipe tells you to fold in ingredients alternately with milk, you should simply incorporate one mixture into another using a large metal spoon and a gentle scooping motion. Mix just until combined; overmixing will make a cake tough.

Rubbing in Use your fingertips to incorporate butter or other fat into flour until the mixture resembles fine breadcrumbs. Do this before adding any liquid.

Sifting Dry ingredients (such as flour, bicarbonate of soda, baking powder, spices and cocoa powder) should be sifted together before being added to a batter. This increases aeration and removes lumps.

Rubbing butter into flour

When rubbing in butter, use only your fingertips so the heat from your hands doesn't soften the fat. Add the liquid gradually, mixing it in with a flat-bladed knife. Add just enough liquid to bind the mixture into a dough.

Crimping pastry

Drape the rolled pastry over a rolling pin and gently ease it into the pie dish. Gently trim the edges. To seal the edges, pinch them with your fingers, as shown, to give a decorative effect, or press down with the tines of a fork.

Making a sponge cake

Grandma always turned out the most beautiful, feather-light sponges. Here are some helpful tips for a perfect basic cake that have been handed down from her generation of home bakers.

1 Preheat the oven to the required temperature. Moisten the base of a spring-form cake tin and cover it with a round of baking parchment or greaseproof paper that has been cut to fit, using the base of the cake tin as a guide.

2 Using a hand whisk or electric mixer, beat the eggs with the sugar until a light, almost white, creamy mixture forms. Sift the flour over the top, then carefully fold the flour in to retain the air that has been beaten into it.

3 Pour the batter into the cake tin, to four-fifths full at the most, to allow for the cake to rise. Level the top of the batter using a wide spatula or cake scraper. Bake in the preheated oven, but don't open the oven door, or the cake may deflate.

4 Remove the cake from the oven. After 5 minutes, run a knife around the side of the tin. Gently turn the cake onto a sheet of greaseproof paper, then place a weight on top and leave it to cool.

5 Remove the base of the tin from the cooled cake and peel away the baking parchment. The cake should be soft and elastic because of the condensed water and sugar in the cake mixture.

6 Using a large knife, carefully cut horizontally through the sponge one to three times, depending on what your recipe requires. If the filling will need support while it rests, place a cake ring around the cake.

Adapting recipes

Grandma's recipes often included generous amounts of fat and salt, but we can still maintain our healthy modern way of eating while enjoying traditional dishes. One approach is to use the richer recipes as treats rather than as everyday fare; another is to reduce the fat in the traditional recipes, whenever possible. Generally, the recipes in this book already contain less fat and salt than Grandma used, but if you'd like to reduce the fat or salt intake further, here's how.

Reducing the fat

You can reduce the quantity of fat – oil or butter in particular – in most meat and vegetable recipes by half, without affecting the way the recipe works. The difference will be the loss of some richness of flavour.

Cut off all visible fat from meat before you start the recipe. If the meat is cooked in a sauce or gravy, you can prepare the dish a day ahead, chill it overnight, then remove the visible fat from the surface before reheating. Before beginning to grill or roast meat, lightly brush both the meat and the grill pan or roasting tin with oil, and then brush the meat again as needed during cooking, rather than basting it with fat.

Remove the skin from chicken before serving – but don't remove the skin before cooking, unless the recipe instructs you to do so, as the skin protects the flesh from drying out. Have some well-reduced chicken stock on hand and brush a little onto the skinned chicken just before serving to give it an appetising gloss and colour.

You can also reduce the quantity of fat in most soup recipes by half. In cream soups, use semi-skimmed milk rather than whole milk or cream. Again, some richness of flavour will be lost, but the recipes will still work. A sprinkle of chopped parsley, chives or other herbs, or a spoonful of reduced-fat evaporated milk swirled through the soup at the last moment, will give added interest and flavour.

Dessert recipes that involve flour mixtures (pastry, dumplings, and steamed or boiled puddings) shouldn't be modified. Simply stick to desserts that don't contain fat, such as fruits, water ices and jellies. For the accompaniment, use reduced-fat ice cream or chilled, whipped, reduced-fat evaporated milk, or make custard using low-fat milk.

Cake and biscuit recipes shouldn't be changed either, as the proportion of fat to the other ingredients is crucial to the texture and the way the mixture sets when cooked. Scones, breads, pancakes and muffins have very little fat, but be careful how much butter you spread on them. Use a non-stick frying pan for pancakes and pikelets, and rather than heating fat in the pan to grease it, brush it lightly with oil or melted butter.

Reducing the salt

In baked goods that don't require yeast, you can generally reduce salt by at least half. In yeasted baked goods, however, don't be tempted to reduce salt as it's necessary for leavening – without salt, the baked goods may become dense and flat.

For most main dishes, salads, soups, stews, casseroles and desserts, you can eliminate salt completely and instead use herbs and spices – such as garlic, pepper, basil, lemongrass or ginger – to add flavour to meals. Instead of using salt at the table, try drizzling lemon juice, lime juice or vinegar on vegetables, fish or chicken. If you do use salt, add it to food at the end of cooking, so you can taste the food's true flavour – and use the smallest amount of salt possible.

Nutritional analyses

Soups and starters

PAGE 38 SOUP OF PASTA AND BEANS
Per serving 1697kJ, 402kcal, 18g protein, 11.5g fat (2.5g saturated fat), 60g carbohydrate (9g sugars), 903mg sodium (2.3g salt), 11.8g fibre

PAGE 41 VEGETABLE SOUP WITH PESTO
Per serving 1803kJ, 430kcal, 15g protein, 20g fat (3.5g saturated fat), 50g carbohydrate (10g sugars), 637mg sodium (1.6g salt), 10g fibre

PAGE 42 PUMPKIN SOUP
Per serving 2022kJ, 490kcal, 5g protein, 47g fat (27g saturated fat), 13g carbohydrate (10g sugars), 197mg sodium (0.5g salt), 4g fibre

PAGE 43 RICH ONION SOUP
Per serving 1899kJ, 450kcal, 13g protein, 8.5g fat (3g saturated fat), 86g carbohydrate (22g sugars), 846mg sodium (2.1g salt), 7g fibre

PAGE 45 SCOTCH BROTH
Per serving 1768kJ, 422kcal, 40g protein, 17g fat (5g saturated fat), 27g carbohydrate (6g sugars), 197mg sodium (0.5g salt), 2g fibre

PAGE 46 POTATO AND LEEK SOUP
Per serving 1350kJ, 321kcal, 7g protein, 12g fat (2g saturated fat), 49g carbohydrate (4g sugars), 346mg sodium (0.9g salt), 4g fibre

PAGE 49 LENTIL SOUP
Per serving 960kJ, 229kcal, 12g protein, 4.5g fat (0.5g saturated fat), 36g carbohydrate (6.5g sugars), 253mg sodium (0.6g salt), 9.5g fibre

PAGE 50 CHICKEN NOODLE SOUP
Per serving 2219kJ, 528kcal, 54g protein, 20g fat (5g saturated fat), 36g carbohydrate (6g sugars), 702mg sodium (1.8g salt), 3g fibre

PAGE 52 BEST-EVER TOMATO SOUP
Per serving 550kJ, 132kcal, 3.5g protein, 6g fat (2.5g saturated fat), 16g carbohydrate (5g sugars), 260mg sodium (0.7g salt), 2.5g fibre

PAGE 53 MINESTRONE SOUP
Per serving 1417kJ, 336kcal, 15g protein, 7g fat (2g saturated fat), 51.5g carbohydrate (5g sugars), 802mg sodium (2g salt), 8g fibre

PAGE 54 PEA SOUP WITH HAM
Per serving 851kJ, 204kcal, 20g protein, 7g fat (1g saturated fat), 17g carbohydrate (5g sugars), 949mg sodium (2.4g salt), 6g fibre

PAGE 57 CREAM OF CHICKEN SOUP
Per serving 2247kJ, 540kcal, 37g protein, 37g fat (21g saturated fat), 16g carbohydrate (5g sugars), 156mg sodium (0.4g salt), 2g fibre

PAGE 58 SALMON MOUSSE
Per serving 2176kJ, 523kcal, 20g protein, 40g fat (16g saturated fat), 22g carbohydrate (2.5g sugars), 1156mg sodium (2.8g salt), 1g fibre

PAGE 60 CHEESE STRAWS
Per serving 256kJ, 61kcal, 1.5g protein, 4g fat (2g saturated fat), 5g carbohydrate (0.2g sugars), 62mg sodium (0.15g salt), < 1g fibre

PAGE 61 STUFFED EGGS
Per serving 278kJ, 67kcal, 4g protein, 6g fat (1g saturated fat), < 1g carbohydrate (< 1g sugars), 104mg sodium (0.26g salt), < 1g fibre

PAGE 62 DEVILLED CRAB
Per serving 1785kJ, 427kcal, 28g protein, 22g fat (10g saturated fat), 31g carbohydrate (9g sugars), 787mg sodium (2g salt), 1.6g fibre

PAGE 65 POTATO PUFFS
Per serving/puff 385kJ, 93kcal, 1g protein, 8g fat (1.5g saturated fat), 4g carbohydrate (< 1g sugars), 23mg sodium (0.06g salt), < 1g fibre

PAGE 66 BLUE CHEESE AND WALNUT DIP
Per serving 803kJ, 192kcal, 11g protein, 15g fat (7.5g saturated fat), 3g carbohydrate (3g sugars), 387mg sodium (0.96g salt), < 1g fibre

PAGE 67 PÂTÉ PINWHEELS
Per serving 253kJ, 61kcal, 1.5g protein, 4g fat (2g saturated fat), 4g carbohydrate (0.2g sugars), 74mg sodium (0.18g salt), < 1g fibre

PAGE 69 SAVOURY SCROLLS
Per serving 742kJ, 176kcal, 7g protein, 6g fat (4g saturated fat), 24g carbohydrate (3g sugars), 269mg sodium (0.7g salt), 1g fibre

Eggs and dairy

PAGE 72 EGG AND BACON PIE
Per serving 2386kJ, 572kcal, 23g protein, 40g fat (16g saturated fat), 35g carbohydrate (1g sugars), 910mg sodium (2.3g salt), < 1g fibre

PAGE 74 HERB OMELETTE
Per serving 1073kJ, 256kcal, 13g protein, 23g fat (9.5g saturated fat), < 1g carbohydrate (< 1g sugars), 171mg sodium (0.4g salt), < 1g fibre

PAGE 75 WELSH RAREBIT
Per serving 2115kJ, 508kcal, 22g protein, 37g fat (22g saturated fat), 23g carbohydrate (2g sugars), 756mg sodium (1.9g salt), < 1g fibre

PAGE 76 CHEESE SOUFFLÉS
Per serving 1226kJ, 293kcal, 13.5g protein, 20g fat (12g saturated fat), 15g carbohydrate (3g sugars), 390mg sodium (0.97g salt), < 1g fibre

PAGE 79 CHEESE AND LEEK TART
Per serving 2194kJ, 526kcal, 15g protein, 35g fat (20g saturated fat), 41g carbohydrate (2.5g sugars), 317mg sodium (0.8g salt), 2g fibre

PAGE 80 SCOTCH EGGS
Per serving 2363kJ, 567kcal, 22g protein, 40g fat (11g saturated fat), 32g carbohydrate (4g sugars), 949mg sodium (2.4g salt), 2g fibre

PAGE 82 EGGS EN COCOTTE
Per serving 787kJ, 190kcal, 8g protein, 17.5g fat (8.5g saturated fat), < 1g carbohydrate (< 1g sugars), 145mg sodium (0.37g salt), < 1g fibre

PAGE 83 BEST-EVER SCRAMBLED EGGS
Per serving 1138kJ, 274kcal, 19g protein, 23g fat (8g saturated fat), < 1g carbohydrate (< 1g sugars), 259mg sodium (0.65g salt), < 1g fibre

PAGE 84 HAM QUICHE
Per serving 2802kJ, 672kcal, 25g protein, 46g fat (26g saturated fat), 43g carbohydrate (3g sugars), 774mg sodium (1.9g salt), 1g fibre

PAGE 87 SAVOURY FRITTATA CAKE
Per serving 1006kJ, 240kcal, 12g protein, 20g fat (6g saturated fat), 3g carbohydrate (1g sugars), 662mg sodium (1.6g salt), 1.5g fibre

PAGE 88 CHEESE PASTIES
Per serving 924kJ, 221kcal, 8g protein, 15g fat (9g saturated fat), 14g carbohydrate (< 1g sugars), 178mg sodium (0.44g salt), < 1g fibre

PAGE 90 MACARONI CHEESE
Per serving 5166kJ, 1233kcal, 44g protein, 66g fat (40g saturated fat), 123g carbohydrate (14g sugars), 794mg sodium (2g salt), 4.5g fibre

PAGE 91 GRATIN OF HAM, CABBAGE AND CHEESE
Per serving 1478kJ, 356kcal, 20.5g protein, 28g fat (16g saturated fat), 6g carbohydrate (5g sugars), 1634mg sodium (4.1g salt), 1.5g fibre

PAGE 92 BAKED TOMATOES AND EGGS
Per serving 629kJ, 150kcal, 8g protein, 11g fat (2g saturated fat), 4g carbohydrate (4g sugars), 78mg sodium (0.19g salt), 2g fibre

PAGE 95 COURGETTE AND PEPPER FRITTATA
Per serving 1589kJ, 382kcal, 25g protein, 30g fat (11g saturated fat), 5g carbohydrate (5g sugars), 514mg sodium (1.2g salt), 1.5g fibre

Lamb, beef and pork

PAGE 98 ROAST SHOULDER OF LAMB WITH FRUITY STUFFING
Per serving 2060kJ, 492kcal, 55g protein, 20g fat (10g saturated fat), 23g carbohydrate (13g sugars), 826mg sodium (2g salt), 1.5g fibre

PAGE 101 FRENCH-STYLE LAMB STEW
Per serving 2216kJ, 531kcal, 53g protein, 23g fat (1.5g saturated fat), 12g carbohydrate (10g sugars), 113mg sodium (0.3g salt), 4g fibre

PAGE 102 LAMB RISSOLES AND ONION GRAVY
Per serving 1684kJ, 404kcal, 26g protein, 25g fat (9g saturated fat), 19g carbohydrate (5.5g sugars), 354mg sodium (0.9g salt), 1g fibre

PAGE 105 QUINTESSENTIAL SHEPHERD'S PIE
Per serving 2403kJ, 575kcal, 36g protein, 31g fat (16g saturated fat), 40g carbohydrate (10g sugars), 403mg sodium (1g salt), 6.5g fibre

PAGE 106 BRAISED LAMB SHANKS
Per serving 2123kJ, 508kcal, 53g protein, 26g fat (9g saturated fat), 11g carbohydrate (7g sugars), 455mg sodium (1.1g salt), 2g fibre

PAGE 108 SCRUMPY LAMB SHANKS
Per serving 2750kJ, 656kcal, 61g protein, 31g fat (1g saturated fat), 34g carbohydrate (29g sugars), 120mg sodium (0.3g salt), 2.5g fibre

Fish, seafood and shellfish

PAGE 192 FISH PIE
Per serving 2551kJ, 610kcal, 41g protein, 32g fat (17g saturated fat), 38g carbohydrate (7g sugars), 453mg sodium (1.1g salt), 1g fibre

PAGE 195 STEAMED FISH WITH SOY AND GARLIC
Per serving 1656kJ, 216kcal, 30g protein, 10g fat (1.5g saturated fat), 1.5g carbohydrate (1g sugars), 650mg sodium (1.6g salt), < 1g fibre

PAGE 196 KEDGEREE
Per serving 1762kJ, 419kcal, 31g protein, 15g fat (6g saturated fat), 44g carbohydrate (2.5g sugars), 908mg sodium (2.3g salt), < 1g fibre

PAGE 198 IMPOSSIBLE SALMON PIE
Per serving 1696kJ, 408kcal, 20g protein, 31g fat (16g saturated fat), 14g carbohydrate (4.5g sugars), 501mg sodium (1.3g salt), < 1g fibre

PAGE 199 GRILLED FISH WITH LEMON BUTTER SAUCE
Per serving 1308kJ, 315kcal, 32g protein, 21g fat (11g saturated fat), < 1g carbohydrate (< 1g sugars), 226mg sodium (0.6g salt), < 1g fibre

PAGE 200 PAN-FRIED FISH WITH BRAISED LENTILS
Per serving 2126kJ, 506kcal, 53g protein, 18g fat (6g saturated fat), 36.5g carbohydrate (5.5g sugars), 289mg sodium (0.7g salt), 7g fibre

PAGE 203 TUNA AND LEMON FISHCAKES
Per serving 2142kJ, 508kcal, 36g protein, 17g fat (3g saturated fat), 56g carbohydrate (2g sugars), 510mg sodium (1.2g salt), 3g fibre

PAGE 204 FISH STEW
Per serving 1333kJ, 316kcal, 48g protein, 7g fat (1.5g saturated fat), 12g carbohydrate (1g sugars), 732mg sodium (1.8g salt), 1g fibre

PAGE 206 CURRIED PRAWNS
Per erving 1437kJ, 343kcal, 33g protein, 20g fat (15g saturated fat), 8g carbohydrate (3g sugars), 387mg sodium (0.9g salt), < 1g fibre

PAGE 207 PRAWN COCKTAIL
Per serving 977kJ, 235kcal, 28g protein, 12.5g fat (2g saturated fat), 1.5g carbohydrate (1.5g sugars), 885mg sodium (0.3g salt), < 1g fibre

PAGE 208 BAKED FISH WITH ONION AND TOMATOES
Per serving 860kJ, 205kcal, 34g protein, 4.5g fat (1g saturated fat), 5g carbohydrate (4.5g sugars), 217mg sodium (0.5g salt), 1g fibre

PAGE 211 BATTERED FISH AND CHIPS
Per serving 3358kJ, 799kcal, 46g protein, 25g fat (3g saturated fat), 99g carbohydrate (4.5g sugars), 334mg sodium (0.8g salt), 5g fibre

PAGE 212 SMOKED FISH WITH CREAMY PARSLEY SAUCE
Per serving 1802kJ, 429kcal, 42g protein, 20g fat (12g saturated fat), 21g carbohydrate (13g sugars), 1537mg sodium (3.9g salt), < 1g fibre

PAGE 215 TUNA AND MACARONI BAKE
Per serving 3686kJ, 878kcal, 50g protein, 42g fat (21g saturated fat), 80g carbohydrate (12g sugars), 837mg sodium (2.1g salt), 3g fibre

PAGE 216 MOULES MARINIÈRE
Per serving 1779kJ, 427kcal, 23g protein, 24g fat (13g saturated fat), 9g carbohydrate (3.5g sugars), 638mg sodium (1.6g salt), < 1g fibre

Vegetables and salads

PAGE 220 ROAST POTATOES AND ROOT VEGETABLES
Per serving 925kJ, 220kcal, 5g protein, 7g fat (1g saturated fat), 38g carbohydrate (11g sugars), 50mg sodium (0.1g salt), 6g fibre

PAGE 223 MUSHROOMS FILLED WITH BACON AND BUTTERY BREADCRUMBS
Per serving 671kJ, 160kcal, 6g protein, 9g fat (3g saturated fat), 16g carbohydrate (1g sugars), 371mg sodium (0.9g salt), 1g fibre

PAGE 224 CAULIFLOWER CHEESE
Per serving 730kJ, 175kcal, 9.5g protein, 11g fat (6g saturated fat), 10g carbohydrate (6g sugars), 143mg sodium (0.36g salt), 2.5g fibre

PAGE 225 POTATO GRATIN
Per serving 1017kJ, 243kcal, 7g protein, 11g fat (7g saturated fat), 30g carbohydrate (4g sugars), 98mg sodium (0.24g salt), 2g fibre

PAGE 227 BUBBLE AND SQUEAK
Per serving 964kJ, 231kcal, 5g protein, 12g fat (3.5g saturated fat), 27g carbohydrate (4g sugars), 42mg sodium (0.1g salt), 3.5g fibre

PAGE 228 RED CABBAGE WITH APPLES
Per serving 310kJ, 74kcal, 2g protein, 3.5g fat (1g saturated fat), 9g carbohydrate (8g sugars), 134mg sodium (0.3g salt), 2g fibre

PAGE 230 MINTED PEAS
Per serving 338kJ, 82kcal, 4g protein, 4g fat (2g saturated fat), 8g carbohydrate (2g sugars), 23mg sodium (0.06g salt), 3g fibre

PAGE 231 CREAMED SPINACH
Per serving 626kJ, 152kcal, 8g protein, 11g fat (6g saturated fat), 5g carbohydrate (5g sugars), 387mg sodium (0.9g salt), 5g fibre

PAGE 232 VEGETABLE PIE
Per serving 2709kJ, 648kcal, 18g protein, 37g fat (19g saturated fat), 65g carbohydrate (16g sugars), 487mg sodium (1.2g salt), 6g fibre

PAGE 235 POTATO LATKES
Per serving 1073kJ, 265kcal, 7g protein, 10g fat (2g saturated fat), 37g carbohydrate (2g sugars), 118mg sodium (0.3g salt), 2.5g fibre

PAGE 236 GLAZED CARROTS
Per serving 199kJ, 48kcal, < 1g protein, 2g fat (1.5g saturated fat), 7g carbohydrate (6.5g sugars), 28mg sodium (0.07g salt), 1g fibre

PAGE 237 OVEN-BAKED CHIPS
Per serving 698kJ, 165kcal, 4g protein, 3g fat (< 1g saturated fat), 32g carbohydrate (1g sugars), 11mg sodium (0.02g salt), 2.4g fibre

PAGE 239 RATATOUILLE
Per serving 312kJ, 75kcal, 2g protein, 4.5g fat (< 1g saturated fat), 7g carbohydrate (6g sugars), 10mg sodium (0.02g salt), 3g fibre

PAGE 240 STUFFED JACKET POTATOES WITH LEEKS AND CHEESE
Per serving 1531kJ, 365kcal, 13g protein, 16g fat (10g saturated fat), 44g carbohydrate (2g sugars), 275mg sodium (0.7g salt), 4g fibre

PAGE 243 PAN-FRIED BRUSSELS SPROUTS WITH BACON
Per serving 662kJ, 160kcal, 6g protein, 14g fat (4g saturated fat), 3.5g carbohydrate (2.5g sugars), 220mg sodium (0.5g salt), 3.5g fibre

PAGE 244 PASTA PICNIC SALAD
Per serving 2122kJ, 503kcal, 18g protein, 15g fat (2.5g saturated fat), 79g carbohydrate (11g sugars), 723mg sodium (1.8g salt), 4g fibre

PAGE 245 RICE SALAD
Per serving 698kJ, 167kcal, 3.5g protein, 3.5g fat (< 1g saturated fat), 31g carbohydrate (4.5g sugars), 101mg sodium (0.26g salt), 1g fibre

PAGE 247 CAESAR SALAD
Per serving 1811kJ, 437kcal, 20g protein, 36g fat (11g saturated fat), 8g carbohydrate (1.5g sugars), 757mg sodium (1.9g salt), <1g fibre

PAGE 248 SALAD OF GREEN BEANS AND BACON
Per serving 707kJ, 171kcal, 6.5g protein, 14g fat (3g saturated fat), 5g carbohydrate (2.5g sugars), 407mg sodium (1g salt), 3g fibre

PAGE 250 COLESLAW
Per serving 276kJ, 67kcal, < 1g protein, 6g fat (<1g saturated fat), 3g carbohydrate (3g sugars), 40mg sodium (0.1g salt), 1g fibre

PAGE 251 TURKEY SALAD
Per serving 1162kJ, 279kcal, 23g protein, 18g fat (3g saturated fat), 6g carbohydrate (5g sugars), 74mg sodium (0.19g salt), 3g fibre

PAGE 252 CREAMY POTATO, EGG AND BACON SALAD
Per serving 887kJ, 212kcal, 6g protein, 11g fat (3g saturated fat), 22g carbohydrate (1.5g sugars), 229mg sodium (0.6g salt), 2g fibre

PAGE 255 EUROPEAN POTATO SALAD
Per serving 595kJ, 142kcal, 2g protein, 6g fat (1g saturated fat), 21g carbohydrate (2g sugars), 15mg sodium (0.03g salt), 1.5g fibre

PAGE 256 BEAN SALAD
Per serving 439kJ, 105kcal, 5g protein, 4g fat (< 1g saturated fat), 12g carbohydrate (4g sugars), 211mg sodium (0.5g salt), 4.5g fibre

PAGE 257 MIXED LEAF SALAD
Per serving 249kJ, 59kcal, < 1g protein, 6g fat (< 1g saturated fat), < 1g carbohydrate (< 1g sugars), 14mg sodium (0.03g salt), 1g fibre

Desserts

PAGE 260 CHOCOLATE PUDDINGS
Per serving 1866kJ, 443kcal, 6g protein, 16g fat (6g saturated fat), 73g carbohydrate (51g sugars), 217mg sodium (0.5g salt), 1.5g fibre

PAGE 263 PAVLOVA
Per serving 1306kJ, 313kcal, 2g protein, 20g fat (12g saturated fat), 33g carbohydrate (30g sugars), 41mg sodium (0.1g salt), < 1g fibre

PAGE 264 BREAD AND BUTTER PUDDING
Per serving 1830kJ, 436kcal, 13g protein, 21g fat (11g saturated fat), 54g carbohydrate (32g sugars), 377mg sodium (0.9g salt), 1g fibre

PAGE 267 PEAR, BROWN SUGAR AND OAT CRUMBLE
Per serving 2447kJ, 579kcal, 4g protein, 15g fat (8.5g saturated fat), 115g carbohydrate (90g sugars), 149mg sodium (0.4g salt), 4.5g fibre

PAGE 268 JAM ROLY POLY
Per serving 1483kJ, 352kcal, 4g protein, 14g fat (9g saturated fat), 56g carbohydrate (27g sugars), 248mg sodium (0.6g salt), 1g fibre

PAGE 271 STEAMED FRUIT PUDDING
Per serving 1787kJ, 425kcal, 6g protein, 18g fat (11g saturated fat), 63g carbohydrate (34g sugars), 282mg sodium (0.7g salt), 1.5g fibre

PAGE 272 LEMON DELICIOUS
Per serving 1147kJ, 273kcal, 6g protein, 12g fat (7g saturated fat), 36g carbohydrate (32g sugars), 146mg sodium (0.3g salt), < 1g fibre

PAGE 274 GOLDEN SYRUP DUMPLINGS
Per serving 2107kJ, 498kcal, 5g protein, 12g fat (7g saturated fat), 99g carbohydrate (68g sugars), 464mg sodium (1.1g salt), 1g fibre

PAGE 275 BAKED APPLES
Per serving 929kJ, 225kcal, 1g protein, 7g fat (5g saturated fat), 41g carbohydrate (39g sugars), 72mg sodium (0.2g salt), 3g fibre

PAGE 276 CLASSIC CHOCOLATE MOUSSE
Per serving 2093kJ, 504kcal, 7g protein, 42g fat (25g saturated fat), 27g carbohydrate (26g sugars), 56mg sodium (0.14g salt), < 1g fibre

PAGE 279 PANCAKES
Per serving 1111kJ, 265kcal, 9g protein, 12g fat (7g saturated fat), 32g carbohydrate (5g sugars), 111mg sodium (0.3g salt), < 1g fibre

PAGE 280 PLUM COBBLER
Per serving 1577kJ, 377kcal, 6g protein, 16g fat (10g saturated fat), 52g carbohydrate (22g sugars), 402mg sodium (1g salt), 3g fibre

PAGE 283 CHILLED BERRY CHEESECAKE
Per serving 2083kJ, 502kcal, 3g protein, 43g fat (26g saturated fat), 28g carbohydrate (18g sugars), 231mg sodium (0.6g salt), 1g fibre

PAGE 284 BAKED CUSTARD
Per serving 824kJ, 197kcal, 8g protein, 7g fat (4g saturated fat), 24g carbohydrate (24g sugars), 88mg sodium (0.2g salt), < 1g fibre

PAGE 287 GRANDMA'S TERRIFIC TRIFLE
Per serving 1628kJ, 389kcal, 5g protein, 17g fat (8g saturated fat), 44g carbohydrate (44g sugars), 153mg sodium (0.4g salt), 1.5g fibre

PAGE 288 CREAMED RICE
Per serving 1192kJ, 285kcal, 8g protein, 7g fat (5g saturated fat), 43g carbohydrate (27g sugars), 76mg sodium (0.2g salt), < 1g fibre

PAGE 289 BANANA CUSTARD
Per serving 1037kJ, 248kcal, 6g protein, 7g fat (4g saturated fat), 40g carbohydrate (35g sugars), 42mg sodium (0.1g salt), 1g fibre

PAGE 291 STEWED APPLES
Per serving 388kJ, 93kcal, < 1g protein, < 1g fat (< 1g saturated fat), 23g carbohydrate (20g sugars), 2mg sodium (0.005g salt), 2g fibre

PAGE 292 RHUBARB AND APPLE PIE
Per serving 1609kJ, 382kcal, 5g protein, 16g fat (10g saturated fat), 58g carbohydrate (28g sugars), 127mg sodium (0.3g salt), 3.5g fibre

PAGE 295 APPLE STRUDEL
Per serving 876kJ, 210kcal, 3g protein, 7g fat (3g saturated fat), 35g carbohydrate (28g sugars), 40mg sodium (0.2g salt), 3g fibre

PAGE 296 TREACLE TART
Per serving 1763kJ, 421kcal, 7g protein, 15g fat (9g saturated fat), 67g carbohydrate (34g sugars), 318mg sodium (0.8g salt), 1g fibre

Breads, cakes, biscuits and other treats

PAGE 300 PERFECT WHITE BREAD
Per serving/slice 605kJ, 143kcal, 4g protein, 2g fat (< 1g saturated fat), 29g carbohydrate (1g sugars), 144mg sodium (0.3g salt), 1g fibre

PAGE 303 IRISH SODA BREAD
Per serving 2591kJ, 614kcal, 16g protein, 20g fat (11g saturated fat), 99g carbohydrate (13g sugars), 999mg sodium (2.5g salt), 3.5g fibre

PAGE 304 SCONES
Per serving 803kJ, 192kcal, 4g protein, 7g fat (4g saturated fat), 29g carbohydrate (2g sugars), 190mg sodium (0.4g salt), 1g fibre

PAGE 305 PIKELETS
Per serving 122kJ, 29kcal, 1g protein, < 1g fat (< 1g saturated fat), 5g carbohydrate (2g sugars), 59mg sodium (0.14g salt), < 1g fibre

PAGE 307 BIG FRUITY TEA BUN
Per serving 826kJ, 197kcal, 4g protein, 4g fat (3g saturated fat), 35g carbohydrate (17g sugars), 41mg sodium (0.1g salt), 1g fibre

PAGE 308 BLUEBERRY MUFFINS
Per serving 883kJ, 210kcal, 4g protein, 10g fat (6g saturated fat), 28g carbohydrate (11g sugars), 165mg sodium (0.4g salt), < 1g fibre

PAGE 311 BASIC BUTTER CAKE
Per serving 2225kJ, 530kcal, 7g protein, 26g fat (15g saturated fat), 72g carbohydrate (41g sugars), 293mg sodium (0.7g salt), 1g fibre

PAGE 312 CHOCOLATE COCONUT SQUARES
Per serving 744kJ, 178kcal, 2g protein, 8.5g fat (7g saturated fat), 26g carbohydrate (23g sugars), 22mg sodium (0.05g salt), 1.5g fibre

PAGE 314 JUST-RIGHT ROCK CAKES
Per erving 527kJ, 126kcal, 2g protein, 4g fat (2g saturated fat), 20g carbohydrate (10g sugars), 140mg sodium (0.3g salt), < 1g fibre

PAGE 315 DATE AND WALNUT LOAF
Per serving 1596kJ, 378kcal, 6g protein, 11g fat (4g saturated fat), 66g carbohydrate (37g sugars), 256mg sodium (0.6g salt), 2g fibre

PAGE 316 DEVIL'S FOOD CAKE
Per serving 2161kJ, 515kcal, 7g protein, 27g fat (16g saturated fat), 64g carbohydrate (39g sugars), 375mg sodium (0.9g salt), 2g fibre

PAGE 319 BOILED FRUIT CAKE
Per serving 2507kJ, 592kcal, 7g protein, 13g fat (6g saturated fat), 114g carbohydrate (91g sugars), 174mg sodium (0.4g salt), 4g fibre

PAGE 320 HONEY CAKE
Per serving 2121kJ, 507kcal, 6g protein, 32g fat (17g saturated fat), 52g carbohydrate (45g sugars), 250mg sodium (0.6g salt), < 1g fibre

PAGE 323 GRANDMA'S NEVER-FAIL SPONGE
Per serving 873kJ, 209kcal, 5g protein, 5g fat (2g saturated fat), 36g carbohydrate (20g sugars), 130mg sodium (0.3g salt), < 1g fibre

PAGE 324 CINNAMON TEACAKE
Per serving 1165kJ, 277kcal, 4g protein, 12g fat (7g saturated fat), 41g carbohydrate (22g sugars), 187mg sodium (0.4g salt), < 1g fibre

PAGE 325 TREACLE GINGERBREAD LOAF
Per serving 1316kJ, 314kcal, 5g protein, 9g fat (2g saturated fat), 53g carbohydrate (31g sugars), 250mg sodium (0.6g salt), < 1g fibre

PAGE 327 CINNAMON STAR BISCUITS
Per serving 369kJ, 88kcal, 2g protein, 4g fat (1g saturated fat), 12g carbohydrate (11g sugars), 5mg sodium (0.01g salt), < 1g fibre

PAGE 328 SHORTBREAD
Per serving 601kJ, 144kcal, 1g protein, 9g fat (5.5g saturated fat), 16g carbohydrate (4g sugars), 65mg sodium (0.16g salt), < 1g fibre

PAGE 331 JAM DROP BISCUITS
Per serving 346kJ, 83kcal, 1g protein, 4g fat (2g saturated fat), 11g carbohydrate (4g sugars), 65mg sodium (0.16g salt), < 1g fibre

PAGE 332 OAT BISCUITS
Per serving 510kJ, 122kcal, 1.5g protein, 7g fat (4g saturated fat), 15g carbohydrate (6g sugars), 86mg sodium (0.2g salt), < 1g fibre

PAGE 333 GINGERSNAP BISCUITS
Per serving 152kJ, 36kcal, < 1g protein, 2.5g fat (1g saturated fat), 6g carbohydrate (4g sugars), 15mg sodium (0.03g salt), < 1g fibre

PAGE 335 MELTING MOMENTS
Per serving 788kJ, 188kcal, 1g protein, 12g fat (8g saturated fat), 18g carbohydrate (9g sugars), 87mg sodium (0.2g salt), < 1g fibre

PAGE 336 CUT-AND-COME-AGAIN COOKIES
Per serving 353kJ, 85kcal, 1g protein, 5g fat (3g saturated fat), 9g carbohydrate (3g sugars), 31mg sodium (0.07g salt), < 1g fibre

PAGE 339 GINGERBREAD MEN
Per serving 615kJ, 147kcal, 2g protein, 6g fat (4g saturated fat), 22g carbohydrate (8g sugars), 110mg sodium (0.27g salt), < 1g fibre

PAGE 340 COCONUT MACAROONS
Per serving 306kJ, 73kcal, < 1g protein, 5g fat (4g saturated fat), 7g carbohydrate (6g sugars), 40mg sodium (0.1g salt), 1g fibre

PAGE 341 CHOC-CHIP BISCUITS
Per serving 354kJ, 85kcal, < 1g protein, 5g fat (3g saturated fat), 10g carbohydrate (6g sugars), 45mg sodium (0.1g salt), < 1g fibre

PAGE 343 JAM AND COCONUT SLICE
Per serving 887kJ, 212kcal, 2g protein, 10g fat (7g saturated fat), 28g carbohydrate (21g sugars), 110mg sodium (0.27g salt), < 1g fibre

PAGE 344 CHOCOLATE PEPPERMINT SLICE
Per serving 775kJ, 185kcal, 1g protein, 10g fat (6g saturated fat), 23g carbohydrate (17g sugars), 50mg sodium (0.1g salt), < 1g fibre

PAGE 347 CHOCOLATE CHERRY SLICE
Per serving 1388kJ, 332kcal, 3g protein, 21g fat (14g saturated fat), 33g carbohydrate (26g sugars), 174mg sodium (0.4g salt), 2g fibre

PAGE 348 LEMON SLICE
Per serving 819kJ, 194kcal, 3g protein, 9g fat (5g saturated fat), 26g carbohydrate (17g sugars), 23mg sodium (0.05g salt), < 1g fibre

PAGE 351 BROWNIES
Per serving 1840kJ, 437kcal, 5g protein, 27g fat (16g saturated fat), 48g carbohydrate (34g sugars), 37mg sodium (0.09g salt), < 1g fibre

Index